Situational Prison C

MW01043264

This book examines the control ... ... prison
from a situational crime prevention perspective. Following the
success of situational crime prevention in community settings,
Richard Wortley argues that the same principles can be used to
help reduce the levels of assault, rape, self-harm, drug use, escape
and collective violence in our prison systems. This pioneering
new study proposes a two-stage model of situational prevention
that moves beyond traditional opportunity-reduction: it attempts
to reconcile the contradictory urges to control prison disorder
by 'tightening-up' and hardening the prison environment on the
one hand, and 'loosening-off' and normalising it on the other.
Combining a comprehensive synthesis and evaluation of existing
research with original investigation and ground-breaking conclusions, *Situational Prison Control* will be of great interest to academics and practitioners both in the areas of corrections and
crime prevention more generally.

RICHARD WORTLEY is Head of the School of Criminology and
Criminal Justice, Griffith University, Brisbane. He was a prison psychologist in the New South Wales prison system for nine years, and
since taking up a university position has taught and researched
in the areas of corrections and crime prevention. Recent articles
have appeared in *Law and Human Behaviour*, *Journal of Applied
Social Psychology*, *Crime Prevention Studies* and *Studies on Crime and
Crime Prevention*. He is currently National Chair of the Australian
College of Forensic Psychologists.

Cambridge Studies in Criminology

Edited by
Alfred Blumstein, *H. John Heinz School of Public Policy and Management, Carnegie Mellon University*
and David Farrington, *Institute of Criminology, University of Cambridge*

The Cambridge Studies in Criminology series aims to publish the highest quality research on criminology and criminal justice topics. Typical volumes report major quantitative, qualitative, and ethnographic research, or make a substantial theoretical contribution. There is a particular emphasis on research monographs, but edited collections may also be published if they make an unusually distinctive offering to the literature. All relevant areas of criminology and criminal justice are included, for example, the causes of offending, juvenile justice, the development of offenders, measurement and analysis of crime, victimization research, policing, crime prevention, sentencing, imprisonment, probation, and parole. The series is global in outlook, with an emphasis on work that is comparative or holds significant implications for theory or policy.

Other Books in the Series:

Life in the Gang: Family, Friends, and Violence, by Scott H. Decker and Barrik Van Winkle
Delinquency and Crime: Current Theories, edited by J. David Hawkins
Recriminalizing Delinquency: Violent Juvenile Crime and Juvenile Justice Reform, by Simon I. Singer
Mean Streets: Youth Crime and Homelessness, by John Hagan and Bill McCarthy
The Framework of Judicial Sentencing: A Study in Legal Decision Making, by Austin Lovegrove
The Criminal Recidivism Process, by Edward Zamble and Vernon L. Quinsey
Violence and Childhood in the Inner City, by Joan McCord
Judicial Policy Making and the Modern State: How the Courts Reformed America's Prisons, by Malcolm M. Feeley and Edward L. Rubin
Schools and Delinquency, by Denise C. Gottfredson
The Crime Drop in America, edited by Alfred Blumstein and Joel Wallman
Delinquent-Prone Communities, by Don Weatherburn and Bronwyn Lind
White-Collar Crime and Criminal Careers, by David Weisburd and Elin Waring, with Ellen F. Chayet

Sex Differences in Antisocial Behavior: Conduct Disorder, Delinquency, and Violence in the Dunedin Longitudinal Study, by Terrie Moffitt, Avshalom Caspi, Michael Rutter, and Phil A. Silva

Delinquent Networks: Youth Co-Offending in Stockholm, by Jerzy Sarnecki

Criminality and Violence among the Mentally Disordered, by Sheilagh Hodgins and Carl-Gunnar Janson

Why Corporations Obey the Law: Assessing Criminalization and Cooperative Models of Crime Control, by Sally S. Simpson

Situational Prison Control
Crime Prevention in Correctional Institutions

Richard Wortley

School of Criminology and Criminal Justice
Griffith University Brisbane Australia

CAMBRIDGE
UNIVERSITY PRESS

PUBLISHED BY THE PRESS SYNDICATE OF THE UNIVERSITY OF CAMBRIDGE
The Pitt Building, Trumpington Street, Cambridge, United Kingdom

CAMBRIDGE UNIVERSITY PRESS
The Edinburgh Building, Cambridge CB2 2RU, UK
40 West 20th Street, New York NY 10011–4211, USA
477 Williamstown Road, Port Melbourne, VIC 3207, Australia
Ruiz de Alarcón 13, 28014 Madrid, Spain
Dock House, The Waterfront, Cape Town 8001, South Africa

http://www.cambridge.org

First published 2002

Printed in the United Kingdom at the University Press, Cambridge

Typeface 10/13pt New Baskerville   *System* LaTeX 2$_\varepsilon$ [TB]

A catalogue record for this book is available from the British Library

Library of Congress Cataloguing in Publication data

Wortley, Richard (Richard K.)
   Situational prison control : crime prevention in correctional institutions /
   Richard Wortley.
      p.   cm – (Cambridge studies in criminology)
   Includes bibliographical references and index.
   ISBN 0 521 80418 3 – ISBN 0 521 00940 5 (pb.)
   1. Prison violence – Prevention.   2. Crime prevention.   3. Prison discipline.
   4. Prison psychology.   I. Title.   II. Cambridge studies in criminology
   (New York, N.Y.)

HV9025.W67 2002   2001037952

ISBN 0 521 80418 3 (hb)
ISBN 0 521 00940 5 (pb)

DEDICATION

To my parents, who always knew the value of education.

Contents

List of figures and tables		*page* x
Foreword		xi
Acknowledgements		xiv

Part I   Theoretical foundations

1	Introduction: why situational prison control?	3
2	Situational theories of prison behaviour	15
3	Situational methods of prison control	36
4	A model of situational prison control	55

Part II   Specific behaviours

5	Prisoner-prisoner violence	79
6	Sexual assaults	101
7	Prisoner-staff violence	117
8	Self-harm	136
9	Drug use	155
10	Escapes	173
11	Collective disorder	190
12	Conclusions: hard and soft situational prison control	211

List of references	226
Index	248

Figures and Tables

FIGURE

4.1   Two-stage model of situational prison control   *page* 57
12.1   Balance between hard and soft control   220

TABLES

4.1   Precipitation-control strategies in prison   58
4.2   Opportunity-reduction strategies in prison   66
5.1   Summary of promising strategies for control of prisoner-prisoner violence   99
6.1   Summary of promising strategies for control of sexual assault   115
7.1   Summary of promising strategies for control of prisoner-staff violence   134
8.1   Summary of promising strategies for control of self-harm   153
9.1   Summary of promising strategies for control of drug use   171
10.1   Summary of promising strategies for control of escapes   188
11.1   Summary of promising strategies for control of collective disorder   209

Foreword

Years ago, I was employed by the Home Office as the research officer for a group of training schools for delinquents in the West of England. These were mostly small, open establishments with (for those days) a relatively liberal regime. One of the greatest headaches for staff was a high rate of absconding and I was asked to undertake a study of the problem. As a newly graduated clinical psychologist, my focus was on the personal characteristics and family circumstances of the boys who ran away. I hoped to identify particular kinds of boys who were more prone to abscond and who could be given the necessary care or treatment to avert this response.

Several years and numerous studies later I had to admit defeat. There seemed to be little that distinguished absconders from other boys. But at the same time I chanced upon some large differences between schools in their rates of absconding. These differences in absconding could not be accounted for by differences in populations admitted, but seemed to be the result of differences in the school environment. I argued that schools were likely to vary considerably in pressures and opportunities to abscond. Thus, staff probably differed in how successfully they dealt with bullying or worries about home, both of which could provide the motive for absconding. Schools also varied in their security, their layout and their geographical position, all of which mediated opportunities to abscond.

A job change took me away from the training schools and I never did undertake the study of school environments that I recommended. Instead, I went on to apply the insights gained from the study of absconding in developing the situational prevention model, largely concerned with reducing opportunities for crime. But I always regretted being unable to continue my work on absconding and bring it to some practical conclusion. I therefore turned with much anticipation to the manuscript of this book by Richard Wortley. Would he reach the same conclusions that I (and others studying juvenile institutions for the Home Office) had reached about the power of the institutional environment to mould the behaviour of inmates? Would he argue that situational changes to prison environments could substantially reduce the incidence of specific problem behaviours? Could situational prevention really contribute to a more secure, trouble-free environment for both prisoners and staff? After all, the prison is the very epitome of institutional control. If situational prevention did have something additional to offer in prisons, how much more might it have to offer elsewhere!

In fact, this book shows clearly how focusing on specific control problems in the prison environment, and studying the related situational contingencies, can yield a host of suggestions for reducing the problems and associated harms. As such, it is an important contribution to the literature on correctional management, but it is much more than this. It is also a highly sophisticated and up-to-date discussion, grounded in a thorough knowledge of social and clinical psychology, of the determinants of problem behaviours and the respective roles of situational and dispositional characteristics.

For me, the book's greatest value, however, lies in its discussion of situational 'precipitators' of crime and other misconduct. For example, Dr Wortley holds that restrictions on prisoners, 'tightening-up', could precipitate some of the behaviours that prison administrators seek to avoid. Situational prevention in prisons must therefore not merely reduce opportunities for undesirable behaviour, but must also reduce precipitators of such behaviour – sometimes by 'loosening-off'. More generally, he argues that situational prevention has neglected precipitators of crime and, by focusing on opportunities, has narrowed our understanding of the situational determinants of crime and has failed to exploit the full range of situational interventions.

Dr Wortley seeks to remedy these limitations by developing a classification of situational interventions to address crime precipitators, which parallels the existing classification of interventions to reduce crime opportunities. While I doubt that precipitators are as important as opportunities, they unquestionably play a role in crime and misconduct (as I found in my study of absconding). I also agree with Richard Wortley that they should be given more attention in situational prevention projects. For this and other reasons, I believe that his analysis of situational control in prisons makes as great a contribution to the literature on situational crime prevention as it does to that on correctional management. Few books can succeed on so many levels.

Ronald V. Clarke
Rutgers University

Acknowledgements

The original idea and impetus for this book came from Graeme Newman and he provided invaluable support and advice throughout the project. Much of the research for the book was conducted while I was a Visiting Library Fellow at Rutgers University. I would like to thank Ron Clarke for providing this opportunity and Phyllis Schultz for helping me find my way around the wonderful Rutgers' Criminal Justice Library. I am further indebted to Ron Clarke for his ongoing interest in the book and his willingness to discuss with me the ideas – some of which challenge his own well-known theories of situational prevention – that are presented. Others who generously gave their time at various stages to discuss ideas or otherwise provide assistance include John Ditchfield, Marcus Felson, Gloria Laycock, Alison Liebling and Linda Zupan. I am grateful also to Carol Ronken who helped to track down numerous references used in the book and assisted with the final formatting of the manuscript. Finally, writing a book takes its toll on family life and completing the task would not have been possible without the understanding and patience of my wife Chris and my children Tom and Sally.

PART I

Theoretical foundations

CHAPTER 1

Introduction: why situational prison control?

This book examines the control of problem behaviour in prison from a situational prevention perspective. This examination of situational prison control is prompted by the accumulating evidence of success for situational prevention initiatives in reducing criminal behaviour in a wide range of community settings (Clarke, 1992, 1997; Poyner, 1993). The situational perspective on crime is a relatively recent criminal justice paradigm (Clarke, 1992, 1997; Cornish and Clarke, 1986) that shifts the attention from the supposed criminal disposition of the offender to the features of the potential crime scene that might encourage or permit criminal behaviour. Situational techniques involve the systematic manipulation of aspects of the immediate environments of potential offenders in an attempt to block or inhibit criminal responses. In this book it is argued that the same principles of situational management used in crime prevention may be usefully applied to the prison setting to help reduce incidents of assault, rape, self-injury, drug use, escape, collective disorder and so forth.

The situational approach depends upon a dynamic view of human action, one that stresses the fundamental variability of behaviour according to immediate circumstances. According to the situational perspective, behaviour can only be understood in terms of an interaction between the characteristics of an actor and the characteristics of the environment in which an act is performed. People behave the way they do because of who they are and where they are. The relationship between situations and behaviour can be examined from a variety of theoretical perspectives. Some authors see situations primarily as 'opportunities' that potential offenders rationally exploit (Clarke, 1997; Cornish and Clarke, 1986). Thus, for example, an offender might succumb to the temptation to steal if they encounter goods

3

that have been left unattended. For these authors, situational prevention involves reducing crime opportunities by making criminal behaviour a less attractive option. Other perspectives propose a more intimate and deterministic relationship in which situations may influence individuals in ways that they may not even be aware and induce them to perform behaviour that they would otherwise not perform (Wortley, 1997, 1998). For example, psychological stress associated with overcrowding might produce heightened levels of aggression and precipitate a violent response. In these cases, prevention may involve a range of strategies that reduce the inclination to offend.

The book adopts an eclectic view of the person–situation relationship and an inclusive approach to situational prevention. Accordingly, a broad perspective is taken here of the situational nature of prison behaviour and of just what situational prison control entails. Notwithstanding the breadth of this interpretation, two general defining features of the situational approach can be identified. First, situational interventions are unashamedly ephemeral in their effect on potential offenders. No particular claim is made for situational strategies to maintain an impact on behaviour once an individual has left the situation in question. The efficacy of situational prevention is based on the situational dependence of behaviour. By this same logic, a potential offender who leaves a 'crime-proofed' situation without offending will continue to be susceptible to situational conditions when he/she enters a new criminogenic situation. That is, situational intervention is about creating safe situations rather than creating safe individuals. In this regard, the situational approach in prison is clearly distinguished from attempts to change prisoner behaviour through therapeutic means such as counselling, therapeutic communities, anger-management programmes, assertion training, and so forth. That is not to say that such programmes do not have a situational element, however. It may be argued, for example, that prison programmes contribute to reductions in prison misbehaviour through their time-structuring properties, irrespective of their content and therapeutic rationales.

Second, situational prevention is unashamedly reductionist in nature. As far as possible, a situational analysis focuses on the relationship between *particular* aspects of the environment and *particular* kinds of behaviour. In the case of situational prison control, this means identifying specific components of, or locations within, the prison environment that are problematic. For example, a situational analysis might seek to discover if disorder is more prevalent in a particular wing, or a particular part of a wing, and if so, what it is about this sub-environment that allows or encourages problems to occur. Similarly, the situational approach also means breaking down the concept of prison disorder into separate kinds of behaviours. The causes of – and solutions to – assaults by prisoners against other prisoners may be very different from the causes of and solutions to assaults by prisoners against guards. Taking this even further, it is probable that there are a number of useful distinctions to be made among various kinds of assaults by prisoners against other prisoners. Assaults associated with theft and those motivated by revenge might require quite different methods of control. The desired endpoint of a situational analysis is an intervention that is tailor-made to meet the conditions of the particular problem under consideration. In this sense, situational prison control is a bottom-up model of prevention whereby overall reductions in problem behaviour are achieved through the accumulation of small successes.

Despite the empirical success of situational methods in community settings, it is likely that a situational approach to prison control will not be universally welcomed. Situational crime prevention remains a controversial – and, it must be said, largely peripheral – model in criminology. The perspective suffers from a serious image problem. In particular, there is a tendency to credit situational prevention as involving little more than a locks-and-bolts approach to controlling behaviour. In equating the situational approach with obtrusive, target-hardening techniques, critics have created a 'straw man' that they proceed to knock down on two counts. The first is theoretical. Situational prevention, it is said, ignores the criminal dispositions of the offender and so can never make more than a trivial impact on criminal behaviour. The second criticism is ideological in nature. Even if situational strategies are shown to work, it is argued, they represent a sinister move towards an Orwellian state, and *ought not* to be employed. Both of these general objections to situational crime prevention are also likely to be raised in the specific case of situational prison control.

The efficacy of situational prison control

Situational crime prevention is invariably attacked by its critics as being simplistic and misguided (Bottoms, 1990; Trasler, 1986). To the extent that situational approaches are shown to work, acknowledgement of that success is grudgingly given. The observation that crime might be controlled by locks and bolts is seen as both trivial and common sense. Moreover, at best such situational strategies are thought to offer no more than pragmatic, stop-gap solutions to crime problems. It is argued that situational prevention does not attack the root causes of crime, and thus it leaves the criminal disposition of the offender intact. Blocking crime avenues at one location, the argument goes, will simply encourage potential offenders to seek out more conducive locations. Thus, the critics contend, situational prevention may displace crime but will not prevent it.

Approached from this position, a situational analysis of prison control might be considered not only superficial, but also somewhat redundant. After all, at first glance the prison would already appear to be the epitome of a regulated, target-hardened environment, purpose-built to maximise control over behaviour. Since Bentham's panopticon vision of 200 years ago, approaches to prison design and management have been driven largely by the desire to monitor and contain prisoner activities. Observation towers, guards, thick walls, bars, razor wire, electronic surveillance, and so forth are all situational elements specifically calculated to reduce opportunities for prisoners to misbehave. In fact, situational prevention has been disparagingly equated with prison-like conditions (Weiss, 1987: 121). What, then, it might be asked, can prison administrators learn from the situational approach?

But traditional approaches to prison security and control are narrow and often crude applications of situational principles. For one thing, despite the appearance of pervasive control, most prisons offer prisoners ample opportunities to misbehave and the prevention and detection of rule violation is at best haphazard. The very fact that prisons have problems with assault and other forms of disorder is evidence of this. Moreover, the thinking behind traditional methods of control is not really situational at all. Sole reliance on coercive and oppressive control methods derives from a conviction that prisoners are inherently unpredictable and dangerous, and must therefore be constrained at all times. That is, traditional approaches to prison control have evolved from static, dispositional models of prisoner behaviour. According to this view, prison regimes might succeed in physically suppressing and containing trouble, but in the final analysis the causes of prison misbehaviour are to be found in the antisocial tendencies of prisoners.

The interaction between situations and behaviour is more subtle and complex than prevention approaches exclusively based on physical containment immediately suggest. Situations affect behaviour in fundamental ways. The problem in promoting this broader picture of situational prevention, however, is that it is based on a counterintuitive premise. Human beings have an entrenched cognitive bias to see individuals as the authors of their own behaviour. Even when someone's actions are unambiguously forced upon them by circumstances beyond their control, observers typically underestimate the role of these outside pressures and construct causal explanations that assume personal agency on the part of the actor (Jones, 1979; Ross, 1977). Fundamental attributional error, as this propensity is called, is accompanied by an exaggerated belief in the stability of the personal characteristics of others and overconfidence that their behaviour is therefore relatively constant from one situation to the next. No doubt the tendency to categorise others in terms of predictable dispositions is an efficient information processing strategy that helps people to deal with the complexity of the world around them. However, this ingrained faith in personal control over behaviour makes the efficacy of situational prevention difficult for people to accept.

The person-centred bias is evident not only in naive accounts of other people's actions, but also in the traditional way psychologists and psychiatrists have sought to explain behaviour. Classic personality and psychodynamic theories locate the determinants of behaviour firmly within the individual. These theories stress the role of internal constructs such as traits, attitudes, needs and drives. Within this framework, personality inventories, projective tests and clinical interviews can be employed to reveal the underlying psychological mechanisms that govern behaviour. Following diagnosis of the problem, the task of modifying misbehaviour requires effecting changes to the individual's basic personality structures.

When applied to the problem of prison control, this approach has meant that a great deal of the research effort has gone into constructing personality profiles of those prisoners considered most likely to be violent, to do themselves injury or to escape. Prevention of particular problem behaviours in prison has been seen in terms of more effective classification systems that identify those prisoners who require special attention. These studies, however, have yielded modest returns. At best, prediction models built upon prisoner characteristics are able to account for 30 per cent of the variance (Carbonell *et al.*, 1985). The large number of false positives these models typically produce (i.e. unfulfilled predictions that certain prisoners will misbehave) means that management decisions tend to be conservative. Many more prisoners than necessary are subjected to special precautionary conditions.

In his seminal book, *Personality and Assessment*, Mischel (1968: 281–301) challenged the dominant view of personality as a cross-situationally consistent and longitudinally enduring predisposition. In fact, Mischel argued, behaviour is highly situationally specific. A person who may be described by others as aggressive does not behave uniformly in an aggressive manner. Rather, aggression is displayed occasionally and only when certain favourable conditions are met. Similarly, most people, if they think for a moment about their own behaviour, will recognise that there is a great deal of variability in the way that they act. They realise that they are neither always confident nor timid, polite nor rude, or honest nor dishonest. Rather, they are aware that, as they move from one situation to the next, how they behave depends upon where they are and whom they are with. They will admit, too, that at times they have done things that they regard as completely out of character and will explain these aberrations as having been caused by particular circumstances at the time. However, it is more difficult for people to see the same variability in others. The behaviour of others often appears more stable because people tend to encounter their friends and associates in similar contexts from one occasion to the next. That is, often what is interpreted as dispositional stability is in reality situational stability.

Mischel was not the first to highlight the crucial role of situations in behaviour, but his cogent articulation of the issue had a major impact on the theoretical debate about the location of the determinants of behaviour. Most modern psychological theories now acknowledge to a greater or lesser extent the importance of the person–situation interaction. Thus, far from being simplistic and atheoretical, the situational perspective reflects contemporary theorising about the fundamental nature of human behaviour. Situational prevention does not ignore the 'root cause' of behaviour; situations *are* a 'root cause' of behaviour.

In fact, there ought to be less resistance to situational thinking in the prison context than has been the case in the crime prevention field. It can be argued that a quasi-situational perspective on prison behaviour predates by forty years the development of situational crime prevention. The classic micro-sociological descriptions of prison life presented by Sykes (1958), Goffman (1961) and others pioneered the idea in criminology that behaviour is profoundly shaped by current circumstances and events. Prison was seen as a generator of – not just location for – aberrant behaviour. Violent and otherwise pathological behaviour of prison inmates was not, these theorists contended, the result of 'imported' deviance, that is, the simple and inevitable consequence of the concentration of so many (supposed) antisocial individuals in one place. Rather, prisoner behaviour, regarded as deviant by the standards of the general community, was a form of adaptation to the social and psychological deprivations of the institutional prison regime – a normal reaction to an abnormal environment. Misbehaviour in prison, then, could be understood as a feature of a defensive and oppositional prisoner subculture produced by the 'pains of imprisonment'.

The deprivation model of prison behaviour has been a major theoretical force behind the argument that the key to changing prison behaviour lies in changing the prison itself. However, despite the undoubted seminal role of the deprivation model in orienting researchers towards broad environmental solutions to prison problems, fully-fledged situational analyses of prison misbehaviour are rare. The theoretical rationales underpinning the deprivation model have remained largely at the socio-cultural level. Prisoner deviance is seen as a sociological phenomenon stemming ultimately from the social organisation inherent in the total institution. Addressing the problems of imprisonment is seen to require at the very least an institution-wide approach and, more likely, changes to the system as a whole. This global, systemic view of prisoner deviance does not readily lend itself to the more fine-grained, individual-level analysis that situational prevention usually entails and that is the primary focus of this book. The deprivation model provides a starting-point for a situational analysis of prisoner behaviour, but further theoretical work is required to develop a true situational model of prison control.

The propriety of situational prison control

Some of the fiercest attacks on situational prevention have been made not because it is assumed that situational techniques will not work, but rather because it is feared that they might. These criticisms question the social and ethical desirability of situational methods. Situational crime prevention has been cited as just another example of the inexorable trend towards increased, pervasive social control (Bottoms, 1990; Garland, 1996; Weiss, 1987). Critics have painted an apocalyptic vision of the target-hardened society constrained and divided by locks, bars, electronic alarms, surveillance cameras and security guards. Any benefits in reduced crime are judged to be not worth the social and human costs involved.

Few critics of situational prevention have commented specifically on the desirability of applying situational measures to prison. (The few exceptions include Bottoms *et al.*, 1995 and Sparks *et al.*, 1996.) However, in general terms social scientists have shown a deep suspicion of any suggestions to increase controls on prisoners and, certainly, few academic commentators would support moves to make prisons even more fortress-like in the way outlined above. On the contrary, the weight of learned opinion is that prisons need to become less oppressive and pay greater attention to prisoners' rights (Bottoms *et al.*, 1995; Clear, 1994; Levinson, 1982; Sparks *et al.*, 1996).

Situational prison control need not be incompatible with these goals. Like the criticism of the efficacy of situational prevention, the attacks on the propriety of situational methods typically centre on target-hardening aspects of the model. But, as has been argued, situational prevention is more than target hardening. The charge that situational prevention will lead to a fortress society in which fearful and distrustful citizens barricade themselves against potential victimisation has been vigorously defended (Clarke, 1997: 37–9; Felson and Clarke, 1997). Many situational interventions employed in the community to restrict criminal activities are unobtrusive and, rather than create social division, actually make people feel safer. Better street lighting is a simple example (Painter and Farrington, 1997). Some interventions do not involve trying to block behaviour at all but, rather, attempt to eliminate environmental conditions that invite a criminal response in the first place. These interventions often involve making environments more pleasant and liveable. Thus, night-club violence may be effectively reduced by modifying the situational factors – excessive alcohol consumption, lack of food availability, lack of entertainment, crowding and so forth – that encourage violent responses (Homel *et al.*, 1997).

Following this argument, when situational principles are applied systematically in prison there is the potential to design a *less* fortress-like environment. Creative and targeted situational interventions may allow a more general easing in restrictions. Improved perimeter security, for example, may reduce the need for restrictive internal controls. Modern technology, often regarded as emblematic of the dehumanising nature of the situational approach, can reduce the reliance on traditional heavy architecture and hard physical barriers (Atlas and Dunham, 1990: 57). Personal staff alarms can permit greater prisoner–staff interaction, the thick, high walls of the traditional prison can be replaced with less obtrusive electronic perimeter systems, viewing windows made from new plastics can replace metal bars and grills, and so on. Further, to the extent that prison disorder is caused by pressures in the prison environment, prison reform and prison control may actually go hand in hand. Put simply, frustrated and angry prisoners are difficult to control and it is in the interests of prison administrators to ensure the needs of prisoners are met.

An added dimension in prison, of course, is the unequal distribution of power. Prisoners are in a vulnerable position and particular care does need to be taken to ensure that abuses do not occur in the name of control. Felson and Clarke (1997) argue that the ethical test for a situational intervention is whether it satisfies liberal-democratic principles of fairness, equity and respect for individual rights. Historically, the treatment of prisoners has frequently violated these standards. However, there is no reason to suppose that situational control has inherent difficulties passing these tests. Any form of treatment can be misused and situational approaches are no more susceptible to abuse than any other control methods. They may even be less susceptible. Attempts to change prisoners' values and behaviours through therapeutic interventions, for example, are arguably more paternalistic, intrusive and disregarding of individual rights than are situational methods of control. Similarly, control methods that depend upon the identification of dangerous or at-risk prisoners are more likely to unfairly discriminate against particular groups than are environmental changes that are applied uniformly across the institution. Maintaining ethical standards of treatment for prisoners is an important matter that requires ongoing attention, but it is not an issue specifically linked with the use of situational control methods.

All that said, it is undoubtedly true that situational control in prison might be coercive and force prisoners to do things that they would prefer not to do. This, at the end of the day, is the inescapable nature of imprisonment. Even the most liberal prison regimes restrict prisoners in fundamental ways (such as not allowing them leave when they please). Some level of coercion is an obvious political reality. Society expects to have a prison system in which prisoners are under control. Moreover, a well-controlled institution is in the best interests of prisoners. Perhaps the most persuasive defence of situational prison control is that those who suffer most from a lack of effective control in prison are prisoners themselves. There is a tradition among many social scientists to write about disorder and control in prison as a battle between oppressed prisoners and an authoritarian regime. Sykes and Goffman fall into this category to varying degrees. The fact is that the greatest risk faced by a prisoner is victimisation from other prisoners. It is now argued by many commentators that one of the unintended consequences of the development of more liberal regimes in the 1970s and 1980s was a power shift from staff to prisoner elites and an accompanying increase in prison violence and disorder (Carroll, 1982; DiIulio, 1987; Ekland-Olson, 1986; Engel and Rothman, 1984; Unseem and Kimball, 1989). On the question of ethics, a fundamental right of prisoners is surely the right to live in a safe and certain environment.

Conclusions and scope of the book

Prisons are enclosed, all-encompassing environments that exert powerful influences on the day-to-day behaviours of prisoners. Too often the influence of the prison environment has been to produce violent and unproductive behaviour from the prison inhabitants. However, it is this very power to influence that gives hope that there may be solutions to many of the control problems that plague prisons. The principles of situational prevention provide the rationale for analysing and modifying the environmental conditions that generate or allow prison misbehaviour and disorder.

A chief attraction of the situational perspective is its 'do-ability'. The behaviour-specific focus means that situational interventions need not involve environmental changes on a grand scale. Situational measures by and large provide relatively quick, practical and cost-effective solutions to immediate problems. Prisons in particular lend themselves to situational interventions. As enclosed environments prisons offer a great deal of control over situational variables. One of the limitations of situational prevention in the community is its ability to deal with highly mobile crimes. Rape, for example, typically does not occur in any designated place unlike, say, thefts from automatic teller-machines. It is difficult, therefore, to crime-proof every location in which rape might occur (although some major hot-spots may be identified and made safer). This is less problematic in prison, where there are a more limited number of locations to consider and a greater ability to make any necessary environmental changes.

Many of the general criticisms of situational prevention are premised on a narrow, target-hardening conception of the scope of the approach. It has been argued in this introductory chapter that situational prevention is much broader than target hardening, and indeed, that many interventions actually depend upon a softening of the environment. With this as a central theme, this book explores the theory and practice of situational prison control, and assesses the empirical validity of situational approaches based on the available research evidence. There is, in fact, very little literature that explicitly applies the situational prevention model to the prison. However, there is a relatively large body of work that is broadly sympathetic to a situational view on prison behaviour and control. There is a long tradition of situational control in prison, even if it has not been recognised as such. Most prison control involves some manipulation of the prison environment, albeit often crude and unsystematic manipulation.

The book is divided into two parts, the first looking at situational prison control in general, and the second analysing specific examples of prison misbehaviour and its control from a situational perspective. The purpose of part I is to set out the theoretical rationales underpinning situational prison control and to propose an integrative framework by which prison control may be conceptualised. The first of the three chapters in this section (chapter 2) reviews major situational theories of behaviour, namely behaviour theory, social learning theory, theories of social influence, frustration-aggression hypothesis, environmental psychology and rational choice perspective. An examination of these perspectives reveals two distinct sorts of situational influences on behaviour. Some situations *regulate* behaviour by providing the opportunity for individuals to behave in a way that will deliver benefits to them. Other situations actively *precipitate* behaviour by prompting or provoking certain actions.

Chapter 3 examines current methods of prison control. While few prison administrators explicitly employ situational theory, unavoidably many attempts to control prisoner behaviour involve situational methods. There are three broad aspects of the prison environment that might be manipulated to control behaviour – the physical environment (architecture and security hardware), the social environment (population characteristics) and the institutional regime (management strategies). A review of these methods reveals two opposing approaches to prison control. One approach to control is to 'tighten-up', that is, to harden the prison environment and clamp down on prisoner freedoms. The other approach involves 'loosening-off' – softening the prison environment and maximising prisoner freedoms.

Chapter 4 presents a model of situational prison control that attempts to integrate theories of situational behaviour and methods of prison control, and to reconcile the apparently contradictory impulses of tightening-up and loosening-off. It is argued that control approaches based on restricting prisoners primarily address regulators of behaviour (i.e. opportunities). Methods that seek to ease restrictions on prisoners derive largely from theories that stress the role of situational precipitators of behaviour. Both of these approaches are incorporated into a two-stage model of situational prison control.

Part II looks at specific control problems. As has been noted, a crucial aspect of the situational approach is its specificity. Hence, a distinctive feature of the book is the breaking down of disorder into specific misbehaviours. Chapters 5–11 examine, respectively, prisoner-prisoner violence, sexual assaults, prisoner-staff violence, self-harm, drug use, escapes and collective disorder. In each case, the chapter begins with an examination of the situational nature of the behaviour in question, then reviews the available empirical research on situational interventions, and finally fits the data to the two-stage control model. The final chapter (chapter 12) provides an overall assessment of the utility of the proposed two-stage control model, and of situational prison control more generally.

Two final comments on the scope of the book are warranted. First, there has been a deliberate attempt in researching for the book to provide an international perspective on prison control. The book is based on no particular prison system but, rather, information has been drawn widely from relevant English-language publications. Inevitably, the majority of citations are American and British, reflecting the volume of research emanating from these two countries. However, research from other countries including Canada, Australia, New Zealand and various European countries has also been used. Where relevant, the country in which research has been conducted is identified. Secondly, the book looks primarily at control in adult male prisons. This is simply because the overwhelming bulk of research is focused on male institutions. The extent to which results are transferable from adult males to females and juveniles is a matter of speculation. In the few places that cited research is based on female or juvenile institutions, this fact is acknowledged.

CHAPTER 2

Situational theories of prison behaviour

Despite the traditional dominance of the person-centred focus in psychology and psychiatry, there is also a long history of the recognition of situational forces. Situational prevention is underpinned by a compelling body of research evidence on the crucial role of the person–situation interaction. This chapter reviews some of the psychological theories with significant situational components – behaviour theory, social learning theory, theories of social influence, frustration-aggression hypothesis, environmental psychology and rational choice perspective – highlighting the implications of these accounts for prison behaviour and its control.

Behaviour theory

Behaviour theory, of course, has always regarded the environment as the prime determinant of behaviour. However, in discussing behavioural explanations of crime, criminology texts have typically focused on the role of historical rather than immediate environments. That is, most attention has been given to the way that behavioural patterns and habits are acquired. In effect, behaviour theory has been treated little differently from traditional personality theories. The impression often conveyed is that individuals learn criminal habits that are internalised and then displayed in a more or less consistent manner. Changing criminal behaviour has been seen to involve for each individual offender the elimination of maladaptive behavioural patterns and the learning of new adaptive ones. Yet the immediate environment is crucial within the behavioural paradigm. When Pavlov conditioned his dogs to salivate at the sound of a bell, he not only demonstrated that reflex behaviour could be learned, but that performance of such behaviour was situationally dependent. The surest way to prevent the dogs from salivating was to avoid ringing a bell.

In its original, radical form, behaviour theory presents a hard deterministic model of human action (Skinner, 1953). According to the principle of determinism, free will is an illusion and human beings simply respond helplessly to the various environmental forces acting upon them. Radical behaviourists are not concerned with what goes on inside people's heads (and for that reason the approach is sometimes called black-box psychology), just with stimulus-response (S-R) relationships. At the situational level, behaviour is subject to two types of environmental stimuli. First, behaviour must be instigated by the presence in the environment of a relevant cue. Then, the continued performance of behaviour is controlled by the consequences the behaviour produces.

Environmental cues

Cues refer to stimuli in the environment that govern if and when behaviour is emitted. Stimuli can be either eliciting or discriminative. Eliciting stimuli are established through classical conditioning and trigger reflex or respondent behaviours (i.e. behaviours that are passive, automatic reactions to a situation). The bell that caused the dogs in Pavlov's study to salivate is an example of an eliciting stimulus. There are many everyday examples where particular environmental conditions become associated with predictable physiological or behavioural responses – viewing erotic images produces sexual arousal, the sight of blood makes many people feel nauseous, the smell of food induces hunger, listening to a familiar piece of music can arouse feelings of nostalgia and so forth. With respect to antisocial behaviour, eliciting stimuli may be particularly important in sex offending. Marshall (1988) reported that one-third of rapists and child-molesters surveyed claimed to have been incited to offend by viewing pornography. Managing behaviour through the control of eliciting stimuli is a technique widely used in clinical psychology. For example, a person trying to keep to a diet might be instructed to ensure that all food is put away in cupboards and not left out in view where it is likely to trigger feelings of hunger.

Discriminative stimuli are established through operant conditioning and signal the likely outcome of a particular behaviour. By indicating imminent rewards and punishments, discriminative stimuli are guides for future action and so initiate operant behaviours (i.e. behaviours that are goal directed and involve the person acting on the environment). Depending upon the nature of the likely outcome – learned through previous experience – behaviour will be pursued or avoided. For example, a green traffic light signals to drivers that they may proceed safely through an intersection; observing a police officer in the rear-view mirror signals that they will nevertheless need to take care not to speed when doing so. Based on this principle, discriminative stimuli may be introduced into an environment to encourage or discourage certain behaviours. So signs that clarify expected standards of behaviour and specify the consequences for non-compliance act as prompts for appropriate behaviour; strategically placed litter bins prompt people not to litter; symbolic territorial boundary-markers (low fences, shrubs, personal items etc.) are signals not to trespass. Such simple tactics can be surprisingly effective. Geller *et al.* (1983) found that honesty prompts attached to self-service newspaper racks reduced thefts by 15 per cent. Watson (1996) found that anti-graffiti signs in college restrooms resulted in an immediate cessation of vandalism, a result maintained in a three-month follow-up.

From a behavioural perspective, the prison environment may be reduced to a complex collection of behaviour-evoking cues. These cues are often subtle and individuals do not need to engage in any cognitive deliberation about them, nor do they even need to be aware of their effects. For example, Berkowitz (1983) found that the mere presence in the immediate environment of a firearm increases the probability of aggression. Berkowitz hypothesised that through their repeated association with violence firearms (and similar symbols of aggression) become eliciting stimuli that conjure aggressive images and moods and facilitate overt aggression. Based on Berkowitz's findings, Veno and Davidson (1977: 403) have suggested that the observation by prisoners of guards armed with weapons and other militaristic paraphernalia may be one factor contributing to prisoner violence.

Consequent determinants

Consequent determinants refer to the effect of behaviour on the immediate environment. Behaviours that produce reinforcing effects are strengthened and those that produce punishing effects are weakened. Behaviours can be strengthened either by positive reinforcement – the receipt of a reward – or negative reinforcement – the removal of something unpleasant. For example, getting a pay on a slot-machine positively reinforces further playing; relief from suffering negatively reinforces a person with toothache to visit the dentist. Similarly, behaviour can be weakened by positive punishment or by the withdrawal of usual rewards (negative punishment). Thus, if the dentist causes a great deal of pain when treating the toothache, the person will be deterred from returning; if the person gets no more pays on the slot-machine, eventually the playing behaviour will cease.

The management of consequences is probably the most common way that people seek to control the behaviour of others. Intuitive approaches to discipline involve the application of basic principles of reinforcement and punishment. The delivery of rewards and the imposition of punishments – the use of carrots and sticks – represent crucial control tools in prison (e.g. Liebling *et al.*, 1999). Perhaps the most significant long-term reward held out to prisoners is the promise of early release via remission or parole. In the shorter term, Vagg (1994: 220–7) found that common sanctions employed in prison included denial of the right to purchase goods, stoppage of earnings, cellular confinement, denial of reading material, removal from work and restrictions on letter-writing. As Vaag's list shows, more often than not privileges in prison are used in negative punishment rather than positive reinforcement. That is, the tendency is to withdraw privileges in the event of undesirable behaviour, rather than to hold out the prospect of rewards if certain specified behavioural targets are met.

Social learning theory

Social learning theory presents a soft deterministic version of the behavioural perspective (Bandura, 1976, 1977). In contrast to the black-box approach of the behaviourists, social learning theorists endow individuals with the capacity for conceptual thought. According to social learning theory, the environment does not act directly to produce behavioural responses (as suggested in the S-R paradigm) but is subject to cognitive mediation (the stimulus-organism-response or S-O-R paradigm). Environmental events must be perceived, interpreted and evaluated, in the process of which a range of perceptual errors, misattributions, flawed inferences and so forth can occur. Behaviour, then, is not the product of an objective reality but is performed in response to an internalised version of the outside environment.

The cognitive basis of social learning theory has a number of important implications for the proposed role of situational factors. Five specific situational effects in social learning are modelling, expectancy effects, vicarious reinforcement, social reinforcement and cognitive disengagement.

Modelling

Modelling refers to the setting of a behavioural example that others are induced to imitate. For example, children who observe a model engaging in aggressive play are likely themselves to also play aggressively (Bandura, 1965). Modelling effects are particularly powerful if the model is of high status or is respected by the observer. For example, Lefkowitz *et al.* (1955) demonstrated that a pedestrian successfully crossing the street against a red light would readily induce others to follow. Imitation was greater when the model had the appearance of a well-dressed businessman than when the model was poorly dressed. Similarly, when work supervisors engage in theft from the organisation, subordinates are more likely to also engage in theft (Adams, 1981; Cherrington and Cherrington, 1985; Hollinger, 1989; Snyder *et al.*, 1991). Models for imitation do not have to appear in person but can be represented symbolically in the mass media. The incidence of suicide has been found to increase immediately following the portrayal of suicide in popular television programmes (Gould and Shäffer, 1989; Phillips, 1989; Phillips and Carstensen, 1990; Schmidtke and Häfner, 1989). Positive correlations have been found between the viewing of television violence by children and concurrent measures of aggression (Leyens *et al.*, 1975; Rosenthal, 1990).

Controlling modelling effects by increasing exposure to prosocial models or reducing the exposure to undesirable models is a popular method of attempting to influence behaviour. Advertisers use celebrities to endorse products in the hope that the public will be induced to imitate the celebrities and also use the product. A similar hope underpins public education campaigns (litter reduction, anti-smoking, seat-belt-wearing) that enlist the aid of sporting personalities and other respected figures. On the other side of the coin, the same principle is used to justify restrictions on the content of television programmes: for example, less sensational coverage of crime and suicide stories in news items (Phillips and Carstensen, 1990; Surette, 1990).

In prison, modelling can help to explain the tendency for young prisoners to emulate the example of older, more experienced prisoners. Perhaps more positively, it is hoped that prison guards can provide prosocial role models. The tendency for media reports of a protest or riot in one prison to spark similar activities in other prisons is an example of the transmission of modelling influences by symbolic means (Davies, 1991: 121).

Expectancy effects

Expectancy effects refer to the tendency for individuals to respond to preconceived beliefs about a situation. In a classic demonstration of expectancy effects, Marlatt *et al.* (1973) found that subjects who were led to believe that they had ingested alcohol, although in reality had been given a placebo, behaved as if they were intoxicated. The subjects responded to their interpretation of the event and on the basis of their expectations about the effects of alcohol rather than to alcohol *per se*.

Expectancies can be altered by providing relevant situational cues. For example, Graham and Homel (1996: 173–4) argued that levels of night-club violence were related to the reputations that the night-clubs had acquired, and that these reputations were in turn partly determined by physical characteristics of the premises. Patrons visited certain night-clubs anticipating that they would be involved in violent incidents and this expectation acted as a self-fulfilling prophecy. Gentrifying the decor of violent night-clubs signals that non-violent behaviour is now expected from patrons. It seems plausible to suggest that certain prisons may similarly have reputations for violence, enhanced by their physical appearance, that in turn makes violence more likely. Similarly, prisoners are more likely to attempt to destroy vandal-proof furnishings than domestic-quality furnishing because of the implied message that vandalism is expected (Wright and Goodstein, 1989: 255; Zupan, 1991: 87–9).

Vicarious reinforcement
Individuals can draw appropriate contingency rules by observing the reinforcing experiences of others. By 'imagining if' they were placed in that situation, individuals learn to anticipate the outcomes of new, untried behaviours. Imitation, then, becomes more likely if a model is observed being rewarded for a particular behaviour (Bandura, 1965). On the other hand, vicarious punishment provides a basis for the concept of general deterrence.

Social reinforcement
In behaviour theory, consequent determinants are typically seen in material terms (money, goods and so on). Social learning theory, on the other hand, emphasises the role of social rewards and punishments. Social rewards include praise and increased status; conversely, social punishments are public condemnation and decreased status. Social reinforcement might be particularly important within delinquent subcultures. Taking part in antisocial activities is a way of achieving acceptance and status within the gang. Given the subcultural dynamics of the prison social structure (Goffman, 1961; Sykes, 1958), a great deal of prisoner deviance may be explained as status-seeking behaviour (Veno and Davidson, 1977: 404).

Cognitive disengagement
According to the cognitive-mediation model, self-generated cognitions in the form of mental imagery and self-talk can produce behavioural effects similar to those produced by actual experience. Erotic fantasies, for example, can readily elicit sexual arousal. Similarly, behaviour can

be self-reinforced and self-punished. Human beings engage in ongoing assessment of their own performance, making judgements of self-adequacy against personal standards of behaviour. Depending upon the outcome of this self-assessment, self-congratulatory or self-condemning cognitions will be produced to help strengthen or weaken the behaviour in question.

Of particular relevance for the situational perspective is Bandura's (1976: 225–7; 1977: 155–8; Bandura *et al.*, 1996) suggestion that internal control mechanisms may on occasions be disengaged, so freeing individuals from the normally constraining effects of self-condemnation. Bandura's concept of disengagement is very similar to Sykes and Matza's (1957) neutralisation theory. Sykes and Matza advanced the concept of neutralisation within a sociological perspective in order to explain the fact that many delinquents seemed to drift in and out of delinquency. They argued that delinquents were not morally committed to their antisocial acts, but, rather, periodically neutralised the internalised moral prohibitions against their misbehaviours. The argument advanced in both neutralisation and social learning theories is that offenders are often able to avoid self-censure by cognitively redefin- ing crime situations in a way that minimises their personal culpability in their own eyes. Bandura (1977: 156) suggested that cognitive disengage- ment techniques can be grouped into four broad categories – those aimed at minimising the wrongness of the behaviour (e.g. 'at least I'm not a child- molester'), those aimed at minimising the degree of personal responsibility for the behaviour (e.g. 'I was drunk and could not help myself'), those aimed at minimising the negative consequences of the behaviour (e.g. 'the house was insured so no one was really hurt'), and those aimed at minimising the worth or blamelessness of the victim (e.g. 'she was just a whore') (see Wortley, 1996: 118–23).

While Sykes and Matza recognised that delinquent behaviour was episodic, they proposed no firm rules for the onset of the drift into delin- quency. Bandura extended neutralisation theory in a crucial way by spec- ifying situational conditions that encouraged cognitive disengagement of self-criticism. Bandura argued that the ability to engage in self-exoneration often depended upon immediate situations and environments that helped people obscure the true nature of their actions. The human conscience is highly malleable and sensitive to the context in which behaviour is per- formed. Given the right circumstances (such as in times of war), ordinary individuals are often capable of great brutality. Bandura suggested, for ex- ample, that social systems in which individuals are treated in anonymous and impersonal ways facilitate neutralisations denying the worth of the victim. On the other hand, it is difficult to derogate and victimise individuals who are in situations that invest them with personal qualities (Bandura *et al.*, 1975). Similarly, the division of labour and lines of authority within organisations facilitates corruption and brutality by allowing individuals to hide behind a collective responsibility (Bandura, 1976: 226). Restructuring arrangements so individuals perform discrete tasks forces them to take personal responsibility for their actions. Given the dehumanising and bureaucratic nature of many prison regimes, the relevance of neutralisation theory to explanations of behaviour in prison is readily apparent.

Theories of social influence

Human beings are social animals whose behaviour is shaped by their interactions and affiliations with other members of the species. Social psychology is concerned with the ways in which people influence one another. Social influences have a crucial role in the development of an individual's core attitudes, beliefs and values. Moreover, a great deal of behaviour is governed by immediate social settings. It is a major principle of social psychology that people behave differently in the company of others than when they are alone. Four social-situational effects are outlined in this section – conformity, obedience, compliance and deindividuation.

Conformity

Conformity refers to the tendency for individuals in groups to adopt group norms and standards of behaviour, even when these contradict personally held beliefs and values. Asch (1955) provided the classic laboratory demonstration of social conformity. Subjects were shown a card on which were drawn three lines of obviously different lengths. They were shown another card on which was drawn a single line equal in length to one of the three lines. Subjects were required to identify the matching line. However, each subject had to announce their judgements in a room of between seven and nine confederate subjects, all of whom first publicly gave the wrong answer. Asch found up to 78 per cent conformity with the obviously incorrect response. Asch further found that conformity levels dropped (though were still apparent) when subjects were permitted to write their answers rather than announce them to the group. Thus, it seems that conformity involves two considerations. Some conformity occurs because of informational social influence. Individuals refer to the group for guidelines for correct behaviour. Conformity also occurs as a result of normative social influence. In this case, individuals accede to group pressure in order to avoid disapproval and to gain acceptance.

Peer pressure to conform is commonly thought to be an important factor in delinquency (Akers *et al.*, 1979; Jensen, 1972; Warr and Stafford, 1991). Parents screen their children's associates in a commonsense attempt to filter out undesirable influences and to prevent their children from getting involved with the wrong crowd. Corruption within organisations is a good example of the power of conformity to induce illegal behaviour. A new employee entering an organisation in which corrupt practices are common faces social pressures from co-workers to also engage in those practices (Altheide *et al.*, 1978; Clark and Hollinger, 1983; Horning, 1970). Greenberg (1997: 98–100) suggested that rotating workers so that stable groups did not form made it difficult for inappropriate group norms to develop.

The prison environment exerts powerful pressures for conformity. Classic sociological descriptions of prison life emphasise the division between prisoners and guards and the formation within the prison walls of two separate societies, each demanding adherence from their members to informal social rules and expectations (Goffman, 1961; Sykes, 1958). The best-known empirical study of prison social dynamics is the Stanford prison experiment (Haney *et al.*, 1973; Haney and Zimbardo, 1998). This research involved the creation of a simulated prison in the basement of Stanford University. Male college student volunteers were recruited to play the parts of prisoners and guards. Zimbardo and his colleagues found that early in the experiment both groups began displaying pathological behaviours – the prisoners became servile and showed signs of psychological distress while many guards became brutal and authoritarian. The researchers explained these results by suggesting that both groups adopted the explicit and implicit social norms associated with their assigned roles. They further argued that conformity to these roles was supported by practices and conditions found in most prisons – the guards' uniform intensified their sense of power and collective identity; the inmates' uniform in contrast was humiliating and dehumanising; the use of numbers rather than names stripped away personal identity; the dependency of inmates on guards for daily needs was emasculating and promoted helplessness.

Obedience

Obedience is the following of a direct command issued by someone perceived to possess legitimate authority. While some degree of obedience is essential to the smooth running of society, psychologists have been interested in the tendency for individuals to comply with unreasonable commands and to perpetrate all manner of cruelty in the process of following orders. The tendency for people to obey the orders of an authority figure was demonstrated empirically in a series of studies conducted by Stanley Milgram (1974). In the prototype study (pp. 13–26), a confederate subject was strapped into what was portrayed as an electric chair. In an adjoining room a naive subject was placed before an impressive-looking but phoney shock generator. The subject was told that the purpose of the experiment was to examine the effects of punishment on learning. The confederate deliberately gave incorrect responses to questions upon which the subject was instructed to administer electric shocks as punishment. Despite the confederate screaming and begging in apparent agony, almost two-thirds of the subjects continued with the experiment and administered the maximum shock levels.

In subsequent studies, Milgram (1974) found that the pressure on subjects to obey could be manipulated in a number of ways. He found that obedience varied with the psychological closeness between the subject and the victim (pp. 32–43). For example, if the subject was moved next to the victim, obedience decreased. On the other hand, if the victim remained silent, obedience increased. Obedience also varied according to the authority conveyed by the experimenter. When the experimenter stood beside the subject he exerted more influence and was more likely to be obeyed (pp. 59–62).

The most commonly cited real-world example of the potency of obedience effects is the routine, brutal treatment of Jews by Nazi soldiers and concentration-camp guards in the Second World War. However, inappropriate obedience can also play a role in crimes of a less extreme nature in civilian contexts. Corruption within bureaucracies often entangles subordinates who, motivated by a misguided loyalty to the organisation, act illegally on the orders of their superiors. Examples of crimes of authority include cases of governmental abuses of power (Kelman and Hamilton, 1989: 25–9), corporate crime (Kelman and Hamilton, 1989: 45–6), police corruption (Fitzgerald, 1989: 211) and prison-officer brutality (Nagle, 1978: 108–19). Milgram hypothesised that obedience to authority is related to broader cultural values and social expectations. He suggested that many societies overvalue obedience and provide insufficient models for the appropriate defiance of orders. Individuals obey unreasonable commands because of a preoccupation with the administrative rather than the moral component of their job and through a sense of loyalty and duty to their organisation. When brutal orders are carried out, Milgram argued, 'typically we do not find a heroic figure struggling with conscience, nor a pathologically aggressive man ruthlessly exploiting a position of power, but a functionary who has been given a job to do and who strives to create an impression of competence in his work' (1974: 187).

Compliance

Compliance refers to the acquiescence to the direct request of others. Compliance is similar to conformity and obedience in that compliant individuals may be induced to perform behaviour that they would rather not perform. However, compliance research is usually concerned with the role of persuasive communication in inducing behaviour-change rather than with the effects of group pressure or authoritarian power. In addition, while the research on conformity and obedience has tended to dwell on the negative aspects of these phenomena and to study how their adverse effects on behaviour might be countered, compliance research has often focused on techniques for inducing prosocial behaviour.

A number of techniques have been found to increase compliance. Compliance with rules increases when people feel that they have contributed to the formulation of those rules. For example, Snyder *et al.* (1991: 46) argued that company theft is reduced when employees are consulted about what constitutes legitimate and illegitimate use of company goods. Similarly, compliance increases when people have actively endorsed a given rule. Iso-Ahola and Niblock (in Roggenbuck, 1992: 191) found that when campers were asked to sign an anti-littering petition, levels of littering decreased. Generally, too, requests made in person are more effective than impersonal requests (Oliver *et al.*, 1985).

Of equal interest to techniques of persuasion are the conditions under which non-compliance or defiance occurs. Perhaps the most widely cited psychological explanation of non-compliance is Brehm's (1966) theory of reactance. Reactance is the psychological state experienced by people when they believe that their freedom of choice is being restricted. According to reactance theory, when individuals feel that they are being manipulated or forced to comply with a request, they may respond by behaving in the opposite direction. Defiance is particularly likely when the attempts to change or restrict behaviour are perceived as unfair or illegitimate (Sherman, 1993: 459–65). The expression of defiance restores their sense of personal freedom. Reactance theory is the basis for so-called reverse psychology.

Compliance research has obvious lessons for prison control. Despite a common impression that prison guards rely on their formal powers to exercise control, in practice interpersonal style is crucial (Bottoms *et al.*, 1995: 93–4; Hepburn, 1989: 197–200; Kauffman, 1988: 52–4; Lombardo, 1989: 93–6; Sparks *et al.*, 1996: 302–11). Control more often involves enlisting the cooperation of prisoners through negotiation and persuasion than rigidly applying rules or employing coercion and force. Guards earn personal legitimacy through treating prisoners in a fair and consistent fashion, and by conveying clear and realistic expectations. Reactance theory suggests that heavy-handed and overly-manipulative attempts to control prisoners may well lead to outcomes opposite to those intended (Goodstein *et al.*, 1984; Martin and Osgood, 1987).

Deindividuation

Deindividuation refers to the reduced self-awareness, and consequent disinhibition, most commonly produced by crowd membership (Diener, 1980; Prentice-Dunn and Rogers, 1982; Zimbardo, 1970). In its extreme form, deindividuation is exemplified by the herd mentality and frenzied behaviour displayed by members of a lynch-mob. Colman (1991) reported on two South African court cases involving murders at the hands of a mob in which expert psychological testimony on deindividuation was accepted as extenuating evidence. In the prison context, gang violence, particularly during prison riots, is the most obvious example of this type of deindividuated behaviour.

Deindividuation is seen to involve interference with two levels of self-awareness (Prentice-Dunn and Rogers, 1982). Public self-awareness refers to the recognition of oneself as a social object. As a member of a crowd, an individual is afforded a degree of anonymity and becomes less concerned with the opinions and possible censure of others. At this level of deindividuation, people may be aware of what they are doing but have a reduced expectation of suffering any negative consequences. Private self-awareness refers to the ability to focus on one's own thoughts, feelings and values. As individuals become immersed in a group they submerge their identities and experience a decreased ability to self-monitor their behaviour. In this state they are particularly sensitive to situational pressures and permit themselves to engage in behaviour that they ordinarily would not perform. At this level of deindividuation, the individual's capacity for self-regulation is fundamentally impaired.

Early research on deindividuation focused largely on the role of public self-awareness. In one study, Zimbardo (1970) abandoned a car in New York and another in Palo Alto (population about 55,000). He found that the car in New York was quickly stripped by looters of all valuable parts while the car in Palo Alto was left untouched. Zimbardo argued that the behaviour of New Yorkers could be explained by the anonymity that they felt living in a large city and the relative freedom from social and legal repercussions that such anonymity provided. Zimbardo (Haney *et al.*, 1973) also partly explained the results of the Stanford prison experiment (described earlier) in terms of deindividuation. The guards' uniforms, which included reflecting sunglasses, provided a disguise for their wearers that helped to screen their identity and promote a sense of anonymity.

The role of private self-awareness has been the focus of more recent research. In a variation of Milgram's (1974) experimental design, Prentice-Dunn and colleagues (Prentice-Dunn and Rogers, 1982; Prentice-Dunn and Spivey, 1986) examined the administration of shocks by small groups of subjects. Private self-awareness was manipulated by varying subjects' levels of physiological arousal and sense of group cohesiveness. The researchers found that subjects in the deindividuated condition (high group cohesiveness and high arousal) delivered longer and more intense shocks to victims than subjects in the non-deindividuated condition (low group cohesiveness and low arousal).

Special care needs to be taken when dealing with crowds to prevent deindividuation. McKenzie (1982) outlined several techniques for interrupting the development of crowd violence, including dividing the crowd into smaller units, removing crowd leaders, and distracting the attention of the crowd away from the focal point. In a study on preventing rioting at an annual motor-cycle race, Veno and Veno (1993) demonstrated the success of cooperative, non-confrontational methods of crowd control. On the other hand, provocative methods of control – sometimes a single triggering incident of overpolicing – can galvanise crowd members and incite collective disorder (Reicher, 1991; Shellow and Roemer, 1987).

Frustration-aggression hypothesis

Frustration is the emotional state produced when an individual is thwarted in their pursuit of goal-directed behaviour. Dollard *et al.* (1939) proposed frustration as the direct and inevitable cause of aggression. They argued that when an animal – including the human animal – is prevented from performing behaviour that has previously delivered rewards, the animal automatically experiences an increased level of physiological arousal. The animal is then driven to reduce the unpleasant effects of this arousal and does so by responding with some form of aggressive behaviour (snarling, scratching, biting etc.). The subsequent reduction in arousal in turn negatively reinforces (rewards) the aggression. In similar future situations the animal will resort to the same response in an attempt to alleviate the feeling of frustration. If the animal is placed in a situation of extreme frustration, its behaviour will become even more vigorous.

There have been a number of challenges and refinements to Dollard *et al.*'s original theory. In particular, the idea that there is an invariable relationship between frustration and aggression has been largely dismissed. Frustration does not always produce aggression. Some people respond to frustration by productively striving to overcome the frustrating situation, while others simply become resigned to defeat. Similarly, aggression is not always caused by frustration. Bandura (1976: 213–17) pointed out that frustration is just one of a number of events that people experience as aversive. Verbal threats and insults, physical assaults, painful treatment, failure experiences, and delay or deprivation of rewards can all increase emotional arousal and facilitate aggressive responses.

In a reformulation of the frustration-aggression hypothesis to bring it into line with social learning principles, Berkowitz (1989) argued that the presence of frustrating stimuli in the environment increases the probability that an individual will become angry and act aggressively but does not necessarily guarantee aggression. Berkowitz emphasised that it was not sufficient for an event to be perceived as frustrating but that it must also be seen as aversive. People can tolerate frustration if they believe that there was no deliberate attempt to harm them or if they agree that the blocking of their goal was fair and legitimate. The precise form the response to frustration takes depends upon an individual's learning history, cognitive interpretation of the event and available behavioural repertoire.

The prison environment contains frustrating and aversive situations for inmates at every turn. In most institutions, inmates do not have control over the simplest aspects of their environment such as turning their cell lights on and off, regulating their individual heating and cooling preferences, or choosing when to associate with others and when to be alone. They must rely on prison staff for many of their everyday needs. Frustration associated with this lack of control may account for much of the violence exhibited by prisoners (Wener et al., 1987: 49; Wener and Olsen, 1978: 20–5; 1980; Wright and Goodstein, 1989: 255).

Environmental psychology

Environmental psychology is 'the study of the interrelationship between behavior and experience and the built and natural environment' (Bell et al., 1990: 7). Thus, environmental psychologists are concerned with the psychological effects of geographic and climatic variables such as temperature, sunshine, wind and humidity, and of the unintended consequences of the products of urbanisation including high-density living, workplace noise, artificial lighting and poor interior design. According to the environmental stress model, many factors in the environment influence behaviour because of their aversive nature and the threat they pose to human well-being (Baum *et al.*, 1981; Lazarus and Folkman, 1984). Taken individually, these environmental stressors may represent little more than background irritation. However, collectively and accumulatively, ambient noxious stimulation may seriously affect psychological functioning. Stress reactions represent the organism's attempt to manage or adapt to aversive conditions and events (the so-called 'fight or flight' response). Responses to environmental stressors may be physiological (e.g. arousal, increased adrenaline activity, physical illness), emotional (e.g. irritability, anxiety, depression) and behavioural (e.g. aggression, withdrawal, suicide). Environmental psychology has played an important role in recent developments in prison architecture. The following section considers the effects of three environmental dimensions particularly relevant to these developments – atmospheric conditions, territoriality and crowding.

Atmospheric conditions
The relationship between weather and behaviour has been a major interest of environmental psychologists. A number of studies have reported a correlation between temperature and violence (Anderson, 1987; Cotton, 1986; Harries and Stadler, 1988). Goranson and King (1970) showed that riots were more likely to occur during heatwaves. Banzinger and Owens (1978) found a correlation between wind speed and delinquency. Rosenthal *et al.* (1985) found that depression was associated with reduced exposure to sunlight in winter. LeBeau (1994) reported a relationship between domestic disputes and the temperature-humidity index.

An extension of natural climate research has been the study of artificial indoor climates. Laboratory studies suggest that as the temperature moves outside an individual's comfort zone there is deterioration on a number of performance variables (vigilance, memory, cognitive tasks etc.) (Fine and Kobrick, 1987; Riley and Cochran, 1984). With respect to social behaviour, curvilinear relationships have been found between temperature and aggression (Baron and Bell, 1975; Bell and Baron, 1977). It seems that moderately warm and moderately cool temperatures increase antisocial behaviours but extremely hot and extremely cold temperatures reduce them. Aggression, then, is facilitated within critical temperature bands. One explanation for this finding is that while people become more irritable when the temperature is uncomfortable, at some point heat has a debilitating effect while cold reduces arousal. In the case of prisons, older-style prisons are notorious for being stiflingly hot in summer and freezing cold in winter (Wright and Goodstein, 1989: 255). Attention by architects to providing adequate heating, airconditioning, insulation, ventilation and access to natural lighting can help to reduce levels of environmental irritation.

Territoriality

Territoriality refers to the tendency to lay claim to an area and to defend it against intruders. Researchers are interested in the effects of territoriality on both territory-possessors and potential intruders. From the perspective of possessors, while invasion of territory may be stressful, the sense of ownership associated with territoriality has positive psychological effects. Home turf is a place where people can relax and feel in control over their lives. People are also more likely to take care of an environment over which they claim dominion (and vice versa). From the perspective of potential intruders, territorial markers – fences, gates, signs, personal possessions and so forth – signal areas that are not to be entered. Even symbolic markers that pose no physical restriction on entry can command high levels of compliance. This concept of 'defensible space' was the basis for the crime prevention work of Oscar Newman (1972).

Territoriality has important implications for the design of residential institutions such as prisons. Altman's (1975) privacy regulation model suggests that residents in communal living settings require sanctuaries to which to retreat in order to reduce the stress and overstimulation associated with excessive interpersonal contact. O'Neill and Paluck (1973) reported a drop in the level of aggression among institutionalised mentally handicapped boys when they were given identifiable territories to call their own. Other researchers have stressed the need for institutions to be designed in ways that promote in residents a sense of ownership of their living areas. Giving residents individual control over lighting and heating has already been mentioned as a frustration-reduction technique, but is also relevant from the point of view of providing the autonomy characteristic of feeling at home. Similarly, territoriality may be fostered by allowing a great deal of freedom in personalising environments with pictures, personal possessions, individual furniture arrangement and so forth (Wright and Goodstein, 1989; 256).

Crowding

Crowding research is concerned with the psychological consequences of high-density conditions. The effects of being crowded are distinguished from the deindividuating effects described earlier of being a member of a crowd. Much of the direct evidence for the deleterious effects of crowding has come from animal research. In both natural and experimentally manipulated environments, many animal species have been found to have a critical upper threshold for population concentration. In perhaps the best-known study, Calhoun (1962) examined the behaviour of rats confined to a fixed-sized environment but otherwise provided with unlimited resources (food, water and nesting material). As the rat population increased, Calhoun found that social order disintegrated and a multitude of physiological and behavioural pathologies developed (abortions, infant mortality, desertion of young, aggression, cannibalism and tumours). Such research has been linked to correlational studies in humans that show that urban population density is associated with increased crime rates (Galle *et al.*, 1972; Gove *et al.*, 1977). Findings of physical, psychological and behavioural problems have been also reported in field studies of specific crowded settings such as college dormitories (Baum and Valins, 1977), night-clubs (Macintyre and Homel, 1997) and naval ships (Dean *et al.*, 1978) as well as prisons (Cox *et al.*, 1984; Gaes and McGuire, 1985; Paulus, 1988).

In considering the application of this research to human conduct, the distinction can be drawn between inside density and outside density. Outside density refers to broad population trends (e.g. people per acre) while inside density typically relates to primary living areas (e.g. people per dwelling). In the prison context, the overall population of a prison relative to the prison size or capacity would be a measure of outside density; the number of prisoners in a cell block would be a measure of inside density. Bell *et al.* (1990) argued that, as a general rule, studies examining the effects of inside density have been the most fruitful.

A further distinction can be made between spatial density – the amount of space per person – and social density – the number of people in a given space. Reducing population density can involve either increasing the amount of space available for a given number of people – reducing spatial density – or decreasing the number of people in a given space – reducing social density. When night-clubs and similar establishments restrict the number of patrons that may enter they are manipulating social density; when prison administrators build more prisons to alleviate overcrowding they are manipulating spatial density. Social density may be varied without altering spatial density. For example, a 500 square feet dormitory housing ten people has the same spatial density as, but greater social density than, ten individual rooms each of 50 square feet (McCain *et al.*, 1980). Generally, high social density is more stressful than high spatial density (Baum and Valins, 1977; Cox *et al.*, 1984). For example, dormitory accommodation in residential settings has consistently been associated with higher levels of violence and antisocial behaviour than single-room accommodation (Atlas, 1982: 335–41; Cox *et al.*, 1984; Sylvester *et al.*, 1977: 54). The social density of a dormitory might be readily reduced without an increase in available space by the utilisation of movable partitions.

Finally, it is also important to note the distinction between density and crowding. Density refers to the physical condition of space limitation. On the other hand, crowding is now viewed as an experiential state relating to the *perception* of spatial limitations. While density is clearly related to crowding, crowding effects can be moderated by a number of social and architectural features in the environment. For example, architectural responses to prison crowding might include increasing the sense of spaciousness through use of colour and light, windows, the provision of special privacy rooms and choice about going to cells during free time (Marrero, 1977; Nacci *et al.*, 1977; Paulus and Nagar, 1989).

Rational choice perspective

Unlike the other theories described in this chapter, rational choice perspective has been specifically formulated as an explanation of criminal behaviour. The perspective was proposed by Cornish and Clarke (1986) not as a separate theory, but as an eclectic model capable of expressing a general situational approach to crime. The organising framework is an adaptation of the expected utility model found in economics and in the psychological decision-making literature. Underpinning rational choice perspective is the assumption that offenders commit crime in order to derive some benefit. Offenders are portrayed as active decision-makers who undertake cost-benefit analyses of presenting crime opportunities and make choices about whether or not to engage in criminal acts. The attractions of criminal behaviour include money, increased status, sexual gratification, excitement and so on. Disincentives include the difficulty involved in carrying out the behaviour and the likelihood of getting caught. Crime occurs when the perceived benefits of offending are judged to outweigh the perceived costs.

The rationality of offenders, however, is qualified. Offenders' decisions are not necessarily sensible in an objective sense. According to Cornish and Clarke, 'offenders seek to benefit themselves by their criminal behaviour; that this involves the making of decisions and choices, however rudimentary these choices may be; and that these processes, constrained as they are by time, the offender's cognitive abilities, and by the availability of relevant information, exhibit limited rather than normative rationality' (1987: 933). The decision an offender makes to engage in crime may well be a poor one and ultimately prove to be self-defeating, but nevertheless it represents the most desirable option at that time *as the offender saw it.*

While rational choice perspective emphasises the role of immediate situations in criminal behaviour, it is not assumed that crime is necessarily opportunistic in the sense of being a spur-of-the-moment reaction to a chance circumstance. On occasions crime opportunities may simply be taken as they fortuitously occur, but opportunities may also be sought out or created by the offender. However, even planned crimes by highly motivated offenders involve situational considerations. The professional burglar, for example, does not steal at random. Rather, he carefully selects targets that experience has shown will deliver maximum pay-off and entail minimum risks.

Clarke characterises the behaviour of offenders as purposive. Thus, an important step in preventing crime is to understand the purpose – the motivation – for the behaviour. Situational prevention based on rational choice perspective involves manipulating the immediate environments of crime in order to increase the cost-benefit ratio of offending as perceived by the potential offender. This approach to prevention is often referred to as opportunity-reduction (Clarke, 1995: 55). According to Clarke and Homel (1997), the decision to engage in a particular behaviour is made with reference to four cost-benefit dimensions – the perceived effort involved (how difficult is the behaviour to perform?), the perceived risks involved (what is the likelihood of being detected and punished?), the anticipated rewards (how attractive are the proceeds?) and the anticipated feelings of guilt or shame (how psychologically or socially distressing will involvement in the behaviour be?).

It can be argued that prisons as a matter of course already employ many opportunity-reduction strategies in the form of high walls, locks, surveillance systems and so forth. However, as will become clearer in subsequent chapters, traditional approaches to prison control by and large lack the problem-solving and micro-environmental character that distinguishes the rational choice approach to opportunity-reduction.

Conclusions

The examination undertaken in this chapter has revealed a wide range of situational variables that might be manipulated in order to influence behaviour, and a variety of theories by which the role of these situational elements may be understood. One way to draw together some of these ideas is to consider a number of basic dimensions that cut across the various perspectives.

First, situations can involve both physical and social variables. Situational forces can refer to the influences of observable, concrete stimuli – for example, tangible rewards and punishments, physical barriers and architectural features – and to influences that take place in the course of interpersonal interaction – modelling, conformity, deindividuation and so on.

Second, situations can vary in size. At one extreme, radical behaviourists generally take a micro-level view, and may reduce a situational influence to the effect of a single environmental element (the sound of a bell in the case of Pavlov). Within other perspectives, situations may be conceived of in more global, macro terms as the combined effect of the encompassing environment. Zimbardo (1970), in his abandoned car experiment, claimed living in New York as a situational influence!

Third, situational effects can vary in intensity. For example, both urban crowding and frustration are thought to generate aversive emotional arousal that an individual may seek to dissipate by an aggressive response. However, urban crowding is conceptualised as a low-intensity, chronic condition while frustration can be an acute sensation that produces more or less immediate effects.

Finally, and most importantly for the arguments to be developed in this book, a distinction can be made between situations that have a precipitating function for behaviour and those that have a regulating function. This separation is made most clearly in learning theories that distinguish between antecedent conditions (eliciting and discriminative stimuli, models and expectancies) that cue or initiate behaviour, and consequent conditions (reinforcements and punishments) that inhibit or encourage behaviour according to the contingent costs and benefits. Rational choice perspective is clearly concerned largely with behavioural consequences. For the most part, the other perspectives covered in this chapter – frustration-aggression hypothesis, theories of social influence and environmental psychology – describe behavioural antecedents concerned with priming or precipitating action.

The distinction between precipitating forces and regulating forces has important implications for crime prevention in general and prison control in particular. As noted in chapter 1, there has been a tendency in the literature to characterise situational prevention as narrowly concerned with blocking crime opportunities and, in particular, with target-hardening techniques relying on the use of physical constraints. The assumption underlying this approach is that offenders enter the crime situation already motivated to offend and so must be deflected from their intended course of action. The theories discussed in this chapter present a much broader interpretation of the situation–behaviour relationship. Situations are conceived not just to provide the physical opportunity for crime to occur, but in many cases actively to induce the propensity to offend. With respect to prisons, this dual role that situations play emphasises the point that misbehaviour is not simply the work of determined individuals exploiting gaps and lapses in prison security (although this undoubtedly occurs); a great deal of prison misbehaviour is unplanned and reactive, generated by the immediate pressures and pulls of the prison environment.

The significance of the distinction between precipitating and regulating situations will be elaborated upon in chapter 4, in which an integrated model of situational prison control will be presented. Before coming to that, however, chapter 3 examines the various situational strategies that have been applied to the problem of prison control over the years.

Situational methods of prison control

Prisons are in the business of control. From the time that the first true prisons were built in the late eighteenth century, prison administrators have been faced with the fundamental problem of how to manage safely and contain securely large numbers of people who have been confined in a restricted space against their will. For the most part, maintaining control has been seen as an uncomplicated matter involving little more than building higher walls and devising more repressive regimes to crush prisoner resistance. Only recently have some of the theoretical insights discussed in the previous chapter been consciously applied to the problem of prison control. However, while prison control strategies have not as a rule been directly fashioned by the theoretical debates about situational prevention, methods of prison control are readily amenable to analysis in situational terms. In many ways, prison control has always and unavoidably been situational.

This chapter describes the various methods of prison control and relates these methods to the theories of situational behaviour outlined in chapter 2. There are three basic situational elements in prison that can be manipulated in an effort to control the behaviour of prisoners – the physical environment of the prison, the characteristics of the prison population and the regimes and strategies put in place to manage the population in that environment.

Control and the physical environment

The physical environment of the prison includes the design and layout, the building style, construction materials, furnishings and security hardware. Conveniently, the history of the prison can be divided into three broad eras or generations (Atlas and Dunham, 1990: 45–9; Nelson, 1993: 26–9;

Wener *et al.*, 1987: 48). These generations describe evolving ideas of prison architecture which, in turn, reflect changing philosophies of human behaviour and approaches to the management of prisoners.

First-generation prisons

The traditional maximum security institution – the stereotypic 'big house' of film and literature – has come to be categorised as the first generation of prison design. First-generation thinking determined the way prisons were built for 200 years. The basic design was established in the first real prisons in the late eighteenth century (such as those of the Auburn and Pennsylvania systems), was employed during the so-called age of the prisons in the second half of the nineteenth century and remained dominant until almost three-quarters of the way through the twentieth century.

The architecture of first-generation prisons is typically heavy and imposing. The prisoners are hidden from the world behind thick, high walls. The buildings are fortress-like and constructed of dull brick and sturdy bars. The yards are honeycombed with internal fences and gates. The furnishings are Spartan and utilitarian. To some extent, these features can be explained in terms of their security functions. But, more than this, these prisons were purposely harsh, forbidding places (Ditchfield, 1990: 76–84; Markus, 1994: 14–16).

A characteristic of first-generation prisons is the radial or linear layout of cells (Ditchfield, 1990: 76–84; Fairweather, 1994: 24). In the radial version, prison wings extend like spokes from a central hub from where prison guards maintained their watch down the various corridors. A variation of this design was Bentham's panopticon, which involved tiers of cells encircling the central hub such that each cell was open to the view of the guards. The radial design supported a separatist regime in which anonymity and non-communication among prisoners were strictly enforced. Prisoners were escorted to their cells wearing hoods over their heads and spent their entire sentences there in total seclusion. The later linear or telegraph-pole designs (of which there are numerous variants) involved cell blocks arranged on either side of a central corridor. These designs emerged as prisoners began to be granted greater degrees of association. The linear designs allowed prisoners to be classified into various categories and housed in separate blocks, minimising the need for prisoner movement.

These architectural features of first-generation prisons reflected prevailing ideologies and beliefs about human behaviour in general and criminal behaviour in particular. The impetus for the first-generation design was a spiritual view of human nature that endowed individuals with free will and the capacity to reform morally (Ditchfield, 1990: 77–8; Marcus, 1994: 14–16). The original prisons were conceived as places in which offenders might come to feel penitence for their sins (hence the term penitentiary) through a monastic existence of solitude, hard work, discipline and silent reflection. When these ideals were generally abandoned by the end of the nineteenth century, the prison system was left to deal with the architectural legacy. Not only did many of these old institutions remain in use, but they so shaped the view of what a real prison was that new prisons continued to be built along first-generation lines long after the original rationale was forgotten. Today, despite the surge in prison building in recent years using alternative designs, most prison systems still have many examples of old, first-generation institutions still on line.

There are a number of control problems associated with first-generation architecture. First, the architecture of traditional prisons is alienating and hostile, and creates a psychologically numbing environment that allows for the brutal treatment of its inhabitants. As noted above, social isolation was an explicit intention of the original first-generation designs. The separate system was ultimately discredited because of its toll on prisoners in the form of high rates of mortality, suicide and insanity (Ditchfield, 1990: 79). The separate system is gone but the continued confinement of prisoners in dungeon-like conditions places strains on the social bonds that govern the way individuals relate to and treat one another. On the one hand, weakened social bonds can alter the view that prisoners have of themselves. Feelings of separateness and anonymity can produce a deindividuated state whereby prisoners become dulled to the consequences of their actions (Zimbardo, 1970). On the other hand, weakened social bonds can affect the perception prisoners and guards have of others. The prison environment can facilitate neutralisations or cognitive disengagements that allow others to be divested of their human qualities and so rendered psychologically acceptable targets for victimisation (Bandura, 1976; Wortley, 1996: 118–23).

Second, traditional prison environments are stressful in many different ways, and may produce tensions that in turn can generate expressive violent outbursts. These older prisons are rarely airconditioned and can be stiflingly hot in summer and freezing cold in winter (Wright and Goodstein, 1989: 255–6). They are inordinately noisy, with the incessant sound of clanking keys, slamming steel doors, heavy footsteps, arguments, orders, and competing radios and televisions reverberating down the cell block corridors (Brodsky and Fowler, 1979: 263; Farbstein *et al.*, 1979: II 5–9; Wright and Goodstein, 1989: 255). The uniform, institutional designs and drab interior decor produce a visual monotony and stimuli deprivation (Suedfeld,

1980: 112–13). Finally, there are limited opportunities for privacy and escape from these stressful conditions. This is particularly so where there are dormitories or multiple-occupancy cells, but even in single-occupancy situations prisoners usually have little control over when they may seek the sanctuary of their cell.

Third, traditional prisons may convey through their overt obsession with security the expectation that prisoners will be violent and destructive, and so invite the very behaviour they seek to prevent (Wright and Goodstein, 1989: 255; Zupan, 1991: 87–9). The castellated architecture of first-generation prisons is typically excessive in terms of legitimate security requirements, designed originally to inspire awe as much as to enforce compliance. However, this emphasis on heavy construction and exaggerated scale also helps reinforce an image of prisoner deviance in both guards and prisoners themselves. In the case of prison guards, the belief that prisoners are deviant can set up a self-fulfilling prophecy. That is, by anticipating troublesome behaviour prison guards may treat prisoners in ways that unwittingly provoke those expected responses. In the case of prisoners the image of deviance may be internalised. Having defined themselves as deviant, prisoners are likely to behave accordingly.

Finally, despite the explicit intention of first-generation designs to facilitate supervision and control of prisoners, in fact they provide limited capacity to observe prisoner activities (Zupan and Menke, 1991: 181–5). They were designed in an era when prisoners rarely left their cells. Now, with relatively high levels of prisoner movement, radial and linear designs have many natural blind spots. Surveillance by guards is intermittent and prisoners are afforded ample locations and opportunities to engage in violent and rule-violating acts without fear of detection. The overriding imperative in these institutions is perimeter security – making sure prisoners do not escape – rather than internal security and prisoner safety. Even the few completed examples of the panopticon failed to ensure adequate supervision of prisoners, for while the guards could observe the prisoners at all times, the prisoners could also observe the guards and always knew when their backs were turned (Ditchfield, 1990: 81).

Second-generation prisons

The second generation of prison design dates from the early 1970s (Atlas and Dunham, 1990: 45; Wener *et al.*, 1987: 48). The traditional radial and linear cell block layouts were replaced by a podular design. Prisoners were classified and divided into small, manageable groups of twenty or so and housed in single cells arranged to form discrete clusters or units. The units were usually, but not always, triangular in shape to maximise visibility. These housing areas were removed from centralised service areas – visiting areas, exercise yards, showers, dining-rooms and so forth – requiring extensive prisoner movement within the prison. To help in this task, second-generation prisons began in earnest to utilise modern technology. Many of the prison guards' activities were performed from a central control room. Newly developed security glazing and closed circuit television (CCTV) provided the ability to observe prisoners at any time, and the passing of prisoners from one section of the prison to another could be regulated by electronically controlled doors.

If first-generation prisons relied on intermittent surveillance, second-generation prisons may be characterised by their emphasis on remote or indirect surveillance. A critical feature of these new prisons was the physical separation of prisoners and guards. While the level of surveillance of prisoners was greatly increased, it occurred from behind transparent screens or via television monitors.

Even more so than first-generation prisons, second-generation designs display a siege mentality to control. They were premised on the belief that prisoners are inherently dangerous and unpredictable, and that their control required anticipating and guarding against the worst at all times. The safety of prison guards was achieved by limiting their need to interact with prisoners. Austere, vandal-resistant fixtures and furnishings were designed to minimise the effects of the expected abuse by prisoners.

In their extreme form, second-generation prisons have been likened to 'electronic zoos' (Nagle, 1978: 122). While they offered high levels of physical control over prisoners' behaviour, this control was achieved at considerable psychological cost. In this regard, they continued or exacerbated many of the negative features of first-generation prisons. The reliance on technology combined with the lack of personal interaction between prisoners and guards made for a sterile, dehumanised environment. The super-precautionary approach to possible violence and vandalism maintained the impression to prisoners that misbehaviour was expected and served to reinforce their sense of deviance. Finally, the control that the guards had over the prisoners' movements necessarily reduced the control prisoners felt over their own lives, and resulted in an environment that was arguably even more frustrating and stressful than that found in traditional prisons.

Third-generation prisons

Third-, or new-generation prisons evolved from the podular designs pioneered in second-generation prisons. However, while the concept of housing prisoners in small units was retained in these new designs, third-generation units differed architecturally in three crucial ways from their predecessor.

First, new-generation designs brought the guards directly into the unit, rather than having them located outside looking in. Guards were now in a position to carry out regular, direct surveillance of prisoners' activities. Direct surveillance provided the capacity for a more proactive, dynamic approach to security (Atlas and Dunham, 1990: 46–9; King, 1987: 121; Krasnow, 1995: 4; Nelson, 1993: 29–31; Zupan and Menke, 1991: 187–90). Moreover, guards and prisoners were forced to interact on a personal level. Accompanying the new-generation architecture was a new functional unit management model based on a cooperative rather than coercive relationship between guards and prisoners. Much of the responsibility for the management of the unit is devolved to the guards who, ideally, have a stable association with a particular unit. Guards are expected to build a positive rapport with prisoners, to play an active role in resolving problems and conflicts that arise among prisoners within the unit, and to become involved in administrative and welfare concerns of prisoners in their charge. Prisoners in turn are encouraged to feel a sense of ownership of the unit and may be given some formal say in its running: they may be consulted, for example, on the admission of new prisoners (Coyle, 1987: 241). Functional units, then, are not simply architectural entities but also involve new management strategies that the innovative architectural features make possible (but do not guarantee).

Second, services that were centrally located in second-generation prisons were now also brought into the unit. The units became true self-contained living areas supporting many of the day-to-day needs of the prisoners. Typically, units had a central lounge area, telephones and their own showers. Programmes and recreational activities were often carried out in the unit. Many units also had their own kitchens allowing prisoners to prepare snacks and sometimes even to cook their main meals. As a result of this centralisation, in a real sense the unit became the prisoners' home.

Third, the hard, institutional finish of second-generation prisons was replaced with a softer, friendlier architecture. Domestic-quality, rather than high-security, fittings and furnishings were used. There was attention to aesthetics, such as colour coordination and incidental decorations, which helped to create as far as possible a pleasant physical environment.

Despite both relying on a podular design, the rationales of second- and third-generation designs are clearly very different. Whereas control in second- (and for that matter, first-) generation prisons is premised on a reactive guarding against the worst, new-generation prisons operate on the basis that normalised environments will produce normal behaviour.

Specifically, the new-generation philosophy is premised on a number of theoretical assumptions that were discussed in the previous chapter. Direct surveillance aims to increase the probability that misbehaviour will be detected and punished. Closer interpersonal contact among prisoners and their guards attempts to inhibit dehumanising neutralisations and encourage unit members to come to know and treat one another as individuals. Decentralisation and unit living are ways to increase in prisoners a sense of control over their environment and thus reduce frustration. Pleasant, 'soft' surroundings are designed to reduce environmental irritation, encourage prisoners to feel a sense of pride and territoriality towards the unit, and convey the message that vandalism is not expected.

Recent developments

New-generation designs have not been a panacea for control problems in prison. In the first place, it would be a mistake to conclude that most prisons now in use are new generation, or even that all prisons now being built are new generation (Fairweather, 1994: 26; King, 1987: 119). In the US new-generation prisons are more common in the federal system than in state and county systems. New-generation designs also tend to be reserved for medium- and minimum-security institutions, and are infrequently used for maximum-security prisoners. In some cases, only part of a prison is built on new-generation lines, giving the option of reserving the units as privilege areas.

There is also evidence of an emerging gap between new-generation theory and practice. Often where new-generation architecture has been provided the ability of the prison to achieve its potential has been compromised by lack of staff training, mismanagement, apathy, understaffing, inadequate funding and prisoner overcrowding (Nelson and Davis, 1995: 16–17; Zupan and Menke, 1991: 193). According to Fairweather (1994: 26), there is a particular strain on the ability to deliver direct supervision. The high staffing ratios required are expensive and staff may be taken from the units to reduce costs. Direct supervision also requires effort and commitment by staff. Maintaining close contact with prisoners in the unit can be intimidating and it is tempting for staff to withdraw behind the familiar barriers. In short, new-generation architecture does not guarantee new-generation management.

Moreover, prison designs are continuing to change and evolve. According to Atlas and Dunham (1990: 56), units are getting larger. In early third-generation prisons, units of 30 prisoners were typical. It is now not uncommon for units to exceed 60 prisoners and they may reach 100. There is also an increasing use of technology and especially electronic aids in prisons. Closed circuit television, personal alarms, electronic locking and electronic perimeter security systems are becoming more common (Atlas and Dunham, 1990: 56–7; Fairweather, 1994: 26; Travis *et al.*, 1989: 38). Atlas and Dunham (1990: 57) argue that many of these electronic aids are unobtrusive and may improve security without significantly detracting from the unit environment. Atlas and Dunham may be right, but the use of such aids certainly signals a trend towards lower staffing ratios and a greater reliance on remote surveillance, and thus indicates fundamental changes to the original concept of unit management.

These developments in prison design seem to have been driven more by economic and political considerations than good science. Prison populations in most Western countries, but in the US in particular, are escalating at an alarming rate (Lillis, 1994; Wees, 1996). With massive injections of prisoners into the prison system, early third-generation designs may be considered a luxury that can no longer be afforded. Furthermore, accompanying this population increase (and probably causing it) is a 'get tough' attitude towards prisoners. Any hint that prisoners are being coddled in soft, new prisons is no longer politically saleable. In the end, as Fairweather (1994: 37) notes, prison design is a balance between 'responsible humanity' and 'irresponsible expediency'.

Control and the prison population

The usual reason for examining the role of population characteristics in prison disorder is to identify demographic and dispositional profiles of prisoners who are thought to be most likely to cause trouble. Clearly, this objective falls outside the scope of the situational approach. However, the characteristics of prison populations are important in a situational analysis of prison control for a different reason. For each individual prisoner other inhabitants of the prison represent an inescapable component of his or her immediate environment. The focus of this section, then, is not on the characteristics of individual rule-violators, but on the overall characteristics of the prison population that might have influenced the behaviour of those rule-violators. Potentially important characteristics of the prison population include size, density, turnover and composition.

Population size

There is a widespread view expressed in the corrections' literature that large prisons by their very nature facilitate disorder. The American Correctional Association (1981), for example, recommends that all prisons built to contain more than 500 prisoners should be sub-divided into discrete units, each to hold fewer than 500 prisoners. The belief that small prisons are easier to control is based on several assumptions. In the first place, it seems logical that the greater the number of prisoners who are forced into close congregation, the greater will be the levels of anonymity and depersonalisation. Weak social bonds between prisoners, it is argued, create a climate in which life is cheap and there is little psychological cost attached to harming others. In addition, large prisons are thought to be more difficult to supervise effectively. It is suggested, for example, that proactive security in prisons often depends upon advanced intelligence from prisoners about impending trouble, and that informal lines of communication between prisoners and guards deteriorate as institutions grow larger.

Despite the apparent preference for smaller prisons, there is an increasing tendency towards larger institutions. In 1990 in the US, 471 (37 per cent) of the country's 1,287 federal and state correctional facilities housed more than 500 prisoners, and 211 (16 per cent) institutions had populations of more than 1,000 prisoners (Stephan, 1997). By 1995 the figures had risen to 646 (43 per cent) with populations exceeding 500 and 360 (24 per cent) with populations in excess of 1,000 prisoners, from a total prison system that had grown to 1,500 facilities. Put another way, in 1995 85 per cent of all prisoners were incarcerated in an institution with a capacity of over 500.

In fact, as later chapters will reveal in more detail, assumptions about the effect of prison size on levels of disorder are not always borne out by the research. However, one obvious problem with the measure is the possible confound between absolute population size and population size relative to available physical space. In other words, prison size may not be particularly problematic as long as an institution can comfortably accommodate the numbers it has. It is this consideration that has led to the investigation of population density as a predictor of prison disorder.

Population density

Crowding has emerged as one of the most commonly researched situational prison variables. As with population size, there is a ready acceptance by commentators that prison crowding and disorder are linked. The American Correctional Association (1981) recommends that for single-cell occupancy each prisoner should be allowed 60 square feet; for multiple-cell occupancy each prisoner should be allowed 50 square feet. The most usual rationale for suspecting such a relationship is the environmental stress model. As prisons become more crowded, prisoners are subjected to more frequent invasion of personal space, reduced levels of privacy, less perceived control over the environment and increased competition for resources. Antisocial behaviour is an expressive manifestation of these increased psychological pressures. Others stress the role of crowding in increasing social fragmentation and a breakdown in the traditional order and its predictability (Hunt *et al.*, 1993: 402–7). Still others have suggested a more indirect relationship between crowding and violence (Marrero, 1977: 32–5). Increased crowding, it is argued, increases perceptions by prisoners of lack of safety and so encourages mistrust and the formation of protective gangs.

While prisoner numbers have grown dramatically in recent years in most Western countries, bringing new facilities on line has helped to contain the overcrowding problem somewhat. For example, in the US between 1990 and 1995 the nation's prison population jumped from 715,649 to 1,023,572, an increase of 43 per cent (Stephan, 1997). Over the same period the rated capacity of the country's prison systems went from 692,783 to 975,719, or from 103 per cent to 105 per cent occupancy. However, overcrowding is not uniformly distributed across the prison systems. In 1995 the federal system was at 124 per cent occupancy, with large prisons (between 1,000 and 2,499 prisoners) at 145 per cent.

The most obvious solutions to prison overcrowding are either to increase capacity or to reduce prison populations. In the current get-tough climate, and given the figures presented above, most attention is clearly being given to the first of these approaches. Whether simply building more prisons as the solution to overcrowding makes good economic and social sense is, of course, another matter. There are two general strategies for reducing prisoner numbers (Skovron, 1988). Front-end strategies are aimed at reducing prison admissions and include alternatives to prison such as probation, home detention and community service. Back-end strategies involve releasing prisoners before their full term through good-time provisions, or remission, parole, works-release and emergency legislation. Of these two approaches, correctional administrations often have some control over back-end strategies, but there may be political impediments to implementing the necessary policies.

Population turnover

A further dimension of the prison population is the rate with which prisoners move through an institution. It has been suggested that violence and misconduct are more likely where there is a transient prison population (Ellis, 1984: 289–91; Gaes and McGuire, 1985: 48–9). Transient populations occur when there is rapid intake of prisoners into the system or a high level of transfer between institutions. It is argued that rapid population turnover is unsettling and makes it difficult for prisoners to form meaningful relationships. These arguments are in direct contradiction of conventional prison wisdom that favours the transfer of prisoners as a control method.

Population composition

Most prison systems have classification procedures that control the distribution of prisoners across the available institutions. The primary aim of classifying prisoners into particular groupings is to facilitate programme delivery. However, the population mix of an institution may also have implications for control. Population dimensions include prisoners' race, age, length of sentence and security needs. The debate with respect to these variables typically revolves around the question of whether control is easier to achieve with homogeneous or heterogeneous populations.

On the one hand it is argued that there are control advantages in keeping like prisoners together. Traditionally, this logic has been applied to the management of young prisoners. Administrators have classified prisoners according to age in order to prevent young, impressionable prisoners from being 'contaminated' or victimised by hardened felons. Similarly, there has been a tendency to separate long-term and short-term prisoners, not just because short-term prisoners may be more vulnerable, but also because long-term and short-term prisoners have different needs. The overriding concern of long-term prisoners is to do their time, and the presence of short-term offenders can be irritating and unsettling (Ditchfield, 1990: 53–5). Finally, racially homogeneous prisons are widely assumed to produce fewer control problems than racially mixed prisons. In particular, racially homogeneous prisons avoid the problems associated with the formation of racial gangs. Racial segregation as a preemptive measure against gang formation is obviously legally and ethically problematic. However, many administrators apparently employ the set-off method – that is, trying to balance gang numbers so that no one gang dominates – to neutralise the effects of the racial mix (Knox and Tromanhauser, 1991: 17).

On the other hand, persuasive arguments are also made in favour of population heterogeneity, especially with respect to age and sentence length. At an individual level, older and long-term prisoners are involved in fewer prison disturbances than are younger and short-term prisoners (Mandaraka-Sheppard, 1986: 171; Walters, 1998; Wolfgang, 1964; Wooldredge, 1998). Older prisoners are supposed to be less physiologically prone to aggression, while long-term prisoners have a greater investment in a stable prison environment. The concentration of young and short-term prisoners is seen to increase the potential for control problems while the presence in an institution of older and longer-term prisoners provides a stabilising influence. Theoretically, there are two reasons for expecting less disorder in prisons with mixed-age and sentence-length populations. First, there is an increased likelihood that young and short-term prisoners will observe and model the more mature behaviour and coping strategies of older and long-term prisoners (and conversely, reduce young and short-term prisoners' exposure to the inappropriate influences of their peers). Second, there are increased social pressures on young and short-term prisoners to conform to the norms set by older and long-term prisoners (and again there are reduced pressures to conform to the behaviour of peers). Note that despite the similarity between these two approaches, modelling and conformity are distinct processes. Modelling involves eliciting from prisoners behaviours that they are disposed to perform or that they are at least ambivalent about; conformity involves pressuring individuals to perform behaviour they would rather not perform.

A special case of the homogeneous/heterogeneous debate involves high-security prisoners. Historically, there are two different approaches for dealing with prisoners considered to be the most dangerous, escape-prone or difficult to control – dispersal or concentration (House of Commons, 1977: 8–10). According to the dispersal model, these prisoners should be spread around a number of maximum-security facilities so that their impact on the system is dissipated. The concentration model, on the other hand, holds that these prisoners should be housed together in one maximum-security prison where special high-security arrangements can be put in place. Arguments against dispersal revolve around the negative effect a small number of disruptive prisoners can have on the overall prison population. Arguments against concentration generally concentrate on the potential of super-security prisons to become unduly repressive, particularly given that classification of dangerousness is far from an exact science. Because the concentration model focuses on the identification of known trouble-makers and the building of special institutions to control their behaviour, it will not be discussed in great length in this book as a general solution to the prevention of prison disorder.

Control and the prison regime

'Regime' is frequently used to describe the internal operations of the prison. Despite the widespread use of the term, regime is a complex and rather abstract concept and in its broadest sense can refer to almost any aspect of imprisonment affecting the prisoner's life. Most formal definitions talk about the prison regime as a set of institutional practices such as the adoption of particular management strategies, the nature of the interaction between staff and prisoners, the enforcement of rules, the application of incentives and sanctions, and the provision of sporting, leisure and therapeutic programmes (e.g. Ditchfield, 1990: 121).

Social scientists have generally attempted to operationalise the concept of regime by examining its supposed effects on prisoners. The deprivation model exemplifies this approach (e.g. Goffman, 1961; Sykes, 1958). To be sure, deprivation theorists have described the features of the 'total institution', but the focus of their analysis has been on the pains experienced by prisoners – their loss of liberty, goods and services, heterosexual relationships, autonomy and security – and the subsequent formation of the prisoner subculture.

Another popular approach has been to break the regime down into dimensions of 'social climate' (Moos, 1968; Wright, 1985, 1991a, 1993). The aim of this analysis is to describe the prevailing 'personality' of the institution along a set of specified dimensions (involvement, support, autonomy etc.). Once again, however, researchers are primarily interested in how institutional practices are experienced at a psychological level by prisoners and staff and whether basic needs are being met. Social climate, then, is an intervening variable rather than a direct expression of the regime.

More recently, and closer to the spirit of the situational approach, DiIulio (1987) has shifted attention from the prisoners' perspective to the institutional practices themselves. The so-called management approach is concerned with the actions of prison administrators. Following DiIulio, Reisig (1998: 231–2) identified eight dimensions or elements of prison management. Organisational communication refers to the channels of communication within the prison – whether communication is restricted to the formal hierarchy or is informal and cuts across levels of authority. Personal relations refer to the nature of the interactions between superiors and subordinates, whether, for example, staff employ mutual or hierarchical forms of address. Similarly, inmate/staff communication refers to the nature of the interactions between staff and prisoners. The next element is discretion, that is, the extent to which staff rigidly follow rules and procedures rather than exercise personal judgement as the situation dictates. Just as it sounds, regimentation of inmate lives refers to the extent to which prison staff enforce a strict routine as opposed to allowing prisoners the maximum practical degree of personal freedom. Response to inmate rule violations refers to whether or not infractions or disruptions are invariably met with official retaliation and formal sanctions. Similarly, response to inmate disruptiveness refers to whether authorities respond to disturbances by negotiating with prisoners or crushing resistance with force. Finally, inmate participation in decision-making refers to the extent to which prisoners are given some say in prison affairs.

With these eight dimensions as a base, DiIulio described three basic regime models – the control model, the responsibility model and the consensual model. This section is organised around DiIulio's classification. While DiIulio's views on prison control are controversial and far from universally endorsed, his classification is useful for current purposes in that it reduces the complex concept of regime into a few broad themes.

The control model

The inspiration for DiIulio's control model – the model that he most favoured – was the Texas prison system of the 1960s and 1970s. He described the system in the following terms:

> In each prison, correctional officers were organized along strict paramilitary lines running from the warden and his assistants, to the major, all the way down to the most junior correctional officer. Official rules and regulations were followed closely and enforced rigorously. In the prison corridors, inmates were required to walk between lines painted on the floors rather than moving at random down the center. Talking too loud was a punishable offense. In short, daily life inside the prisons was a busy, but carefully orchestrated, routine of numbering, counting, checking, locking, and monitoring inmate movement to and from work activities and treatment programs.
>   (1987: 105)

In terms of specific management elements identified by Reisig (1998), the control model relies on a strictly hierarchical pattern of organisational communication where commands flow downwards via official channels (DiIulio, 1987: 104–9). Consistent with this military-like approach, personal relations between levels of staff are characterised by respectful formality. A similar formality is shown in inmate–staff communication. Individual discretion by staff is minimal – guards run the institution 'by the book' – and the daily routine of prisoners is highly regimented and predictable. If inmates do break the rules, or are disruptive, the official response is swift and certain. It goes without saying that prisoners are considered to have no role in the management of the institution.

The selection and training of guards reflects the paramilitary nature of the regime. Prescriptive educational levels for recruitment were not emphasised since this might exclude potentially good officers. The training is hands-on and practical, conducted on-the-job by experienced officers rather than in the classroom.

Training and programmes are also provided for prisoners, but these too reflect the no-nonsense ethos of the institution. The emphasis is on basic education and vocational skills. The same level of discipline and order is expected during programme participation as it is elsewhere in the prison. Programme attendance does not excuse an inmate from putting in a full day's work. Programmes and even visits are considered privileges and may be cancelled if the prisoner misbehaves.

It should be made clear that while DiIulio stressed the importance of strong and decisive management, he was not advocating the brutal treatment of prisoners or unfettered exercise of power by guards. On the contrary, he argued that such regimes were characteristic of weak administrations. Rather, he argued that strict and predictable control was the best guarantee of a humane, safe and productive environment for prisoners and staff.

There are clear links between the management approach adopted in the control model, and first- and second-generation prison designs. Prisoners are viewed as inherently dangerous and unpredictable, and as needing to be watched and contained at all times. Theoretically, the control model shares features of the opportunity-reduction approach to prevention. The control model aims to reduce prison disorder by monitoring prisoners so closely, keeping them so busy and enforcing rules so strictly that they are unable to engage in misbehaviour. The model discourages casual contact between prisoners, restricting their ability to plan escapes, mount attacks, organise disturbances and traffic contraband. One of the chief successes of the control model, according to DiIulio, is its effectiveness in restricting the activities of prison gangs. Prisoners are simply not permitted the freedom of association that might permit stable groupings to form.

The responsibility model

The responsibility model was based on DiIulio's analysis of the Michigan prison system. In contrast to the Texas system,

> prisons are to be run in ways that impose minimum constraints on inmates . . . Tight security is 'counterproductive' because inmates ought to be given a chance to behave in acceptable ways. Rather than having their every move monitored inmates ought to be given the greatest measure of freedom consistent with basic security requirements and then be held strictly accountable for their actions.
>
> (1987: 119)

The paramilitarism of the control model is replaced in the responsibility model with a less formal approach (pp. 118–21). Where the control model relies on a strict chain of command, the responsibility model favours the devolution of authority to unit managers. Relations between staff members, and between staff and inmates, are casual and egalitarian. Guards exercise considerable discretion and are encouraged to use individual judgement rather than a strict adherence to the rulebook. Rather than having their days ordered and managed by the administration, prisoners have considerable free time and are given choice in the activities in which they participate. Minor rule violations may be overlooked or dealt with informally and the official response to disruptive behaviour is likely to involve negotiation with inmates. Participation of inmates in prison affairs is encouraged and formal structures for this purpose – grievance committees and the like – may be established.

Because the responsibility model reflects a 'human-relations' approach to management, considerable emphasis is placed on the hiring and training of appropriate staff. Affirmative action policies may be adopted in recruitment to increase the number of women and minority groups on the staff. Higher educational qualifications are required than is typically the case for the control model. Extensive pre-service training is offered, comprising a broad curriculum of psychology, counselling and criminal justice theory, in addition to operational matters.

The responsibility model is generally more treatment-oriented than the control model. Inmates may choose from a wide range of programmes that often may be taken in lieu of a work assignment. Extensive visiting privileges and telephone access are the norm. Moreover, the overall approach is to encourage prisoners to take responsibility for their own behaviour and to develop social relationships. Where the control model sets out to divide and fragment prisoners, the responsibility model explicitly attempts to foster a sense of community.

Of the three models he proposed, DiIulio was clearly least impressed with the responsibility model. Leaving his personal assessment aside for the moment, the responsibility model is broadly consistent with third-generation thinking on prisoner control. Control of behaviour in the responsibility model is based on psychological principles such as conveying appropriate expectancies, reducing frustrations and inhibiting neutralising cognitions.

The consensual model

The consensual model is based on the California system. DiIulio (rather disparagingly) conceptualised the consensual model as a sort of compromise or combination of the control and responsibility models. On the one hand:

> Like Michigan, California has developed elaborate classification procedures and inmate grievance mechanisms. As in Michigan, California inmates have

participated in a variety of inmate councils and been offered what are commonly considered to be a wide range of rehabilitative programs. Though not to the extent of Michigan, California has generally favored less rather than more restrictive correctional environments and has come down on the side of liberality in its policies governing inmate grooming, movement, property rights, and other matters.   (1987: 128)

On the other hand:

California's officer force has been organized along paramilitary lines. While grooming standards for officers have been more relaxed than in Texas, California has had a similar emphasis on a 'spit and polish' appearance. While California officers have been less formal in relations with their superiors and more informal in dealing with the inmates than officers in Texas, there has been a far greater emphasis on the chain-of-command and the organizational hierarchy than in Michigan.   (1987: 128)

Apart from these derivations from the control and responsibility models, the consensual model is defined by the emphasis given to 'management by consent':

If there is a single unifying principle of California's approach to correctional administration, it is the notion that prison government rests ultimately on the consent of the governed – that is, the inmates. Prison workers in each state expressed the view that the inmates were capable of seizing control of the prison if they so desired. This opinion was expressed most frequently in California and least frequently in Texas.   (1987: 129)

According to DiIulio, management by consent grew as a strategy specifically to handle prison gangs (1987: 131–7). To secure control, administrators in California were obliged to broker deals with the system's most powerful gangs. The combination of control and responsibility elements reflects an attempt on the one hand to impress inmates with a display of paramilitary professionalism, and on the other hand to elicit the cooperation of inmates through offering a degree of latitude in the prison routine. Prison management is a balancing act. Over-reliance on a paramilitary approach may inflame tensions; allowing prisoners too much freedom will shift the power away from the authorities where it belongs.

Conclusions

While theories of situational prevention are relatively recent in criminology, prison administrators have always relied on manipulating some aspect of the prison environment in order to maintain control. In reviewing the array of control strategies that have been employed in prison, the same situational dimensions outlined in the previous chapter – physical/social, micro/macro, chronic/acute and precipitating/regulating – may be identified.

Thus, strategies of prison control have involved both changes to the built environment, and attempts to alter the patterns of interaction among and between staff and prisoners. Developments in prison design and architecture and the use of security hardware are examples of physical approaches to control. Efforts to reduce crowding, to alter the composition of the prison population and to apply unit management principles all reflect a concern with the social dimension of control.

Control, too, has involved both broad, institution-wide measures, as well as highly specific, targeted interventions. As an enclosed environment there is a sense in which the whole prison may be considered a single 'situation'. On these grounds, almost any aspect of prison conditions – overall level of crowding, the availability of programmes, the general degree of prisoner autonomy – may be regarded as situational. Perhaps closer to the spirit of situational prevention, however, are interventions that are directed at particular control problems. Selective use of CCTV, structured application of incentives and sanctions, and the use of vandal-resistant furnishings are examples of a more micro-situational approach.

Control strategies have also ranged from low-intensity, background measures that have long-term, cumulative effects, to sharp, intensive measures that deliver an instant impact. The soft architectural features of new-generation prisons – the use of harmonious colours, noise-dampening surfaces, filtered lighting, airconditioning – are designed to prevent chronic stress that might increase interpersonal tensions and in this way contribute to prison violence. A sudden and dramatic increase in security is a more immediate method of tackling the problem of violence.

Finally, control strategies have been directed both at prison conditions that are seen to generate disorder and those that allow disorder to occur. Attempts to control overcrowding, to soften and normalise the institutional environment and to liberalise the prison regime are based on the rationale that a great deal of prison misbehaviour is precipitated by the prison environment and as such can be prevented before it starts. Emphases on hardened environments and tight security, on the other hand, exemplify a reactive approach to control where the aim is largely defined in terms of regulating behaviour by reducing the opportunities to offend.

Differing approaches to prison-officer safety illustrate these two rationales. The traditional way to protect prison officers from assaults by prisoners is to minimise the need for personal contact between the two groups through the installation of bars, bullet-proof glass, automatic doors, video cameras and so forth. The alternative strategy adopted in third-generation prisons is to do just the opposite – to reduce the physical barriers that separate prisoners and guards and encourage greater interpersonal contact between the two groups in the hope that prisoners and staff will come to know one another as individuals.

This final distinction between control of the precipitators of disorder and control of the regulators of disorder is particularly challenging because of the inherently contradictory nature of many of the suggested strategies. The dilemma is apparent in the above example concerning the protection of staff. The two suggested approaches are not just antithetical, but from the perspective of each approach the other may be viewed as actively counterproductive. Restrictions aimed at reducing opportunities to misbehave increase the sense of alienation; normalising the environment to reduce alienation increases opportunities to misbehave. There have been some attempts to combine these apparently divergent approaches. Third-generation prisons, for example, rely on both restricting prisoners' behaviour through the adoption of strict unit rules and increased surveillance, and reducing tensions through softer architecture and an emphasis on personal relationships. DiIulio's consensual model also grapples with this problem. How hard and soft approaches to control might be reconciled within a single situational model is the subject of chapter 4.

A model of situational prison control

In criminology, rational choice perspective (Cornish and Clarke, 1986; Clarke, 1992, 1997) is the dominant model for explaining the relationship between situations and offending behaviour. According to the rational choice account of crime, potential offenders weigh up the costs and benefits of illegal behaviour as they judge them to be at the crime scene and then act on the basis of the outcome of this calculus. Rational choice perspective, in turn, provides the rationale for the opportunity-reduction approach to situational crime prevention. Within this approach, crime prevention is viewed in terms of increasing the perceived costs and reducing the perceived benefits of offending so that criminal behaviour might be judged by the potential offender to be an unattractive option.

However, the distinction made in chapter 2 between situational precipitators and situational regulators represents a significant point of departure from these conventional accounts of situational behaviour and its control. The identification of these two sorts of situational influence suggests that rational choice perspective and the opportunity-reduction model are telling only half the story. It was argued that situational theories of prison disorder rely not just on the role of the perceived outcomes of action (i.e. cost-benefit analysis), but also on the role of situational factors that initiate behaviour an individual may otherwise not have undertaken. Similarly, approaches to situational prison control have involved both concerns with restricting opportunities for misbehaviour (manipulating situational regulators) and with reducing the institutional pressures to misbehave (controlling situational precipitators).

Accommodating these two perspectives on control, however, poses some conceptual difficulties. There is clearly the potential for conflict between

55

strategies aimed at controlling precipitators of disorder and those aimed at regulating the contingencies associated with disorder. Each approach may imply quite different and even contradictory solutions to the problem of prison control. On the one hand, control is typically sought by softening and normalising the prison environment and reducing the pressures on prisoners that induce misbehaviour. This approach is exemplified in third-generation prisons and in shifts towards more liberal prison regimes. On the other hand, control is sought generally by hardening the prison environment and reducing the opportunities for prisoners to misbehave. This is the approach that characterises first- and second-generation prisons and provides the rationale for more restrictive and authoritarian regimes.

The contrast between these soft and hard positions on prison control has been a recurring theme in the corrections' literature (e.g. DiIulio, 1987; Levinson, 1982; Rucker, 1994). This chapter proposes a two-stage model of situational prison control for integrating these two approaches. The model, shown in figure 4.1, is based on a temporal sequencing of precipitating and regulating situational influences. In the first stage of the model, a range of psychological processes are proposed that may actively induce individuals to engage in conduct that they may not have otherwise performed. The behaviour may be avoided entirely if relevant precipitators are adequately controlled. In the event that behaviour is initiated, then, in the second stage of the model, performance of that behaviour is subject to consideration of the consequences that are likely to follow. The absence of appropriate disincentives or constraints will permit or encourage behaviour while appropriate disincentives or constraints will prevent or discourage behaviour. However, there are two loops in the model. Over-attention to the control of precipitating factors may necessarily preclude the use of adequate opportunity-reducing strategies, and so permit the performance of unwanted behaviour. Alternatively, over-control at the opportunity-reduction stage may be equally counterproductive and feed back to increase precipitating pressures on behaviour.

What is proposed in this chapter is a general conceptual framework linking the situational theories of behaviour outlined in chapter 2 and the approaches to prison control discussed in chapter 3. It is not the intention in this chapter to consider in any systematic way how well the model might explain specific forms of prison disorder, or to provide extensive empirical evidence for the propositions and predictions contained in the model. These tasks will be left to the following chapters. At this stage, then, the model might be considered a theoretically plausible hypothesis of prison control that reviews of the available research in the subsequent chapters will test.

Situational precipitators

Based on the theories outlined in chapter 2, four general ways that situations can precipitate action are listed in figure 4.1 and expanded upon in table 4.1. Situations can present cues that *prompt* the individual to perform antisocial acts, they can exert social *pressure* on an individual to misbehave, they can reduce self-control and *permit* individuals to engage in behaviour that they would otherwise self-censure, and they can produce emotional arousal that *provokes* a violent response (Wortley, 1997: 66–74; 1998: 175–9). These categories in turn suggest four broad strategies for controlling situational precipitators – controlling prompts, controlling pressures, reducing permissibility, and reducing provocations – each involving four techniques.

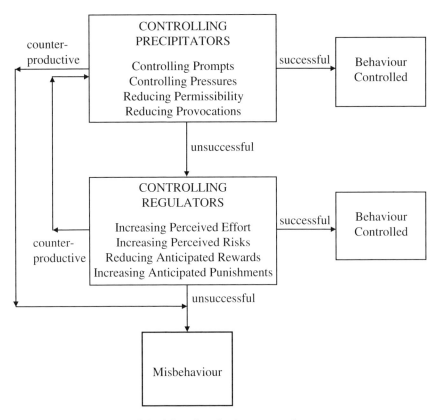

Figure 4.1 Two-stage model of situational prison control

Controlling prompts

Situations may present salient cues to prisoners that prompt misbehaviour. The concept of prompting is based on learning theory's stimulus-response (S-R) principle that holds that virtually all action must be initiated by an appropriate cue in the immediate environment. Even if an antisocial pattern of behaviour has been learned and internalised by an individual, situational conditions govern if and when this behaviour is performed. In every-day terminology, environmental cues may be said to tempt us, jog our memory,

Table 4.1. *Precipitation-control strategies in prison*

Controlling prompts	Controlling pressures	Reducing permissibility	Reducing provocations
Controlling triggers: • Weapons effect • Allowing mementos	*Reducing inappropriate conformity:* • Mixed-age populations • Dispersing trouble-makers	*Rule setting:* • Guards as moral agents • Unit induction	*Reducing frustration:* • Personal control over lights, heat etc. • Non-provocative commands
Providing reminders: • Warning signs • Overt indications of security	*Reducing inappropriate obedience:* • Support for whistle-blowers • Participatory management	*Clarifying responsibility:* • Ownership of living spaces • Alcohol restrictions	*Reducing crowding:* • Reduced prisoner numbers • Use of colour, windows, light etc.
Reducing inappropriate imitation: • Guards as exemplars • Removal of troublemakers	*Encouraging compliance:* • Negotiation with prisoners • Grievance mechanisms	*Clarifying consequences:* • Sense of community in units • Confrontation in unit meetings	*Respecting territory:* • Personal decorations • Room keys
Setting positive expectations: • Domestic-quality furnishings • Conferring trust	*Reducing anonymity:* • Small prison size • Limiting guards' uniforms	*Personalising victims:* • Prisoner–guard contact • Humane prison conditions	*Controlling environmental irritants:* • Noise-absorbing surfaces • Airconditioning

create expectations, set examples for us to follow, evoke moods, stimulate us and alert us to impending consequences. In theoretical terms, environmental cues include eliciting stimuli, discriminative stimuli, models and expectancy cues. The four corresponding prevention techniques described in this section are controlling triggers, providing reminders, reducing inappropriate imitation, and setting positive expectations (table 4.1).

CONTROLLING TRIGGERS

Controlling triggers is directed at automatic responses to situational conditions. Some aspects of the prison environment may trigger reflex negative reactions. For example, the weapons effect described by Berkowitz (1983) suggests that objects such as guns and guards' uniforms that previously have been associated with violence may elicit feelings of aggression in prisoners. Drab, institutionalised cells may trigger feelings of depression, especially if the cell is used for suicide-risk prisoners. By the same token, cues may be introduced into the prison to stimulate positive reactions. For example, photos and personal mementos might provide comfort to prisoners by evoking pleasant memories and moods, and so may help to counter feelings of loneliness and depression. Arguably, access to hetero-erotic photographs and literature might reduce the incidence of homosexual assault.

PROVIDING REMINDERS

Providing reminders is another way to prompt appropriate behaviour by signalling the likely outcomes of transgression. Strategically placed warning signs give ongoing instructions about what behaviour should be performed. The consequences need not be formal punishments. For example, signs may be posted warning of the serious health dangers of needle-sharing and unprotected sex. Reminders do not need to be written signs. Overt security measures such as visible CCTV cameras provide timely prompts to prisoners not to misbehave.

REDUCING INAPPROPRIATE IMITATION

Reducing inappropriate imitation involves two broad strategies. On the one hand, attempts may be made to reduce the influence of negative role models. It is this rationale that underpins the common tactic in prisons of transferring known troublemakers who might incite imitative behaviour. Alternatively, positive models might be used to encourage desirable behaviours. One of the roles that prison guards can fulfil is to model positive standards of behaviour for prisoners. Mature prisoners may also fulfil this role.

SETTING POSITIVE EXPECTATIONS

Finally, desirable behaviour may be prompted by setting positive expectations. Prisoners are likely to respond to the expectations held of them, whether these expectations are positive or negative. Domestic-quality furnishings in third-generation prisons provide expectancy cues that prompt prisoners to take care of their living environment. Positive expectancies can also be conveyed via the nature of the guards' interactions with prisoners. Talking to a prisoner in a way that signals that a hostile reaction is expected may elicit this very response. Displaying a degree of trust towards prisoners may be equally self-fulfilling.

Controlling pressures

Situations may exert social pressure on individuals to perform inappropriate behaviour. Human behaviour is strongly influenced by the expectations and demands of those around them. Four social pressures were identified in chapter 2. Individuals are subject to pressures to conform to group norms, to obey the instructions of authority figures, to comply with social persuasion and to immerse their identity in a crowd. The four prevention techniques corresponding to these pressures are: reducing inappropriate conformity, reducing inappropriate obedience, encouraging compliance and reducing anonymity.

REDUCING INAPPROPRIATE CONFORMITY

There are a number of measures that can be taken in prison that are aimed to reduce inappropriate conformity. Following the logic of the deprivation model, treating prisoners as individuals and permitting them a degree of autonomy may reduce the pressures on prisoners to form self-protective cliques. More direct tactics include manipulating the composition of the prison population. For example, young prisoners in mixed-age prison populations may conform to the more mature behaviour of older prisoners. Within a prison, altering patterns of interaction and contact among prisoners – for example, dispersing troublesome prisoners and placing them in units with more stable prisoners – may help to encourage prosocial conformity.

REDUCING INAPPROPRIATE OBEDIENCE

Inappropriate obedience to authority by prisoners is most likely to occur with prison gang structures. The influence of the gang hierarchy may be weakened by isolating gang leaders or transferring gang members to other institutions (Knox and Tromanhauser, 1991: 17). Given the militaristic nature of most prison regimes, reducing inappropriate obedience also applies to prison guards. There are many documented cases of brutality carried out by guards who claimed to be obediently following the commands of superiors (e.g. Nagle, 1978: 109). Even a single dissenter within an authoritarian structure may positively influence others in an organisation not to succumb to unreasonable demands. Clear organisational codes of conduct and departmental policies that provide active support for whistle-blowers may also help to provide models for appropriate behaviour. Less militaristic and hierarchical regimes, for example, some elements of participatory management and rotating leadership positions with relative frequency, may also reduce authoritarian influences (Kelman and Hamilton, 1989: 321–38).

ENCOURAGING COMPLIANCE

Encouraging compliance involves the use of strategies to secure adherence to rules and requests. Of course, a great deal of compliance in prison is the result of obedience to authority backed by the formal power of the state. For the most part, following lawful commands is obviously both appropriate and essential to the smooth running of the prison and needs to be distinguished from the issue of inappropriate obedience discussed above. However, attempts to gain compliance in prison just as often involve persuasion and personal influence as the issuing of direct orders. Requests and commands that are perceived as fair, consistent and legitimate by prisoners are more likely to be followed than those seen as capricious and unreasonable (Bottoms *et al.*, 1995: 93–4; Kauffman, 1988: 52–4; Lombardo, 1989: 93–6; Sparks *et al.*, 1996: 302–11). The negotiation with prison gangs described in DiIulio's (1987: 131–7) consensual model is an example of securing compliance. Introducing some degree of prisoner participation in management (e.g. through a formal grievance mechanism) is another way of having prisoners commit to rules and regulations (Bloomberg, 1977).

REDUCING ANONYMITY

Reducing anonymity involves avoiding situations in which individuals are made to feel anonymous or deindividuated. Following the logic of Zimbardo's (1970) abandoned car study, feelings of anonymity may be less problematic in smaller prisons than in large, impersonal prisons. The Stanford prison experiment (Haney *et al.*, 1973) further suggests that the wearing of uniforms by guards may encourage a sense of collective identity in their wearers and weaken feelings of personal accountability. More informal modes of dress and the wearing of identifying nametags may help to break down the sense of licence that anonymity and symbols of authority confer. Limiting prisoner turnover might also reduce levels of anonymity. Anonymity is particularly problematic during collective disorder. Provocative methods of crowd control may only serve to heighten prisoner arousal and induce deindividuation.

Reducing permissibility

Situations may facilitate neutralisations or cognitive disengagements and thus interfere with individuals' ability to keep a check on their actions and permit them to engage in normally proscribed behaviours. Situations that encourage individuals to overlook the ethical basis of their behaviour, obscure their personal contributions to the event, misconstrue the consequences of their behaviour and portray potential victims in a dehumanised fashion all interfere with self-censuring and self-control mechanisms (Wortley, 1996: 66–74). The corresponding prevention techniques are rule setting, clarifying responsibility, clarifying consequences and personalising victims.

RULE SETTING

Rule setting seeks to reduce uncertainty about the moral illegitimacy of a given behaviour by denying potential transgressors neutralisations that allow them to contrast their behaviour with the more heinous behaviour of others, focus on the corruption of those in power, redefine their actions using more palatable language or claim that their actions are serving a higher moral principle. Issuing prisoners with rulebooks on admission provides them with a catalogue of permissible and impermissible behaviours. Similarly, unit induction procedures should include a clear outlining of rules so as to leave little room for prisoners to exploit ambiguity in their own favour (e.g. 'I didn't know it was wrong'). Clear rules also need to be conveyed to visitors emphasising the impermissibility of passing contraband to prisoners. Individuals often rely on those around them for guidelines for correct behaviour and may come to accept corrupt and antisocial practices as normal (e.g. 'everybody does it'). Guards may play an important role here in maintaining community standards in prison and conveying these standards in their reactions to prisoners' behaviour.

CLARIFYING RESPONSIBILITY

Clarifying responsibility targets neutralisations in which individuals seek to avoid self-blame for their actions by citing external causal agents, blaming others, claiming a lack of behavioural alternatives, or using groups, organisations or superiors to diffuse their personal contribution to antisocial acts.

Restricting prisoners' access to alcohol is an obvious example of reducing the potential for chemically induced disinhibition (e.g. 'I couldn't help it'). However, other strategies operate at the moral-reasoning level. Prisons in which few programmes and activities are available provide prisoners with ready excuses for misbehaving (e.g. 'it's their fault if there is nothing else to do'). Neglecting prisoners' concerns about safety (e.g. refusing protection) allows prisoners to blame prison administrators in the event of an escape (e.g. 'I had no choice'). Prisoners are also likely to feel little responsibility towards property over which they have little sense of ownership (e.g. 'it doesn't belong to me'). Vandalism in prison may be reduced by promoting in prisoners a sense of possession over their living areas by allowing more freedom to personalise these areas with pictures, personal possessions, individual furniture arrangements and so forth. Clarifying responsibility can also apply to the behaviour of guards. Following Bandura's (1976: 226) argument that the division of labour within organisations facilitates corruption by allowing individuals to hide behind a collective responsibility (e.g. 'I'm just part of the group'), prison guards can be assigned a case-load making them responsible for the welfare of specific prisoners.

CLARIFYING CONSEQUENCES

Clarifying consequences is based on the principle that individuals may seek to deny causing harm by portraying the outcome of their actions as being less serious than it really is, denying that any harm was caused, or even claiming that the consequences were positive. The general control strategy involves exposing individuals' attempts to gloss over the negative consequences of their behaviours. (Clarifying consequences differs from providing reminders in that it focuses more on the moral dimension rather than on the narrow consequences to oneself.) One of the benefits of unit management is the sense of community that is developed and the recognition that one's own behaviour impacts on others. This message can be reinforced formally in unit meetings in which staff and other prisoners can confront a misbehaving prisoner with the effects of his or her misbehaviour on unit members.

PERSONALISING VICTIMS

Personalising victims is based on the principle that people find it easier to victimise those who can be stereotyped as sub-human or unworthy, those who can be portrayed as deserving of the fate that has befallen them, or even those who are simply outsiders or anonymous. The general control strategy involves creating a prison environment that minimises depersonalisation and strengthens the emotional attachment among and between prisoners and guards. Reducing population turnover may allow prisoners to form more stable social relationships. The emphasis on prisoner–guard contact in third-generation prisons is based partly on the rationale that it is more difficult to be abusive towards people who have come to be known as individuals. More generally, prison conditions that respect the dignity of prisoners reduce the capacity of potential aggressors to characterise victims in a depersonalised way. Referring to prisoners by numbers, making them wear sub-standard clothing and housing them in squalid, overcrowded conditions all contribute to this dehumanising process.

Reducing provocations

Finally, situations may provoke emotional arousal that can trigger an antisocial response. Aversive emotional arousal can be generated by frustration – having goal-directed behaviour blocked – and environmental conditions such as crowding, intrusions on territory and privacy, excessive noise and temperature extremes. The resulting stress and frustration increase adrenaline activity and irritability that organisms may attempt to resolve with an aggressive behavioural response. Four techniques for reducing provocation are reducing frustration, reducing crowding, respecting territory and controlling environmental irritants.

REDUCING FRUSTRATION

The prison environment offers many opportunities for reducing frustration. Boredom, waiting for the use of telephones and disputes over television programmes are frustrations easily remedied by situational interventions (e.g. better programming, more televisions and telephones etc.). Similarly, giving prisoners more control over day-to-day aspects of their lives – for example, providing individually controlled light and heating switches in cells – reduces their frustrating dependency on others. More generally, aggression may be provoked by many forms of aversive treatment. Taunts, insults and physical mistreatment by guards and other prisoners are all likely to provoke aggressive responses in prisoners. Better-trained and more experienced staff may be less likely to provoke aggressive responses in prisoners.

REDUCING CROWDING

Reducing crowding ideally involves actual reduction of prisoner numbers relative to available space. Prison building programmes aim to reduce overcrowding, although new prisons seem to fill as fast as they are built. Back-end release strategies (parole, good-time provisions, home release) are one way that prison administrators can contribute to reductions in prison numbers. Failing this, some reductions in the experience of crowding may be achieved through the use of colour, light and interior design to increase the sense of spaciousness. Partitions and other methods of sub-dividing the prison population can be used to reduce social density without needing to reduce spatial density.

RESPECTING TERRITORY

Respecting territory involves encouraging in prisoners a sense of ownership over their immediate environment and providing havens for them to meet personal space and privacy needs. Giving prisoners a sense of ownership over their living quarters not only encourages them to take care of the area (as suggested previously under clarifying responsibility) but may also contribute to lower levels of prisoner-prisoner violence. Single-cell accommodation gives prisoners a place to call home. Allowing them to decorate their cells and providing them with cell keys enhances this sense of territoriality. While territorial possession is associated with positive psychological states, invasion of territory is stressful and can provoke an aggressive response. Officers need to take special precautions when entering prisoners' cells and carry out any necessary searches with some sensitivity to the prisoners' territorial concerns.

CONTROLLING ENVIRONMENTAL IRRITANTS

Controlling environmental irritants seeks to minimise chronic stress-inducing aspects of the built environment. The use of sound-absorbing surfaces to reduce noise pollution, the use of non-institutional colour schemes to reduce visual monotony and the installation of airconditioning to regulate temperature extremes are examples of how this objective might be operationalised. Many of these features are found in third-generation prisons.

Situational regulators

In the event that behaviour is precipitated, performance of that behaviour is regulated by consideration of the consequences that are likely to follow. Regulators may take the form of rewards and punishments, or environmental conditions that place more direct physical constraints on behaviour. Regulating behaviour is the usual focus of situational crime prevention and the logic of this approach is comprehensively described by rational choice perspective and the opportunity-reduction model of situational prevention

Table 4.2. *Opportunity-reduction strategies in prison*

Increasing perceived effort	Increasing perceived risks	Reducing anticipated rewards	Increasing anticipated punishments
Target hardening: •Vandal-proof furnishings •Hardened plastic screens	*Entry–exit screening:* •Screening visitors •Searches on leaving workshops	*Target removal:* •Restrictions on personal property •Protection for vulnerable prisoners	*Increasing costs:* •Formal charges •Non-replacement of vandalised property
Access control: •Control gates •Closing wings during the day	*Formal surveillance:* •CCTV •Drug testing	*Identifying property:* •Property-marking •Prison issue	*Removing privileges:* •Denial of parole •Expulsion from units
Deflecting offenders: •Staggered cell release •Structured activities	*Surveillance by employees:* •Direct supervision in units •Civilian staff	*Reducing temptation:* •Single-cell accommodation •Supervision of outside workers	*Increasing social condemnation:* •Unit meetings •Utilising prisoner self-interest
Controlling facilitators: •Plastic cutlery •Restrictions on fruit juice	*Natural surveillance :* •Defensible space principle in units •Shared cells for suicide risks	*Denying benefits:* •PIN for phone cards •Ignoring manipulation	*Making an example:* •Punishing ringleaders •Publicising punishments

Adapted from Clarke and Homel, 1997.

(Clarke, 1992, 1997). In the latest version of the opportunity-reduction model, Clarke and Homel (1997) proposed four categories of opportunity-reduction; increasing perceived effort, increasing perceived risks, reducing anticipated rewards and inducing guilt or shame (relabelled removing excuses in Clarke 1997). However, the model of opportunity-reduction described here differs in two ways from Clarke and Homel's. First, the category inducing guilt or shame has been omitted. Wortley (1997: 75; 1998: 183–5) has argued that many of the proposed strategies within this category do not involve opportunity-reduction in the normal sense of that term, but are directed at psychological processes that 'ready' the potential offender to perform illegal acts. This category, then, is more logically conceptualised as precipitation-control and has been subsumed in the current model largely by reducing permissibility. The second change is the inclusion of a new category increasing anticipated punishments. The rationale for this new category is suggested by learning theory and complements the existing reducing anticipated rewards category. The four strategies associated with these categories are shown in table 4.2.

Increasing perceived effort

This category involves strategies designed to make prison disorder more difficult to carry out. Approaches to increasing perceived effort range from the use of heavy security measures that will physically block the most determined of offenders to relatively unobtrusive measures aimed at deflecting incidental transgressors. The four techniques within this strategy are target hardening, access control, deflecting offenders and controlling facilitators.

TARGET HARDENING

The first strategy, and perhaps the most widely known of all opportunity-reduction techniques, is target hardening. Target hardening is the 'locks-and-bolts' face of situational prevention and has long been an intrinsic part of prison control. Target hardening aims to obstruct potential offenders carrying out their intended actions by putting physical barriers in their way. Prisons are by nature target-hardened environments. The use of reinforced materials to deter vandalism, the installation of hardened plastic screens to protect guards and perimeter security systems are just some of the many examples of target hardening in the prison context.

ACCESS CONTROL

Access control is also widely practised in prison and involves controlling the movements of prisoners and restricting their entry into certain areas. For example, prisoners are typically required to have a prisoner officer open a locked gate in order for them to move from one section of a prison to another. Often, too, some sections of the prison are completely shut off to prisoners at certain times of the day. Closing wings during the day, for example, reduces the chances of prisoners stealing from cells while the occupants are at work.

DEFLECTING OFFENDERS

Deflecting offenders seeks to divert likely offenders from potential trouble spots. The staggered release of prisoners from their cells is an attempt to prevent possible trouble associated with a sudden congregation of prisoners.

Similarly, staggering mealtimes is a way of reducing congestion in the dining-room. The provision of programmes and activities in prison may also be interpreted as a method of deflecting prisoners from trouble by dispersing them throughout the prison and imposing structures on their time.

CONTROLLING FACILITATORS

Controlling facilitators involves denying access to objects that might assist in an illegal endeavour. For example, replacing metal prison cutlery with plastic alternatives makes the cutlery a far less useful weapon. Restrictions on fruit juice in many prisons are designed to prevent prisoners brewing home-made alcohol. Removing shoelaces and belts from suicide-risk prisoners is designed to make self-harm more difficult to accomplish.

Increasing perceived risks

Increasing the perceived risk seeks to deter crime by enhancing the probability that illegal behaviour will be detected. Being monitored and watched is a ubiquitous part of a prisoner's life. This does not mean, however, that there are not many opportunities in most prisons for misbehaviour to go undetected or considerable scope for improving surveillance procedures. The four specific techniques under this category are entry–exit screening, formal surveillance, surveillance by employees and natural surveillance.

ENTRY–EXIT SCREENING

Entry–exit screening involves carrying out checking procedures to prevent contraband being brought into the prison, or to prevent the movement of contraband within the prison. Thus, staff and official visitors may be searched before entering the prison. Similarly, prisoners' visitors may be screened before visits and prisoners searched after visits. Prisoners are also regularly searched when they return from court or from outside programmes. Within the prison, prisoners may also be searched as they move from one location in the prison to another, for example, after leaving workshops, to ensure that they are not carrying homemade weapons.

FORMAL SURVEILLANCE

In prison most aspects of the prisoners' lives are subjected to formal surveillance. Observation towers, guards on their rounds, roll-calls, cell checks and CCTV are all aspects of the formal surveillance regime in prison. Also included under this strategy is drug testing, since this too is designed to keep tabs on the prisoners' behaviour.

SURVEILLANCE BY EMPLOYEES

A further strategy is surveillance by employees. In the prison context, the distinction between this and the previous strategy would seem rather blurred, since prison employees are usually employed precisely to carry out surveillance. Nevertheless, a distinction can be made between staff activities explicitly directed at monitoring prisoners, and activities for which monitoring is an ancillary aspect. Thus, the interaction between guards and prisoners in functional units both reduces tensions between these two groups and provides guards with an opportunity to carry out more direct supervision of prisoners. The incidental surveillance role of civilian staff such as teachers, psychologists and so on can also be classified under this strategy.

NATURAL SURVEILLANCE

Natural surveillance attempts to capitalise on the observations of misconduct by people going about their daily lives. As with the above strategy, the concept of natural surveillance is perhaps more useful in a community setting than a prison. Nevertheless, the elimination of blind spots may be conceptualised as an example of increasing natural surveillance. There are also opportunities to involve prisoners in the surveillance task. For example, the defensible space principle in functional units encourages prisoners to care for and protect their own territory. The open-plan design of functional units also forces a high degree of interpersonal interaction among prisoners and between prisoners and staff that increases natural surveillance. Putting suicide-risk prisoners in shared-cell accommodation rather than in single cells reduces the opportunities for engaging in self-harm.

Reducing anticipated rewards

Reducing anticipated rewards involves making the outcome of contemplated behaviour less desirable. Rational choice perspective assumes that most crime is purposive, that is, individuals seek to benefit themselves in some way. Reducing anticipated rewards, therefore, requires an understanding of what is motivating the misbehaviour. The four techniques associated with this strategy are target removal, identifying property, reducing temptation and denying benefits.

TARGET REMOVAL

One way to reduce anticipated rewards is through target removal. If assaults in prison are motivated by theft, then one strategy is to remove from prisoners commodities that are likely to be stolen. The same rationale explains the removal of vulnerable prisoners to protection areas to reduce opportunities for their victimisation.

IDENTIFYING PROPERTY
The benefits of theft can also be reduced by identifying property. Prison-issue goods are usually clearly identified in some way: clothes are a distinctive colour, library books are stamped, radios have serial numbers and so forth. Similarly, prisoners' possessions will be less desirable objects of theft if they are clearly marked and able to be identified. Keeping a register of personal possessions issued to prisoners further facilitates checking.

REDUCING TEMPTATION
Another strategy is reducing temptation. This strategy assumes that some misbehaviour is a spur-of-the-moment decision to capitalise on a chance opportunity. Impulsive escapes by prisoners working unsupervised outside the prison walls may fall into this category. The temptation to sexually assault another prisoner or to steal personal property is reduced if single-cell accommodation is provided rather than shared cells or dormitories.

DENYING BENEFITS
Finally, denying benefits seeks to render worthless ill-gotten gains or to ensure that misbehaviour does not achieve its desired goal. Phone cards with personal identification numbers (PIN) are able to be used only by the owner and so are of little value as objects of theft in prison (La Vigne, 1994). A more controversial tactic may be to withhold rewards from prisoners who exhibit manipulative or attention-seeking behaviour. An example of this tactic is to refuse to transfer a prisoner whose acting-out behaviour is specifically calculated to obtain a transfer. The problem with this tactic is deciding whether the behaviour is truly manipulative, or whether it is an expression of genuine fear or depression. Ignoring suicide threats is never recommended.

Increasing anticipated punishments
A new opportunity-reduction category is proposed that is based on the concept of punishment outlined as part of learning theory in chapter 2. Whether this category is transferable to community settings is perhaps debatable, since many punishments for crime occur well after the performance of the behaviour and so do not really qualify as situational. However, within the confines of the prison walls there is sufficient control over environmental contingencies to operationalise punishment strategies at a more-or-less

situational level. Four ways to increase punishments for misbehaviour are increasing costs (based on positive punishment), removing privileges (negative punishment), encouraging condemnation from peers and significant others (social punishment) and having the potential offender observe the punishment of other misbehaviours (vicarious punishment).

INCREASING COSTS

To increase costs is probably the most common control mechanism in prison. Virtually all forms of prison misbehaviour are liable for punishment if detected. Typical prison punishments include warnings, transfers, fines and formal criminal charges (Vaag, 1994: 220–7). However, increasing costs does not necessarily involve formal sanctions. For example, not replacing recreation equipment that has been deliberately broken by prisoners is an informal way of punishing vandalism.

REMOVING PRIVILEGES

Removing privileges involves taking away things that prisoners value. Note that removing privileges is conceptually distinct from denying benefits. Denying benefits is a neutral intervention in that no rewards are delivered as a result of the behaviour; removing privileges is a punishment since the individual is worse off as a result. Again, this tactic is ubiquitous in prison, and includes expulsion from a desirable unit and return to general discipline, denial of parole, loss of remission, suspension of canteen privileges and so forth.

INCREASING SOCIAL CONDEMNATION

Increasing social condemnation seeks to enlist the support of the prison community to shape the behaviour of recalcitrant prisoners. The usual picture of prison society would suggest that just the opposite is likely to occur, that is, that other prisoners will actively encourage dissent and misbehaviour. But this need not be the case. When the behaviour of a trouble-maker threatens the harmony and conditions of the general community, then other prisoners have good reason to seek to have the behaviour changed. Once again, units have proved to be a powerful forum for exerting social control. Disruptive unit members may be challenged at a unit meeting, or be subjected to condemnation in the course of informal social interaction. Prisoners have a particular interest in ensuring that fellow inmates behave if the former are negatively affected by the misbehaviour. For example, in the case of the non-replacement of damaged equipment described earlier, all prisoners are made to suffer for the actions of a few, and these few are likely to become unpopular. Similarly, all prisoners have a stake in ensuring low escape rates if authorities are known to respond to escapes with tightened security procedures. The danger in using other prisoners in these ways, of course, is that social condemnation may escalate into outright intimidation and coercion. Prisons have an unsavoury history of using other prisoners as enforcers.

MAKING AN EXAMPLE

Making an example is based on the premise that seeing or hearing of others punished for a behaviour serves to inhibit the performance of that behaviour. Ensuring that punishments are widely publicised within the prison may increase the general deterrence value. It is partly to set an example that recaptured escapees are confined to maximum-security conditions. The targeting of gang leaders for punishment is also designed to set an example to other members.

Counterproductive control

As figure 4.1 indicates, erring too far in either the direction of precipitation-control or opportunity-reduction can be counterproductive. A comparison of strategies listed in tables 4.1 and 4.2 reveals numerous points of potential tension between the respective approaches, presenting prison administrators with ongoing dilemmas about whether it is better to tighten-up or loosen-off in order to maintain control.

Too-hard control

The idea that overt constraint generates prison disorder has its theoretical roots in the symbolic interactionist explanations of the prison experience advanced by sociologists such as Sykes (1958) and Goffman (1961). According to these accounts, attempts to control prisoners through coercion succeed only in strengthening the prisoner subculture and entrenching prisoner resistance. While theoretical explanations may differ, the general view that strict control is counterproductive has come to be adopted as the standard position of most social scientists in the field. According to the situational analysis outlined here, there are a variety of ways that excessive or otherwise inappropriate opportunity-reduction can precipitate misbehaviour. Too-hard control can transform into each of the four categories of situational precipitators shown in table 4.1.

COUNTERPRODUCTIVE CONTROL THAT PROMPTS

First, attempts to reduce opportunities for disorder can inadvertently prompt prisoners to misbehave. There are a number of ways that this can occur. In some cases, attempts to exercise authority can subvert attempts at controlling triggers. If an object used to help control behaviour has associations with situations that have elicited antisocial responses in the past, then the object may itself elicit an antisocial response. The weapons effect described by Berkowitz (1983) is an example of this. The wearing by prison guards of firearms, uniforms and other militaristic paraphernalia that are used to assert control may in fact evoke feelings of aggression from prisoners and encourage the very sort of behaviour the weapons etc. are designed to deter.

Obtrusive opportunity-reduction can also interfere with attempts at setting positive expectations. Overt attempts to control behaviour can convey to potential offenders the self-fulfilling message that violent and destructive behaviour is expected. For example, target hardening suggests that the solution to prison vandalism is to guard against inevitable abuse of property by prisoners by using vandal-resistant fittings and furnishings. However, according to the logic of the expectancy effect, target hardening in this way may only exacerbate the problem.

COUNTERPRODUCTIVE CONTROL THAT EXERTS PRESSURE

Second, excessive constraint can increase social pressures to perform antisocial behaviour. Over-reliance on punitive approaches to control can defeat attempts at reducing inappropriate conformity. The typical reaction of groups under external threat is to increase intra-group cohesion and to exert greater pressure on individual members to conform to group norms (Forsyth, 1990: 387–8). In addition, in-group/out-group differentiations become more sharply drawn. Members of a cohesive group develop a strong sense of in-group righteousness and a corresponding belief in the moral illegitimacy of the threatening outsiders. To accentuate the differences between 'us' and 'them' the group may even adopt norms and behaviours that are explicitly oppositional to those of the outgroup with whom they are in conflict, and that, in turn, serves to entrench and escalate the tension between the parties (Forsyth, 1990: 388). The danger, then, is that the more repressive the prison regime, the more likely prisoners are to maintain a unified resistance. This, of course, is the very pattern of negativistic prison behaviour (albeit described in somewhat different theoretical terms) that Sykes, Goffman and others identified and described more than forty years ago.

Similar negativism at an individual level may occur when restrictive methods of control are employed instead of using more subtle attempts to encourage compliance. In this case, the psychological mechanism is re-actance. While prisoners expect to have their personal freedoms curtailed in prison, some restrictions can be more psychologically threatening than others. When attempts to persuade prisoners to obey rules or comply with instructions are perceived to be unfair, illegitimate, manipulative or unnecessarily coercive then the reaction may be one of defiance rather than compliance.

Opportunity-reduction strategies can also clash with the objective of reducing anonymity. The role of uniforms as elicitors of aggression has already been discussed, but Haney *et al.* (1973) argued that a further problem with regimented prison dress is the tendency for it to promote a sense of anonymity both among guards and prisoners. This sort of weakening of personal identity is a chronic problem in many prisons. However, more acute levels of deindividuation can also be generated by inappropriate attempts to exercise control. Under certain conditions, prisoner solidarity can progress to deindividuation. One of the key determinants of deindividuation (in addition to group membership) is arousal (Forsyth, 1990: 462). Accordingly, responding to instances of collective action by prisoners with control tactics that further inflame emotions and heighten the sense of righteous rage of group members can induce extreme deindividuation. Under these circumstances the situation may escalate into a full-blown riot.

COUNTERPRODUCTIVE CONTROL THAT FACILITATES PERMISSIBILITY

Third, inappropriate attempts to constrain behaviour can facilitate the weakening of personal controls. Many prison environments provide the ideal conditions for inducing moral neutralisation. In particular, control strategies relying on hardening targets in prison may run counter to strategies aimed at increasing victim worth. High walls, security guards, bars and so forth not only create physical barriers between potential offenders and victims, but also create psychological barriers. Harsh, depersonalising environments designed to restrict violent behaviour can in fact divest individuals of their human qualities and render them psychologically more acceptable as targets for victimisation.

COUNTERPRODUCTIVE CONTROL THAT PROVOKES

Fourth, attempts to over-control behaviour can generate aversive emotional arousal and provoke disorder. Tightly run prison regimes can make the task of reducing frustration difficult. Restrictions on prisoners' movements and activities by definition involve blocking goal-directed behaviour. The need to pass through gates to move from one section to the next, having basic functions such as heating and lighting centrally operated and restrictions on the possession of goods are just a few examples of control strategies that are inherently frustrating. In some cases the resulting aggressive response to frustration may be such as to overwhelm the attempts at control that produced it.

Obtrusive environmental constraints may also interfere with respect for territory, thus contributing to environmental stress and in this way increasing levels of antisocial behaviour. There is an ongoing tension between the surveillance needs of staff and the privacy needs of inmates. Constant observation of prisoners' activities and frequent body and cell searches involve invasions of territory and personal space.

Too-soft control

Claims about counterproductive control work both ways. Looking at the problem from the other direction, too much concern with controlling situational precipitators of disorder in prison may also backfire. Not all commentators are convinced by the 'less-is-more' argument raised in favour of control through loosening-off. A few researchers have refuted the orthodoxy that prison disorder is the product of too many restrictions on prisoners (DiIulio, 1987, 1991; Ekland-Olson, 1986; Farmer, 1988; Unseem and Kimball, 1989). On the contrary they have argued that far from reducing prison violence, the liberalisation of prison regimes in the past thirty years is responsible for an increase in disorder. Reflecting these concerns, Buchanan *et al.* (1988) in their *Disruptive Maximum Security Inmate Management Guide* warned:

> each attempt at normalization bears examination to determine the impact that the feature will have on inmate management and control. Any effort to create a 'soft environment' that will impede inmate supervision and the management of disruptive behavior should be strongly opposed. (p. 95)

The arguments about counterproductive effects of loosening-off are essentially the mirror of those raised in connection with tightening-up and need not be laboured. For example, just as it may be argued that the use of uniforms encourages abuse of authority, so too it might be argued that doing away with uniforms reduces the capacity of guards to assert legitimate authority. Clearly there are limits to the degree of trust, individuality, privacy and autonomy that can be extended to prisoners before security and control concerns are compromised. Taken to absurdity, for example, the expectancy principle argues against the need for any form of opportunity-reduction lest it imply an affronting lack of faith in human nature. Similarly, at some level having goal-directed behaviour blocked – that is, not getting we want – is simply a reality of life both inside and outside of prison and a crucial experience in the learning process. And while some prisoners might find continual surveillance an intrusion on privacy, the other side of the coin is that lack of adequate supervision is a major failing in many prisons and a significant contributor to the high levels of prisoner victimisation and suicides.

Conclusions

Typically, approaches to prison control aimed at reducing the precipitators of misbehaviour and those aimed at reducing the opportunities for misbehaviour have been cast as polar alternatives. Each approach is seen to derive from fundamentally different assumptions about the nature of human behaviour and the causes of prison disorder. A choice is demanded between the proposition that prison disorder is essentially reactive and needs to be mollified, or that it is purposive and needs to be deterred. Adopting one approach is seen to necessarily preclude the adoption of the other or, more seriously, to actively work to the detriment of the other.

It has been argued in this chapter that situational precipitators and opportunities need not be viewed as competing explanations of behaviour, but rather seen as complementary explanations. Both provide valid accounts of prison disorder but each describes a different situational source of that disorder. That is, precipitation-control and opportunity-reduction can be understood not so much as opposing logics, but as strategies directed at different stages of the person-situation interaction. While there is a potential for counterproductive interventions, these can be explained within the model and guarded against. The issue is not the choice between hard and soft control but rather the appropriate balance between these two approaches.

The chapters that follow examine the situational control of specific kinds of prison misbehaviour, namely, prisoner-prisoner assaults, sexual assaults, prisoner-guard assaults, self-harm, drug use, escapes and collective disorder. In examining these behaviours, the utility of the proposed two-stage model of prison control outlined in this chapter is assessed against the available empirical research.

PART II

Specific behaviours

CHAPTER 5

Prisoner-prisoner violence

Prisoner victimisation of other prisoners is arguably the most common form of prison violence. It is also the form of prison disorder that has attracted most empirical attention. With the dominance of the deprivation model among social scientists since the 1950s, much of this research has focused on the contribution of prison conditions to prisoner violence. While not quite situational, this research nevertheless provides a relatively large database (compared with other forms of misbehaviour) from which a situational analysis might be constructed.

Nature of the problem

Definition and incidence

Prisoner-prisoner violence is taken to include all incidents of fighting, assaults (with or without weapons) and homicides where prisoners were both the assailant and the victim. In 1995, nearly 26,000 prisoner-prisoner assaults, resulting in eighty-two deaths, were recorded in US prisons (Stephan, 1997). While the number of assaults is considerably higher than the level recorded in 1990 (21,184), because of the dramatic increase in prisoner numbers over this period there has actually been a slight drop in the assault rate (31.3 versus 28.4 per 1,000 prisoners). Looking back further, assault and death rates have fallen considerably from the record highs recorded in the early 1980s (Lillis, 1994).

But, as Cooley (1993) points out, reported assaults are the tip of the iceberg. The actual assault levels may be five times the official rate. This dark figure further underscores the potential offered in the prison environment to carry out offences unobserved. Based on research in the Canadian prison

79

system, Cooley conservatively estimated the rate of assault in prison to be more than three times that of the general community and about twice that of a matched community sub-sample. Using self-report methods, O'Donnell and Edgar (1996: 9), in a British study, found that 44 per cent of young prisoners had been threatened with violence by other prisoners and 30 per cent had been assaulted in the month preceding the study. For adults the figures were 26 per cent and 19 per cent respectively. Maitland and Sluder (1998), in a survey conducted in a US prison, found that during their current sentence, 6 per cent of prisoners had been threatened with a weapon, 7 per cent had been bitten, 10 per cent had property extorted, and 59 per cent had been subject to verbal harassment.

Patterns

Most prisoner-prisoner assaults are committed by single assailants and do not involve weapons. In a study of four prisons, Atlas (1983) found that single-assailant assaults accounted for between 65 per cent and 98 per cent of all incidents, and that between 53 per cent and 82 per cent of all assaults were carried out by unarmed assailants. Where assailants are armed, the choice of weapon is limited by what is readily available within the prison environment. Knives are the most common weapon (Cooley, 1993; Jayewardene and Doherty, 1985; Porporino et al., 1987; Sylvester et al., 1977: 14, 27). For example, Sylvester et al. (1977) found 75 per cent of prison homicides were carried out with knives or stabbing weapons, 7 per cent involved strangulation, 6 per cent blunt objects, 6 per cent firearms and 4 per cent arson. Homicides are somewhat more likely to involve multiple assailants than are assaults, suggesting a more premeditated pattern. Porporino et al. (1987) reported that in the cases for which the information was available, half of prison homicides were carried out by multiple assailants.

Motivation

Varied reasons for attacks by prisoners on other prisoners have been found. O'Donnell and Edgar (1996: 74–5) interviewed victims and perpetrators of assaults and found that the most common reasons given for an attack were retaliation, to settle a conflict, to enforce debts, to enhance status, to achieve some material gain or to relieve boredom. Porporino et al. (1987) found that 14 per cent of prison homicides were associated with the drug trade, 11 per cent were motivated by revenge, 7 per cent were attacks on sex offenders, 6 per cent involved prison debts, 6 per cent occurred during an altercation, 4 per cent were attacks on informants and 4 per cent arose from homosexual affairs (in over 40 per cent of cases no cause could be determined). Other researchers (e.g. Edgar and O'Donnell, 1998a; Wener and Olsen, 1978: 23; 1980) have emphasised the spontaneous nature of many assaults, with violence often the result of prisoners quarrelling about access to telephones, television programmes, the use of sporting equipment, places in queues and so forth.

Summarising the various motives for prison-prisoner violence, Bowker (1985: 12) distinguished between expressive and instrumental assaults by prisoners. Expressive assaults are heat-of-the-moment affairs, sparked more often than not by some trivial altercation. Instrumental assaults, on the other hand, are carried out in quest of some definable gain – power, status, revenge, material goods and so forth – and tend to involve a degree of planning.

Bowker's classification can be interpreted within the general situational model of prison disorder proposed in chapter 4. Expressive assaults equate with the precipitation stage of the model. With these assaults, the prisoner is generally viewed to be reacting to pent-up tensions and frustrations generated by incarceration, and/or to be responding to a more immediate and specific provocation or behavioural trigger. Strategies in these cases involve reducing pressures and frustrations and as such may be conceptualised as precipitation control. Instrumental assaults typically involve the calculated exploitation of a presenting opportunity and so fit the second stage of the model. The prisoner carries out the assault because he judges that the likely benefits will outweigh the potential costs. The required control strategy in this case involves increased surveillance, the elimination of blind spots and so forth.

Situational context
SEASONAL VARIATIONS
The effect of temperature on assault rates has been explored in a number of studies. With a few exceptions (Dietz and Rada, 1983; Walters, 1998) studies have reported relatively high assault rates for the summer months (Atlas, 1982: 344–6; 1984; Ganjavi *et al.*, 1985; Megargee, 1977; Porporino *et al.*, 1987; Steinke, 1991; Sylvester *et al.*, 1977: 12). At the other end of the scale, some studies have also found high assault rates in mid-winter (Atlas, 1982: 347), a finding possibly related to the increased levels of enforced association among prisoners. Generally, however, these studies did not find that assault rates were related to daily ambient temperatures. That is, hot summer days did not produce significantly more assaults than mild summer days. It seems that to the extent that temperature does provoke aggression, there is either a critical threshold operating,

or the stressful effects are cumulative and take some time to manifest themselves.

There is scattered and sometimes conflicting research that looks at other climatic and seasonal variables. Atlas (1984) failed to find any effect for the lunar phases. Ganjavi *et al.* (1985) found no association between rainfall and assaults, while Atlas (1983) found rainfall did reduce assaults on hot days, a result he attributed to associated cooling effects. Ganjavi *et al.* (1985) further found that violence was positively correlated with wind in winter and negatively correlated in summer, again suggesting that prisoner comfort levels may be important. They found no consistent patterns for humidity, hours of sunshine or snow.

SECURITY LEVEL

There are more assaults and homicides in high- and medium-security institutions than in low-security institutions (Jayewardene and Doherty, 1985; MacDonald, 1999; McCorkle *et al.*, 1995; Porporino *et al.*, 1987). Assaults in medium- and maximum-security institutions are also more likely to involve a weapon (Cooley, 1993). At first glance, these findings might suggest that the increased level of opportunity-reduction in maximum-security institutions is not effective in reducing assaultive behaviour and may even provoke it. The problem with this research, of course, is the confound between security level and prisoner characteristics. Presumably, high-security prisoners are not only subjected to more intense scrutiny (although even this assumption may not be necessarily true), but are also judged to be in more need of this security.

TIME

Assault rates have been found to increase on certain days of the week or at certain times of the day, although the exact pattern of the temporal distribution may vary from one institution to another. Homicides are generally more frequent on weekends (Jayewardene and Doherty, 1985; Porporino *et al.*, 1987). Several studies have found most homicides occurred during the evening (Jayewardene and Doherty, 1985; Porporino *et al.*, 1987; Sylvester *et al.*, 1977: 12), although Dietz and Rada (1983) found most assaults occurred during the day shift. On balance it does not seem that certain days or times of the day are inherently stressful. Instead, these studies suggest that assault rates are affected by particular aspects of individual institutions – for example, the timing of the movement of prisoners from one location to another, lower staffing levels or the change of shifts – that might generate provocations or increase opportunities.

LOCATION

Similarly, preferred assaults sites have been found to vary considerably from one study to another, reflecting variations in the characteristics of the institutions under investigation. Sylvester *et al.* (1977: 13–14) found 25 per cent of prison homicides occurred in participants' cells, one-third in the cell block or dormitory, with common areas such as recreation areas and gyms the next most likely location. In their examination of prison homicides Porporino *et al.* (1987) found that 45 per cent took place in cells, 14 per cent in the common room, 14 per cent in yards, 12 per cent in corridors and 8 per cent in showers. Quinsey and Varney (1977), in a study of a maximum-security psychiatric unit, found that 40 per cent of assaults occurred in corridors, 25 per cent in patients' rooms and 8 per cent in the showers. Wener and Olsen (1978: 37–40) found that assaults usually took place in multipurpose areas, television areas and bedrooms. Dietz and Rada (1983) found most assaults occurred in high-density areas such as dining-rooms and dayrooms. Harris and Varney (1986), in a ten-year study of assaults on a maximum-security psychiatric unit, found the most common location off-ward was the exercise yard, while few assaults occurred in workshops and recreation areas. In the wards most assaults occurred in the corridors (59 per cent), sunroom (19 per cent), patients' room (13 per cent) and showers (6 per cent). Atlas (1982: 341–4; 1983), in a study of four prisons, found the most common assault sites were cells (from 27 per cent to 44 per cent of all assaults) and architectural 'blind' areas such as halls, showers and outside areas (14 per cent–24 per cent), although up to 14 per cent of assaults were judged to occur in areas of direct supervision. Steinke (1991) examined infraction reports from a large (500-capacity) medium-security prison for inmates experiencing some behavioural and/or psychiatric problems. In general, assaults on another inmate were more likely to occur where inmates congregated, in places like corridors and showers, and least likely to occur at job or educational sites. Jayewardene and Doherty (1985) found that workshops were the only area where homicides did not occur. In general, the location of assaults matches prisoners' perceptions of safe places. O'Donnell and Edgar (1999) found that prisoners felt least safe in the showers, the segregation unit and travelling to and from wings, and most safe in individual cells, the library and the chapel.

Despite the variation in assault sites across different prisons, two general trends emerge from the research that are consistent both with Bowker's classification and the proposed two-stage model. First, as usually predicted, many assaults occurred in areas of poor supervision, which, depending upon individual prison regimes, typically included cells, showers and corridors.

Atlas (1983), for example, reported that in the prisons he studied there were danger areas that were well known to inmates and were colloquially referred to as 'muggers alley'. He also found that the design of the interiors of cells made surveillance difficult. Moreover, he reported that the assaults that occur in these unsupervised areas were more likely to involve weapons and to involve multiple assailants (Atlas, 1982: 343–4; 1983). The implication is that these assaults were premeditated and involved a degree of planning aimed at reducing the chances of detection.

The second category of assaults occurred in areas that are well supervised but where inmates congregated in free association with little imposed structure. These areas include gyms, recreation rooms and dining-rooms. These assaults usually involved single assailants and typically did not involve weapons. This pattern suggests spontaneous behaviour that is triggered by the immediate pressures of the situation. For example, Atlas (1982: 341–4) found that the design of dining-rooms, where inmates are required to queue and inmate circulation is poorly planned, encouraged assaults by increasing the chances of jostling. For this kind of assault, deliberations about risk of detection and likely consequences if caught are of secondary consideration.

The logical obverse to these two trends is that assaults have been found least likely to occur in areas that combine both adequate supervision and structured activity that regulates prisoner interaction. These areas included workshops, education sites and organised sporting facilities.

Controlling prisoner-prisoner violence

The physical environment

HOUSING TYPE

The housing arrangements provided for prisoners – whether they are accommodated in single cells, multiple-occupancy cells or dormitories – involve both precipitating and regulating elements. Single cells reduce social density, help prisoners to meet privacy needs, aid in the surveillance task and offer prisoners better opportunities to defend themselves.

Research has consistently found that inmates prefer single cells, and feel safer in them (O'Donnell and Edgar, 1999; Wener and Olsen, 1978: 14–19). The behavioural evidence generally backs up the veracity of this perception by prisoners. Lower assault rates are usually reported where there is cell accommodation rather than dormitory accommodation (Atlas, 1982: 335–41; Cox et al., 1984; Lester, 1990; O'Donnell and Edgar, 1996: 87; Sylvester et al., 1977: 54). However, at least one study has shown that there appears to be no great advantage in having single-cell occupancy over double-cell occupancy as long as prisoners have been appropriately classified and a secure locker for personal possession is provided (Atlas, 1982: 340).

Not all researchers are convinced of the advantages of cells over dormitories. Some of the negative effects of dormitories can be ameliorated with the help of secure lockers, single bunking, adequate space and partitioned cubicles (Atlas, 1982: 340–1; Cox *et al.*, 1984). Gaes (1994: 343) argued that there is little relationship between assaults and dormitory accommodation. He pointed out that almost all available studies have employed cross-sectional designs. He argued that these studies generally do not control adequately for selection bias. It is typically the most trusted inmates who earn the right to go to individual cells, and so are less likely to be involved in trouble.

FUNCTIONAL UNITS

By and large, the empirical evidence indicates that new-generation architecture and unit management reduce prisoner assaults on one another (Bayens *et al.*, 1997; Farbstein *et al.*, 1996, 19–22; Farbstein and Wener, 1989, IV 1.3; Farmer, 1988; King, 1991; Robson, 1989; Senese *et al.*, 1992; Sigurdson, 1985, vi; 1987a, v; 1987b, i; Wener *et al.*, 1987). It must be said, however, that research in the area is not extensive and that which has been conducted often has methodological problems.

Farbstein and Wener (1989) surveyed fifty-two prisons and jails using a detailed postal questionnaire. Institutions were rated on a five-point scale according to how well unit management principles were in place and comparisons were conducted between institutions at each extreme of the scale. Administrators of pure unit management institutions rated their institutions to be safer and reported less incidents of assault (an average of 13 versus 32 a year) than the other institutions (p. II 2.3). In a follow-up stage of the study, Farbstein and Wener conducted on-site case studies of seven institutions. Institutions were matched on age of the facility, staffing ratios, programme availability, inmate type and hardness/softness of the environment. There was a spread of supervision styles in the sample – four direct supervision, two indirect supervision and one hybrid. Data were collected using behavioural observations, questionnaires and interviews with staff and prisoners. Results were not entirely supportive of the value of direct supervision (pp. III 5.5–13). Questionnaires revealed that while prisoners in direct supervision believed staff–prisoner relations were more positive and that response times of staff to emergencies were better, the chances of prisoner-prisoner attacks were judged to be greater. Staff believed that surveillance was better in direct supervision, but also felt that it was more difficult for prisoners to contact an officer. However, there are a number of methodological problems with this study that limit the conclusions that might be drawn. First, while Farbstein and Wener attempted to match institutions, they reported that the institutions with direct supervision tended to have softer architectural features and furnishings. Further, it seems that the direct supervision facilities had a greater problem with overcrowding. Finally, official assault rates are not reported.

King (1991: 143) also employed self-report in his comparison of a US new-generation high-security prison (Oak Park Heights) with a British dispersal prison (Gartree). He found that supervision levels were perceived to be higher in the new-generation facility, with 51 per cent of prisoners claiming to have had their cells searched and 43 per cent claiming to have been strip-searched at Oak Park Heights compared with 5 per cent and 3 per cent respectively at Gartree. Similarly, 73 per cent of Oak Park Heights prisoners regarded their movement in the prison to be very restricted compared with 39 per cent at Gartree. Nevertheless, prisoners at Oak Park Heights were significantly more likely than Gartree prisoners to feel very safe (30 per cent versus 3 per cent) or quite safe (53 per cent versus 42 per cent). In comparing the respective institutions, King characterised Gartree's history as 'troubled and turbulent' while Oak Park Heights had 'experienced no significant control problems'.

Senese *et al.* (1992) did examine official figures and reported fewer assaults in a podular design prison than in a traditional prison (20 incidents versus 45 over six months). However, there seemed to be little effort made in the study to control for other differences between the two institutions and, in fact, the respective characteristics of each were not reported. To overcome this problem, Bayens *et al.* (1997) employed a longitudinal design tracking disorder rates in a single facility for five years either side of the introduction of unit management in 1988. They found significant reductions in prisoner-prisoner violence after the change to unit management. Fights between inmates fell from 148 to 57 and assaults from 114 to 61 for the two five-year periods respectively, at the same time that the inmate population doubled. One advantage of a longitudinal design is that the institution acts as its own control. However, one disadvantage is that the assault rates may be affected by other changes over time.

CONTROL OVER THE ENVIRONMENT

It has been argued that it is frustration in association with a lack of control over the environment – no choice when cell lights are on or off, inability to regulate individual heating and cooling preferences, no choice in television programmes, having to queue for meals and so forth – rather than the oppressive nature of the environment *per se* that accounts for much of the violence exhibited by prisoners (Wener and Olsen, 1978: 20–5; 1980; Wright and Goodstein, 1989: 255). For example, Wener and Olsen (1978: 23) reported that 57 per cent of assaults they studied occurred as a result of fights over the use of telephones, often fuelled by frustration experienced by prisoners who were required to wait for long periods to make a call. There are simple situational solutions to many of these problems, such as putting comfort control switches inside cells, providing more televisions, staggering meal times and regulating the length of telephone calls.

AIRCONDITIONING

Given the interest shown in the effects of climate on behaviour, it is surprising that the logical question of whether the stresses of natural climate extremes can be reduced through artificial means has rarely been raised. In one of the few studies to address this question, Atlas (1982: 346; 1984) reported some evidence that assault rates are lower for airconditioned areas and areas with easy access to showers.

BLIND SPOTS

The geographic analyses outlined earlier showed that instrumental assaults usually took place in areas that were difficult to supervise (e.g. Atlas, 1982: 341–4; 1983; Sylvester *et al.*, 1977: 12–13). The obvious implication to be drawn from such findings is that violence may be reduced by eliminating architectural blind spots to increase surveillance capabilities. Strategies might include the more effective use of windows and hardened plastics, improvements to lighting and employment of technological aids such as CCTV. It should be noted, however, that there are no studies that have examined the effects on violence of increasing levels of surveillance.

Population characteristics

SIZE

The assumption that prisoner-prisoner assaults occur more frequently in large prisons has received mixed empirical support. Megargee (1976, 1977) reported a weak positive relationship between prison size and assault levels among prisoners, and Sylvester *et al.* (1977: 55) described a similar pattern for murders. Ganjavi *et al.* (1985) found that assaults correlated with prison size only in medium-security institutions and during summer months. However, others have failed to find any relationship between prison size and inmate violence (Gaes and McGuire, 1985) or have reported that assaults are less likely in large prisons (Farrington and Nuttall, 1980; McCorkle, *et al.*, 1995).

As Farrington and Nuttall (1980: 222–3) have pointed out, the seeming contradictions in the research findings may be partly explained by the differing ways in which assault levels are expressed, that is, whether reported as incidents per institution, or as incidents per prisoner. In general, it seems that while assaults and murders occur more frequently in large prisons than in small ones, rates of interpersonal violence in large prisons (the proportion of assaults to overall prisoner numbers) are lower than in small prisons. Farrington and Nuttall argued that offending rates are the more appropriate index and that therefore prison size cannot be considered as a direct generator of prisoner violence.

Lower assault rates in large prisons may be the result of compensatory measures adopted to counteract the size problem. For example, staff in large prisons may come to employ more effective control strategies or become more vigilant. It may also be the case that overall prison size may be less relevant than the number of other prisoners with whom the prisoner comes into day-to-day contact. Thus, part of the success of functional units in reducing violence may be due to the breaking down of large prison populations into more intimate, manageable sub-populations.

CROWDING

Like the research on prison size, empirical studies are almost evenly divided between those that have found a positive relationship between crowding and prisoner-prisoner assaults (Cox *et al.*, 1984; Gaes, 1985; Gaes and McGuire, 1985; McCain *et al.*, 1980; Marrero, 1977; Megargee, 1976, 1977; Ruback and Carr, 1984) and those showing no relationship (Atlas, 1982: 330–5; DiIulio, 1987: 74–5; Ekland-Olson *et al.*, 1983; Fry, 1988; Innes, 1987; McCorkle *et al.*, 1995; Pelissier, 1991; Porporino and Dudley, 1984). A number of studies have reported qualified results, finding, for example, that crowding is a significant predictor of violence only in the case of young prisoner populations (Jan, 1980; Nacci *et al.*, 1977). At least one study (Walters, 1998) found that prisoner violence decreased as crowding increased.

One of the most widely cited studies supporting the deleterious effects of crowding is that by Megargee (1977). Megargee's study involved tracking discipline problems in a medium-security prison over a three-year period. Changes in prisoner density were also tracked. Aside from normal fluctuations in prisoner numbers, during the study period renovations at the institution reduced available space at certain times. Megargee reported a significant relationship between assault rates and density levels. However,

Megargee acknowledged that the renovations caused other pressures that also might have contributed to higher levels of violence. For example, when a dormitory was closed for renovation, prisoners needed to be transferred to another section of the prison, intruding upon established territories and disrupting friendship ties.

Research in this area generally is vulnerable to a range of confounding influences. Crowding effects may be mediated by a range of institutional factors, such as variations in staff–prisoner ratios, programme availability, prison design and so forth. Extraneous variables such as these cause particular difficulties in studies employing cross-sectional designs that compare different institutions (e.g. McCorkle *et al.*, 1995), as opposed to those utilising longitudinal designs that examine trends over time in a single institution or system (e.g. McCain *et al.*, 1980; Megargee, 1976).

The crudeness of the crowding index employed as the basis of comparison is also problematic. Typically, the level of institutional crowding is determined simply by comparing daily numbers with stated capacity. An over-capacity measure may convey little of the day-to-day experiences of crowding by prisoners. As a macro-level, 'outside' measure, over-capacity takes no account of any uneven distributions of crowding within institutions, and does not distinguish between the effects of spatial density and social density. Some authors use housing type (single cell versus multiple occupancy) as a finer-grained measure of crowding (social density). Similarly, the relatively high incidence of assaults in areas where prisoners are permitted to congregate can be taken to infer acute crowding effects (Atlas, 1982: 341–4; 1983; Dietz and Rada, 1983).

AGE COMPOSITION

At an individual level, involvement in assaultive behaviour in prison is negatively correlated with prisoner age for both males (Walters, 1998; Wolfgang, 1964; Wooldredge, 1998; Wright, 1991b) and females (Mandaraka-Sheppard, 1986: 171). Younger prisoners are also more likely than older prisoners to believe prison is a violent place and to be fearful of attack from other prisoners (Hemmens and Marquart, 1999). There is some evidence that increasing age diversity within a prison helps to reduce assault rates. A longitudinal study purporting to demonstrate this principle was conducted by Mabli *et al.* (1979). They traced the changes in prisoner composition at federal institutions in El Reno, Oklahoma and Texarkana, Arkansas. El Reno was a maximum-security prison for young offenders (from eighteen to twenty-six years old) and had chronically high levels of violence. Texarkana was a medium-security prison for older prisoners (90 per cent older than 28 years) that had relatively low levels of violence. Randomised transfers between these two institutions resulted in the proportion of prisoners over the age of 28 at El Reno increasing from 0 per cent to 36 per cent, and the proportion of prisoners aged under twenty-eight at Texarkana increasing from 10 per cent to 42 per cent. Effects were measured in terms of monthly serious prisoner-prisoner assault rates. It was found that there was a 'steady, long-term downward trend' in violence at El Reno, while at Texarkana there was 'a more erratic, initial upsurge in violence, coupled with a later leveling-off'. The authors took these findings as providing broad support for the positive effects of age heterogeneity in reducing violence.

This interpretation of the findings, however, is open to question. In the first place, rather inconveniently for the researchers, other changes were taking place at El Reno at the same time as the transfers – the introduction of unit management and an increase in programmes – that may also have contributed to reductions in violence. In addition, the study does not rule out changes in assault rates that might have occurred simply through changes in the relative numbers of troublesome prisoners in each prison. That is, the rate of offending at El Reno may have fallen simply because there were fewer potential trouble-makers than before. Finally, at best the study demonstrates that young prisoners benefit from mixed-age prisons. Older prisoners experienced less violence when they were housed in the age-homogeneous prison.

RACIAL COMPOSITION

Evidence suggests that in the US assaults are more frequent in race-heterogeneous institutions (Ellis *et al.*, 1974). In particular, racial heterogeneity is associated with gang violence. However, as Gaes and McGuire (1985: 60–1) pointed out, the effect of various mixes of race is still poorly understood. They found that assaults decreased as the white to black ratio of prisoners increased. They interpreted these findings as tentative evidence that prisoner-prisoner assaults decreased as racial groups approached equal size. That is, the problem in race-heterogeneous prisons may be greater when one racial group is in a minority and is thus vulnerable to victimisation.

GENDER COMPOSITION

There have been a number of examples of mixed-gender correctional facilities (referred to as co-corrections). Co-correctional facilities are thought to foster healthier social relationship patterns and lessen the dehumanising effects of confinement. Lower levels of violence are expected through the creation of a more normalised prison environment.

Most evaluations of co-corrections come in the form of descriptive case studies (Almy *et al.*, 1980; Campbell, 1980; Heffernan and Krippel, 1980; Lambiotte, 1980). These studies are almost universally positive in their assessment of the value of co-corrections, especially in reducing levels of prisoner violence, but they contain little in the way of hard data. The alternative possibility is that the mix of genders will create jealousy and competition among prisoners and actually increase violence. Again the evidence is anecdotal, but Campbell (1980: 89), recounting the Fort Worth experience with co-corrections, claimed that this did not occur.

PRISONER TURNOVER

Although numerous writers have speculated on the link between transience and violence in prison (e.g. Ellis, 1984: 289–91) only a few studies have examined the effect of turnover of prisoners on assault levels. Porporino and Dudley (1984) found that violence levels were higher for institutions with more frequent prisoner transfers and releases. Wright (1991a) found that prisoners newly arrived in an institution had higher levels of disciplinary infractions (including assault) than longer-term prisoners, suggesting that a period of adjustment is required after arrival into a new environment. However, Gaes and McGuire (1985) found no evidence of a relationship between prisoner turnover and violence.

The prison regime
STAFF EXPERIENCE

Logically it would be expected that there would be less violence in institutions with experienced staff. In fact the research has either found no effect for staff experience or an inverse relationship. Using staff turnover as a measure of staff experience, McCorkle *et al.* (1995) found no significant effect on prisoner assault rates. Walters (1998) conducted a nine-year longitudinal study of violence in the Federal Bureau of Prisons. Using the percentage of staff with less than one year of service as a criterion of inexperience, he found a negative correlation with violence levels (although the measure of violence included prisoner-staff assaults). In accounting for this finding, Walters argued that correctional systems might compensate for the hiring of new staff by introducing other measures (for example, additional training, changes in policy etc.). Alternatively, the findings may indeed mean that new and enthusiastic employees are simply more effective and less provocative than the old hands.

STAFF–PRISONER RATIO

Similarly, it might be expected that there would be fewer assaults in institutions with relatively high staff–inmate ratios on the grounds that higher ratios are likely to mean greater levels of supervision. When comparing institutions, no relationship between overall staffing levels and assault rates has been established (Gaes and McGuire, 1985; MacDonald, 1999; McCorkle *et al.*, 1995; Walters, 1998). McCorkle *et al.* (1995) also found no relationship between changes in staff–prisoner ratios over a six-year period and changes in assault rates over the same time. However, Gaes and McGuire (1985) found that the higher the proportion of custodial staff to non-custodial staff the more non-weapon assaults took place between prisoners. This result lends support to the argument that the deinstitutionalising effect of the presence of non-custodial staff may be more important than the extra surveillance custodial staff provide.

STAFF RACIAL COMPOSITION

McCorkle *et al.* (1995) found that assaults between prisoners increased with the white to black ratio of staff. McCorkle *et al.* argued that when the racial mix of staff differs significantly from that of the prisoners then racial tensions within the prison are likely to increase. A major problem for correctional administrators, they contend, is the tendency to place prisons in rural areas where it is difficult to attract good staff and, in particular, where few racial minorities reside. 'In the interests of running orderly prisons', they conclude, 'officials need to rethink strategies aimed at attracting and retaining minorities into correctional work' (p. 328).

SECURITY CRACKDOWNS

Although the instinctive response of correctional authorities to a perceived lack of institutional control is usually the tightening-up of institutional discipline and security measures, few studies have actually examined empirically the effect of such practices. A case study of a crackdown on gang violence is provided by Ralph and Marquart (1991). They described the entrenchment of gangs and the disintegration of order in Texas prisons that accompanied the end of the 'building tender system' – the use of prisoners to control other prisoners – and the strategies employed by administrators to regain control. The order to end the building-tender system arose from the Ruiz trial in 1980 (Ekland-Olson, 1986). This was a class action suit against the Texas Department of Corrections. It was chiefly concerned with complaints about overcrowding, but during the course of the trial, evidence of abusive methods employed by staff was also revealed. As well as demanding a reduction in crowding levels, the court also ordered changes to disciplinary procedures, increased staff–prisoner ratios and the cessation of the use of prisoners in administrative and control capacities. Ralph and Marquart (1991) argued that the court decision resulted in a power vacuum that produced a dramatic increase in violence as gangs became more entrenched. Leaving aside the ethical concerns, under the building-tender system Texas had one of the lowest prison homicide rates in the country. However, in 1984–5 – a period known as the 'war years' – 90 per cent of the fifty-two murders were gang-related. Successful control tactics included the establishment of a special prosecutors office that specialised in gangs and secured a number of long sentences; stronger laws, for example, making it a felony for any inmate to possess a weapon and reducing judicial discretion; and placing all known gang members in administrative segregation. This latter strategy resulted in up to 1,500 gang members at any time being taken out of general discipline and locked down for twenty-three hours a day. Nevertheless, these tactics resulted in a dramatic decrease in assaults and murders. For example, between 1986 and 1990 there were only nine gang-related murders.

The history of the US Penitentiary in Marion provides another example of the effects of a security crackdown on prisoner violence (Holt and Phillips, 1991). Between 1963 and 1978 Marion operated as a traditional maximum-security prison. Between 1978 and 1983 Marion began to receive a greater concentration of dangerous prisoners and security was generally strengthened. However, this move was accompanied by an escalation of violence that increased in 1982–3 after there were some efforts to normalise the prison environment. This led to the introduction in 1983 of a strictly controlled prison regime. In particular, there was an emphasis on close supervision of prisoner movement, so prisoners were required to spend most of the day in their cells or cell house, with out-of-cell time tightly controlled. The result of this tightening was a significant fall in inmate murders and assaults. Before the introduction of the tighter measures there were fifteen prisoner murders; after the tighter security there have been five prisoners killed. Assault rates (assaults per 10,000 inmates) went from a high of 59.9 before the crackdown to a low of 8.3 after the crackdown.

There is some research that cautions about the effects of overcontrol. Mandaraka-Sheppard (1986), in her study on English women's prisons, found that perceived levels of punishment severity positively correlated with levels of institutional violence (pp. 178–80). Similarly, Wright (1991a) found that disciplinary infractions in ten male prisons increased with perceived levels of authoritarian control. However, as both researchers acknowledge, the direction of causation is not clear from these findings. Severe punishments may have been imposed because levels of violence were high.

PROTECTION FOR VULNERABLE PRISONERS

One obvious strategy to reduce assaults is to protect or separate vulnerable prisoners from known predatory prisoners. Atlas (1982: 101) reported on a study by Bohn on controlling violence at the Federal Correctional Institution in Tallahassee. The project involved identification of extremely aggressive prisoners (13 per cent of the population) and reallocation of these prisoners to a separate dormitory within the same institution. Prison-wide, there was a reduction in assaults over two years of 46 per cent. Further, while assaults in the special dormitory rose initially, levels eventually dropped to those of the wider institution. It should be noted, however, that despite the apparent success of this approach the segregation of supposed violent prisoners presents some philosophical problems from a situational perspective. Arguably this strategy depends more upon a dispositional approach to behaviour than on situational concepts. Moreover, a common danger in separating out violent offenders (apart from error associated with the prediction of future behaviour) is that, so identified, these prisoners will become subject to excessive controls.

CONTROLS ON PERSONAL PROPERTY

Assaults are often carried out in pursuit of some other material gain. The importance of understanding the motivation for assaults is shown in the study by O'Donnell and Edgar (1996). In an investigation of victimisation of prisoners by other prisoners, it was found that the object of some assaults was to steal the phone card carried by the victim (p. 88). O'Donnell and Edgar suggested that assaults might be reduced by the simple expedient of marking each phone card with the owner's name and lodging the card when not in use with the wing-officer.

A similar problem over phone disputes, but an alternative solution, was described in a study by La Vigne (1994). She reported on the introduction of a computerised phone system on Rikers Island. The computerised system required a card with a PIN to access the phone line, then automatically checked the inmates' current phone-call entitlements before connecting; blocked specified phone numbers; and terminated calls precisely after six minutes. This procedure not only resulted in a reduction in the abuse of phone entitlements and a significant financial saving, but also reduced violence associated with phone use by nearly a half. Under the previous phone system, in which calls were supposedly logged and timed by staff but which in practice was poorly supervised, powerful prisoners allocated phone times in return for favours or payment. This situation resulted in fights and even homicides. The computerised system greatly reduced the potential for exploitation. While prisoners could still steal cards, without the PIN the cards were worthless.

PROGRAMME AVAILABILITY

Prison programmes include treatment interventions, education classes, vocational training, work assignments and sporting and leisure activities. Most prison programmes do not have the explicit objective of facilitating control but are usually justified in terms of their presumed rehabilitative or therapeutic effects. However, at a situational level prison programmes may assist in the control task because of their time-structuring properties and their imposition of routine on prisoners. As Ditchfield (1990: 115) noted, conventional wisdom among prison administrators holds that 'an idle prisoner is a dangerous prisoner'.

The geographic research by Atlas (1982, 1983) and others cited earlier indicates that assaults are less likely to take place in areas within the prison where structured activities are undertaken. Similarly, at an aggregate level, the research supports the contention that programme participation is related to lower levels of prisoner violence (Ellis, 1993; Ellis *et al.*, 1974; Gaes and McGuire, 1985; Gerber and Fritsch, 1995; Linden *et al.*, 1984; McCorkle *et al.*, 1995; Regoli and Poole, 1983; Saylor and Gaes, 1992; Wooldredge, 1994, 1998; Wright, 1991b). Positive findings have been reported across a range of programme types. Wooldredge (1998) surveyed prisoners about their victimisation by other prisoners. He found that being a victim of assault was negatively related to the amount of time spent in educational classes, although hours spent in a job and in vocational training were not significant. Linden *et al.* (1984) found that prisoners enrolled in college education programmes in prison had lower disciplinary infractions than other prisoners (although assault rates were not specifically reported). Saylor and Gaes (1992) reported a similar finding for enrolment in vocational programmes (but again, assaults were not isolated from other infractions). Ellis (1993) found that inmates participating in a work squad carrying out basic cleaning and maintenance tasks around the prison were involved in fewer incidents of assault than previously. At a perceptual level, Wright (1991b) found that prisoners who assault other prisoners are more likely to rate the prison environment as lacking activity, social stimulation and structure. There is no research, however, that examines whether reductions in assault depend upon some necessary programme characteristics. Thus, the extent to which these positive results may be attributed to time-structuring (keeping busy) or to some deeper psychological change (e.g. a sense of achievement) is unknown.

Not all studies support the efficacy of programmes. A number of studies have failed to find a relationship between programming and violence (Brown and Spevacek, 1971; Frey and Delaney, 1996; Gendreau *et al.*, 1985; Langenbach *et al.*, 1990). Others have reported a positive relationship. Wooldredge (1998) found that being a victim of assault was positively related to the amount of time spent in recreational activities, a result he attributed to the increased opportunities for violence in sport. Adams *et al.* (1994) found that inmates involved in educational and vocational programmes had more disciplinary infractions (although assault levels are not specified) than other inmates. The authors speculated that programme involvement might have provided prisoners with more opportunities to offend, or may have exposed them to greater scrutiny by custodial staff (pp. 444–5).

VISITS

It has been argued that family visits have the potential to reduce prison violence by reducing the pains of imprisonment (Bowker, 1982: 73; Cooke, 1991; Whatmore, 1987). Few studies have examined this proposition empirically. Lembo (1969) found no statistical link between visits and infractions, but through interviews found that prisoners believed visits helped them to avoid misconduct. Wooldredge (1994) found a lower incidence of violence among prisoners who received at least monthly visits, although it is not clear from the study whether violent prisoners simply have fewer family ties. On the other hand, Wooldredge (1998) found that prisoners who received regular visits were more likely to be victims of assault. He argued that receiving visits was a signal to other inmates of conventional social ties and that this may have marked visit-receivers as outsiders in the prison social structure.

PAROLE AND REMISSION

A common justification for parole and other forms of early release is that they are crucial behavioural control weapons for prison administrators. A number of studies have tested this assertion. Atlas (1982: 348) examined the effect of a legislative requirement in Florida for the Parole Commission to review all prisoners and retroactively to apply new parole guidelines. During the ten-month review of prisoners, assault rates in many facilities dropped to zero, only to rise again when the review was complete. The greatest declines in assault rates occurred in institutions with the greatest number of parole-eligible prisoners. A similar finding was reported by Memory *et al.* (1999). They examined prison disciplinary infractions before and after the introduction of truth-in-sentencing legislation in North Carolina (that is, where parole and time off for good behaviour were effectively abolished). The researchers found a significant increase in assaults after the truth-in-sentencing changes. As one inmate in the study commented, under the new regime 'I don't have anything to lose' if convicted of a disciplinary offence (p. 62).

Other studies, however, have not found parole to be an effective management tool. Stone and Hoffman (1982) compared the behaviour of prisoners given a presumptive (determinate) parole date with prisoners under normal parole conditions. If parole operated as a significant incentive, it would be expected that prisoners for whom release decisions had not been made would feel more inhibitions about misbehaving than prisoners with fixed release dates. The data indicated no difference between the two groups in their levels of misconduct, although the relevance of the study to the current argument is diminished by the fact that assault rates are not specifically provided. In another study Sorensen and Wrinkle (1996) compared assault rates for death-sentenced (n=93) and life-without-parole prisoners (n=323) with assault rates for life-with-parole prisoners (n=232). They found no significant differences between the two groups. The authors concluded that the assumption that prisoners without the prospect of release are more dangerous than those with the possibility for release are unfounded, and so there was no basis on which to continue the restrictive regimes to which death-sentenced and life-without-parole prisoners are typically subjected. Of course, the fact that these prisoners are subjected to more restrictive regimes in the first place may well account for their relatively low assault rates.

INCENTIVES

There are other incentives in additional to parole that are available to prison administrators. Liebling *et al.* (1999) reported on the introduction of a comprehensive incentive system (Incentives and Earned Privileges) by the Prison Service in Britain. The system involved tying rewards such as access to private cash, number of visits, time out of cell, wearing of own clothes and employment in desirable jobs to good behaviour and performance. The results of the evaluation were mixed. The researchers found general endorsement of the scheme by staff who believed it to be a useful management tool and that overall there was a positive improvement in prisoners' behaviour. However, prisoners believed that the scheme had a detrimental impact on staff fairness, relations with staff, regime fairness and consistency of treatment, and that the effect on prisoners' behaviour was neutral or negative. Analysis of pre- and post-scheme assault and head-injury figures showed no significant improvement. Liebling *et al.* concluded that the incentive scheme strengthened staff control and that the failure to find any significant impact on prisoner behaviour may have been the result of inconsistencies in the application of the scheme at ground level.

Conclusions

Despite the relatively large body of research examining prisoner-prisoner violence, there are limitations fitting the findings to the proposed two-stage model of prison control. Generally, the available research is methodologically weak, and contradictory findings are common. Moreover, little of the research comes explicitly from a situational perspective, with most researchers focusing on broad, institution-wide measures. A few studies have examined prisoner-prisoner violence at a micro-level – for example, the geographic analyses of violent incidents by Atlas (1982, 1983) – but the implications of such findings often have not been fully exploited. Thus, while research suggests that assaults may be reduced by eliminating architectural blind spots and increasing surveillance capabilities (say, by using CCTV), there are no pre-test/post-test studies that actually confirm this.

Notwithstanding these limitations, the research findings are consistent with the view that the prison environment both generates and allows prisoner-prisoner violence. Likewise, strategies for reducing prisoner-prisoner violence involved both controlling the precipitators and regulators of behaviour. Categorisation of promising strategies reviewed in this chapter is shown in table 5.1. The table lists all interventions for which there was at least some empirical support. Because few studies in this area satisfy the rigorous conditions of quasi-experimental designs, there has been no attempt to grade the research beyond this. A listing in the table does not imply that the efficacy of the intervention is uncontested.

There is little to be found in the reviewed research that bears on the issue of counterproductive control. The breakdown of control in Texas prisons after the abandonment of the building-tender system (Ekland-Olsen, 1986; Ralph and Marquart, 1991) offers some insights into the dangers of dis-empowering prison guards and ceding control to prisoners (although the court-mandated reforms that led to the crisis were not misguided attempts to improve control but were motivated by civil rights concerns). On the other hand, the disproportionate level of violence in maximum security might

Table 5.1. *Summary of promising strategies for control of prisoner-prisoner violence*

Strategy	Precipitation-control category	Regulation-control category
Single-cell accommodation	Respecting territory Reducing crowding	Target hardening
Partitioned dormitories	Respecting territory Reducing crowding	
Functional units	Setting positive expectations Rule setting Personalising victims Controlling environmental irritants	Formal surveillance Natural surveillance
Increasing control over the environment	Encouraging compliance Reducing frustration	
Airconditioning	Controlling environmental irritants	
Elimination of blind spots		Formal surveillance Natural surveillance
Small/sub-divided prisons	Reducing anonymity	
Reduced population density	Reducing crowding	
Reduced prisoner congregation	Reducing crowding	Deflecting offenders
Age-heterogeneous populations	Reducing inappropriate imitation Reducing inappropriate conformity	
Race-homogeneous or race-balanced populations	Reducing inappropriate imitation Reducing inappropriate conformity	
Gender-mixed populations	Reducing frustrations Setting positive expectations	
Slow prisoner turnover	Reducing anonymity Personalising victims	
Presence of non-custodial staff	Reducing frustration	
Matched staff-prisoner racial composition	Reducing frustration	

Table 5.1. (*cont.*)

Strategy	Precipitation-control category	Regulation-control category
Security crackdowns		Controlling facilitators
		Formal surveillance
		Increasing costs
		Removing privileges
Segregation of vulnerable prisoners		Target removal
Removal/marking of personal property		Target removal
		Identifying property
		Denying benefits
Prison programmes/work	Reducing frustrations Clarifying responsibility	Deflecting offenders
Visits	Reducing frustrations	
Good-time provisions		Removing privileges
Incentives	Encouraging compliance	Removing privileges

indicate the presence of counterproductive stress and frustration, but the confound with prisoner type makes this conclusion speculative. These cases aside, there are no obvious examples of interventions that have backfired, although this probably says more about the limitations of the research than the principle of counterproductive control.

CHAPTER 6

Sexual assaults

In the corrections' literature, sexual assault by prisoners on other prisoners is generally treated as a special case of prisoner-prisoner violence. Following this tradition, a separate chapter has been devoted to sexual assault in this book. It is likely that there are unique situational characteristics of sexual assault that suggest control strategies different from those already discussed.

Nature of the problem

Definition and incidence

A fundamental difficulty in interpreting research in this area is the failure of many researchers adequately to define sexual assault either to the participants of the research or to the readers of the research findings. In one of the few attempts to specify what constitutes sexual assault in prison, Heilpern (1998) offered the following definition to the prisoners in his study:

> sexual assault [is] physical contact of a sexual kind, where your involvement is forced upon you, such as unwanted anal sex, oral sex, wanking or fondling. The force may be by threat of, or actual, physical harm. (pp. 16–17)

This chapter adopts the parameters of sexual assault set out by Heilpern. As Heilpern's definition makes clear, sexual assault is broader than might be conveyed by the term 'rape'. Aggressors may employ intimidation as well as physical force, and need not necessarily effect penetration. The definition includes cases where prisoners are forced to provide sex in return for protection from other predators. However, consensual homosexual relations and sexual behaviour willingly performed in return for goods or services fall outside the definition and are not directly considered in this chapter.

As Tucker (1982: 67) pointed out, however, in the prison context the line between coercive and consensual homosexual behaviour is often blurred.

Partly as a result of the definitional issues discussed above, there are two contradictory views put forward in the literature concerning the incidence of sexual assault in prison. One view is that sexual assault is rampant or at least widespread (Davis, 1968; Donaldson, 1995; Heilpern, 1998; Lockwood, 1980; Struckman-Johnson *et al.*, 1996; Weiss and Friar, 1974; Wooden and Parker, 1982), the other that sexual assault is relatively rare (Cooley, 1993; Moss *et al.*, 1979; Nacci and Kane, 1983, 1984; Power *et al.*, 1991; Saum *et al.*, 1995; Tewksbury, 1989). At one extreme, Donaldson (1995) estimated that 300,000 male prisoners are sexually assaulted each year in American correctional facilities. Other surveys have revealed less dramatic but nevertheless high levels of victimisation. In a study of six New York state prisons, Lockwood (1980: 18) found that 28 per cent of all prisoners, and half of the white prisoner population, had been targets of sexual aggression. Struckman-Johnson *et al.* (1996) reported similar results, with 22 per cent of prisoners identifying as victims of sexual assault in a study of the Nebraska prison system. In an Australian study, Heilpern (1998: 29) found that 26 per cent of a young-prisoner sample (<25 years) reported having been sexually assaulted in prison, with 7 per cent reporting that it was at least a weekly occurrence and 1 per cent that they were raped daily.

However, Saum *et al.* (1995: 414) argued that there is considerable mythology surrounding prison rape. The image of endemic prison rape, they contend, is based largely on anecdotal accounts and sensationalist reporting in the popular media. Many studies showed less than expected rates of sexual aggression. In terms of officially recorded incidents, Nacci and Kane (1984) found only two sexual assaults per month were reported in the US Federal Bureau system, at that time housing more than 31,000 prisoners. Given the acknowledged underreporting of sexual assault – Davis (1968) found that only 3 per cent of sexual assaults he investigated were reported – most studies have utilised self-report methods. But even in self-report studies, often surprisingly low levels of sexual assault have been found. Nacci and Kane (1984) found that 1 per cent of prisoners surveyed reported having to perform sex to protect themselves from other prisoners. A further 9 per cent of prisoners said that they had been targets of sexual aggression, and 29 per cent said that they had been propositioned for sex. Tewksbury (1989) found 7 per cent of respondents had been approached for coercive sex but none reported having been raped. In a sample of 117 Canadian inmates, Cooley (1993) found only one case of sexual assault. Saum *et al.* (1995) found that none of their sample of 101 prisoners admitted to being raped, only one-third said that they had heard of others being raped and 4 per cent claimed to have witnessed a rape.

Irrespective of the objective risk of sexual assault, prison rape has an entrenched place in prison folklore and looms as a terrifying prospect for many prisoners (Tewksbury, 1989). Even if they have little direct experience of rape in prison, prisoners often accept the popular image that rape is widespread, with 39 per cent of respondents in Saum *et al.*'s study believing that rape occurred in their institution at least once a week. Heilpern (1998: 30) found that 71 per cent of his sample were fearful of being raped, with 16 per cent worried about the prospect on a daily basis.

Patterns

Looking at patterns of sexual assault, Struckman-Johnson *et al.* (1996) found that 52 per cent of cases involved anal sex, 14 per cent genital contact and 8 per cent oral sex. Roughly half of the incidents were perpetrated by a lone offender, while 10 per cent involved groups of more than six. The average number of assailants was three. In about half the cases the assaults were carried out by assailants unknown to the victim. Force was used in over 75 per cent of sexual assaults and 27 per cent involved a weapon. The victim sustained physical injuries in about one-third of cases.

Lockwood (1980: 40–4) broke down sexual assaults according to the aggressor's first move. In 36 per cent of incidents, there was a sexual overture accompanied by offensive remarks or gestures, in 32 per cent of cases the incident began with a polite proposition, in 18 per cent of cases the victim was physically attacked and in 13 per cent of cases the assailant began with verbal threats. Lockwood argued that violence associated with sexual assault is about equally divided between cases in which the victim is assaulted by an assailant as planned, and cases in which the victim responded to a suspected sexual advance with violent retaliation.

In the US (though less so elsewhere) the pattern of sexual assault has a significant inter-racial component. At an individual level blacks are disproportionately represented among assailants, and whites among victims, and a predominance of cases involve both a black assailant and a white victim (Lockwood, 1980: 28–31; Nacci and Kane, 1984; Scacco, 1982; Struckman-Johnson *et al.*, 1996). For example, Lockwood (1980: 105) found that 78 per cent of aggressors were black in a prison population where only half the prisoners were black. Struckman-Johnson *et al.* (1996) found that 78 per cent of victims were white and 18 per cent black in a population where the racial breakdown was 62 per cent white and 33 per cent black.

Apart from race, key victim characteristics include possession of feminine attributes, signs of homosexual orientation and evidence of lack of a supportive network. These characteristics reflect two considerations on the part of aggressors. First, victims may be selected because they are considered to be physically attractive. Secondly, victims are chosen because they are assumed to be physically weak and unlikely to resist or retaliate.

With respect to the feminine physical attributes of victims, Davis (1968) found that in comparison to aggressors' victims tended to be younger (21 versus 24), lighter (141lbs versus 157lbs) and somewhat shorter (5′8″ versus 5′9″). Nacci and Kane (1984) found victims often possessed a number of physical and behavioural cues associated with feminine characteristics. Compared with the general prison population, victims tend to be taller (contradicting Davis), more slender, to have longer hair, to be rated as more passive in interpersonal relationships and to generally give the impression of being more effeminate.

A relationship has also been claimed between homosexuality and sexual assault. According to Nacci and Kane (1983, 1984) prisoners who engage in consensual homosexual behaviour, associate with those who engage in homosexual behaviour or openly discuss homosexual behaviour are more likely to be selected as sexual assault targets. Similarly, Wooden and Parker (1982: 18) found that 41 per cent of homosexual prisoners in their sample had been forced to have sex during their sentence. This compared with 9 per cent victimisation levels among heterosexual prisoners. Donaldson (1995) estimated that homosexual prisoners were three times more likely to be sexually assaulted than non-homosexual prisoners were.

Finally, signs that a prisoner has few connections in the prison subculture are a further cue to potential aggressors. This does not mean that victims are necessarily naive first offenders. Davis (1968) found that 33 per cent of victims had been charged with serious felonies. Lockwood (1980: 25) found that 65 per cent of victims had served previous sentences, a finding replicated by Nacci and Kane (1984). Prisoners who have been involved in incidents that identified them as weak and not to be respected are likely to be targets for victimisation. Once a prisoner has been a victim of sexual assault there is a tendency for continued victimisation. Heilpern (1998: 29) found that over one-third of prisoners who reported being victims of sexual assault were assaulted on at least a weekly basis. Struckman-Johnson *et al.* (1996) found that on average victims of sexual assault had experienced nine incidents of forced sex. However, incidents establishing a reputation for weakness need not necessarily involve sexual assault – there is also strong correlation between sexual and non-sexual victimisation (Heilpern, 1998: 31).

Motivation

In terms of offender motivation, the desire for sexual gratification, heightened by the sexual deprivations of imprisonment, would seem an obvious cause of sexual assault in prison. Interviews conducted by Lockwood (1980: 126–8) confirmed that for many prisoners homosexual behaviour in prison is motivated primarily by the need for sexual release. In the words of one interviewee who had recently sexually assaulted another prisoner:

> You get a letter from your girlfriend, and you think about all the other girls. And then it starts to build up until your head is filled with thoughts, but all you see around you is men, men, men. So you just say I have got to get . . . I am going to start messing with the homos. I am going to start messing with the queens.
>
> (p. 127)

This account from a rape victim (Tucker, 1982) also highlights the sexual basis of the behaviour:

> A surprising number of the men who fucked my ass were doing things like kissing the back of my neck, calling me by various girls' names, or whispering tenderly in my ear. These men as often as not stayed in me a while after climaxing and I came to welcome this as a relief from the interminable thrusting and hurt. (p. 60)

However, a number of commentators have argued that prison sexual assaults are motivated more by aggression needs and the desire to enhance status and power in the prison than sexual needs (Cotton and Groth, 1984: 130; Donaldson, 1995; Heilpern, 1998: 80–2; Nacci and Kane, 1984; Rideau and Sinclair, 1982: 5; Wooden and Parker, 1982: 22–4). That is, sexual assault should be seen as a way of expressing violence, rather than violence being a way to express sexual desire. In this context, the relationship between sexual assault and the more general problem of inter-gang violence has also been highlighted (Bowker, 1980: 8; Lockwood, 1980: 28–31; Nacci and Kane, 1984). One argument that has been advanced in this regard is that black gangs target white victims as a form of retribution for racial injustices in society as a whole.

Notwithstanding the debate about the role of sexual deprivation, there is broad agreement that sexual aggression in prison is generally perpetrated by prisoners who in other circumstances would not regard themselves as homosexual (Davis, 1968; Donaldson, 1995; Heilpern, 1998: 80; Rideau and Sinclair, 1982: 9; Wooden and Parker, 1982: 15–16). There is, in other words, a significant situational component to the behaviour. Conceptualisation of the situational forces contributing to sexual aggression in prison follows the now familiar pattern of precipitating and regulating factors. On the one hand, some researchers see sexual aggression as yet another example of dysfunctional behaviour generated by a brutal and repressive prison system, and have emphasised the need to humanise and normalise the prison environment. On the other hand, other researchers have focused on the exploitive nature of the behaviour and have stressed the need to improve surveillance, increase deterrence and generally offer greater protection to potential victims.

Situational context

SECURITY LEVEL

Nacci and Kane (1984) found a greater incidence of sexual assault in high-security, long-term facilities. While this finding is consistent with the findings for other forms of violence, Nacci and Kane argued that it was not necessarily to be expected that sexual assault would be more common in maximum-security situations. While long-term facilities afford more opportunities to offend, the heavy Bastille-like architecture might also have been expected to inhibit sexual desires.

STAGE OF SENTENCE (VICTIM)

Lockwood (1980: 25) found that most assaults (77 per cent) occur within sixteen weeks of arrival at the institution. Lockwood argued that newly arrived prisoners to an institution are in a position of relative weakness in that they generally have not yet established protective alliances. Lockwood found that attacks are typically preceded by a testing-out period where the aggressor seeks to establish whether the new prisoner is sexually available. The threat of victimisation increased if prisoners did not become members of a group or clique.

LOCATION

Not surprisingly sexual assaults, when compared to other forms of violence, have been found to be much more likely to occur in cells, dormitories and showers. For example, in one prison studied by Atlas (1983), 77 per cent of sexual assaults took place in cells (39 per cent for other assaults) and 17 per cent occurred in the showers (nil for other assaults). Similarly, Lockwood (1980: 27–8) found that more than half of sexual assaults took place in the living areas of those involved. Where prisoners occupied single cells, the attacks usually took place in public places in the living area such as showers and toilets (since prisoners were usually locked in while they were in their cells). However, where prisoners were housed in dormitories, self-report data suggested high levels of assault in these sleeping areas. Just the same, Lockwood found that 16 per cent of sexual assaults took place in relatively well-supervised areas such as workshops and classrooms. These incidents, however, were generally at the less serious end of the scale (gestures, whispered threats etc.).

Controlling sexual assault

The physical environment

HOUSING TYPE

Higher levels of sexual assault are associated with shared rather than single accommodation. Despite the prevalence of sexual assaults in prisoners' cells, Lockwood (1980: 27) found single cells gave a degree of protection to prisoners as long as they were locked in. Dormitories, on the other hand, offered little protection. Similarly, Atlas (1983) found the assault rate was slightly higher for dormitory areas than for cells. Dorms were also perceived by prisoners as less safe. Power *et al.* (1991), in a study of 559 Scottish prisoners, did not find a single case of sexual assault, a result he attributed partly to 'single cell occupancy of Scottish prisons [that] greatly reduces the opportunity for such behaviour' (p. 1508). Prisoners and guards consistently suggest single-cell accommodation when they are asked for sexual assault prevention strategies (Lockwood, 1980: 145; Struckman-Johnson *et al.*, 1996).

FUNCTIONAL UNITS

A number of evaluations of unit management have specifically looked at sexual assault. Most of the available studies, however, are in the form of audits that describe the introduction of unit management at a particular institution. These studies outline implementation problems, staff perceptions and incidents of misbehaviour since the opening of the institution. However, no comparison data is provided. Thus, Sigurdson (1985: vi) reported that Manhattan House of Detention did not have a single incident of sexual assault in its first year of operation. Similarly, neither Larimer County Detention Center (Sigurdson, 1987a: v) nor Pima County Detention Center (Sigurdson, 1987b: i) had any sexual assaults in the first years of operation (three-and-one-half years and two years respectively). Likewise, Farbstein *et al.* (1996: 19), in their audits of Dakota County Jail, Hillsborough County Orient Road Jail and Norfolk County Sheriff's Correctional Center, found that sexual assault was virtually non-existent. But, as impressive as these results might be, the lack of some basis for comparison severely limits the conclusions that can be drawn.

The only study examining sexual assault that has included comparison data relied on perceptions of staff and inmates rather than official sexual assault rates. In this case, Farbstein and Wener (1989: III 5.5–8) found that staff perceived that the risk of sexual assault was lower in functional unit institutions than in traditional prison, but that prisoners perceived a greater risk of sexual assault in functional units. The authors speculated that the higher perceived risk among prisoners was related to overcrowding and double-bunking in the functional units.

BLIND SPOTS

As noted earlier, sexual assault is a particularly secretive activity and takes place in areas of poor supervision (Atlas, 1983; Lockwood, 1980: 25–8). Shower areas and cells are especially dangerous places. As with other forms of prisoner-prisoner violence, eliminating blind spots and improving supervision of problem areas is an obvious control strategy, although there are no studies that specifically examine the efficacy of improving surveillance capabilities.

Population characteristics

AGE COMPOSITION

The popular image of prison rape typically involves the victimisation of young prisoners by older felons. It might be supposed, therefore, that for sexual assault age homogeneity would be associated with lower levels of victimisation (opposite to the relationship found for other forms of prisoner-prisoner violence). Few studies have addressed this issue, but the available evidence suggests that segregation of young prisoners offers no protection from sexual assault. Davis (1968) found that the average age of prison rapists was 24, four years below the prison-wide average. Lockwood (1980: 104–5) found that 46 per cent of sexual aggressors were less than 19 years of age. Ekland-Olson (1986) found that the relationship between youth and sexual aggression is even stronger than the relationship between youth and other forms of prison violence.

RACIAL COMPOSITION

As noted earlier, blacks are more likely to be assailants in sexual assault incidents and whites more likely to be victims, a pattern that most commentators attribute to gang behaviour (Carroll, 1982: 124; King, 1992: 69; Lockwood, 1980: 28–31; Nacci and Kane, 1984). Not surprisingly, then, at an institutional level Lockwood (1980: 25) found that rapes occurred more frequently in racially heterogeneous institutions.

However, while they acknowledged a link between racial gangs and sexual assault, Nacci and Kane (1984) disputed the common conclusion that rapes are directly motivated by racial tension and the desire for revenge. As Nacci and Kane pointed out, simply establishing a relationship between race and sexual assault does not prove that race was a causal factor. It may be, for example, that whites are selected because they are perceived as easy targets. The racial analysis also overlooks the incidence of sexual aggression in other countries where racial conflicts are not a major feature of prison life. Nacci and Kane found that the rate of victimisation of whites was higher for white assailants (88 per cent) than for black assailants (82 per cent). That is, while there were fewer white assailants than black assailants, when whites did perpetrate sexual assault they were more likely than blacks to select a white target. The conclusion that Nacci and Kane drew from these figures was that whites are more acceptable victims for reasons incidental to race. For example, whites might be perceived generally to be less able to retaliate. These conclusions were supported by self-report data. The higher overall incidence of black assailants was attributed to the fact that there was a greater incidence of black gang rapes. That is, there seemed to be a greater tendency for blacks to draw together in order to deal with the dangers of prison.

MIXED-GENDER PRISONS

It was argued in the previous chapter that co-corrections might reduce levels of prisoner violence by normalising the prison environment and reducing institutional tensions. The rationale for mixed-gender prisons to reduce sexual assault is more direct. It is assumed that the introduction of women prisoners into the usually all-male world helps heterosexual prisoners to re-tain their sexual orientations (Lambiotte, 1980: 222). The benefits of mixed-gender prisons do not depend upon sexual contact between prisoners (which is usually outlawed) but on the development of social relationships and the reinforcement of gender identity. Case studies on co-correctional institutions invariably note reductions in homosexual behaviour in gen-eral and sexual assault in particular as direct benefits of the programme. However, as with prisoner violence more generally, the evidence presented in support of co-corrections is entirely anecdotal, and is based on the percep-tions of staff and prisoners (Campbell, 1980; Heffernan and Krippel, 1980; Lambiotte, 1980).

The prison regime
FURLOUGHS AND CONJUGAL VISITS

Increased use of prison leave and conjugal visits are often recommended by researchers (French, 1978; Heilpern, 1998: 188–92; Ibrahim, 1974: 44; Jones and Schmid, 1989: 60; Money and Bohmer, 1980; Rideau and Sinclair,

1982: 27; Rothenberg, 1983; 81; Scacco, 1975: 106–7, 113; Schaffer, 1991) and prisoners (Hopper, 1989; Lockwood, 1980: 148; Struckman-Johnson *et al.*, 1996) as methods of combating sexual assault. It is assumed that providing opportunities for consensual sex outside the prison environment will help to reduce sexual frustrations and so too will reduce pressures to sexually assault other prisoners. Moreover, conjugal visits are also thought to help to maintain outside relationships and through this to reduce prison tensions. Prisoners have reported that the intimacy with loved ones made possible through conjugal visitation was as important as the sexual release (Carlson and Cervera, 1991; Hopper, 1962, 1969).

Assumptions about the benefits of conjugal visits, however, are largely untested. Hopper (1962, 1969, 1989) reported on the pioneering conjugal visiting programme in Mississippi and found that prisoners and staff believed that homosexual violence was reduced. However, the research did not involve direct measures of sexual assault. On the other hand, Nacci and Kane (1984) found no relationship between home visits and abstinence from prison homosexual behaviour, although again sexual assault was not specifically measured. Nacci and Kane believed that prison sexual assaults were generally not carried out with the primary purpose of obtaining sexual gratification and those interventions that simply attempted to alleviate sexual frustrations were unlikely to succeed. Lockwood (1980: 148) argued that many sexual aggressors do not have wives or girlfriends so would not be eligible for such programmes in any case.

REACTIONS OF OTHER PRISONERS
One of the ironic aspects of prison homosexuality is its acceptance by other prisoners. While it might be expected that an inmate code that values exaggerated images of masculine toughness might condemn homosexual behaviour, as long as it is recognised that a prisoner's homosexuality is caused by the deprivations of imprisonment (that is, that the prisoner is not a 'real' homosexual), then it can be regarded as normal or at least understandable. It is from this position that sexual assaults in prison carry no particular stigma but, on the contrary, may be status-enhancing (Nacci and Kane, 1984; Wooden and Parker, 1982: 14).

The attitudes of other prisoners clearly have an important situational role in prison sexual assaults. The tacit support of such assault by other prisoners increases the difficulty of reducing the behaviour. However, some recent research on prisoner attitudes gives some sign of hope. Saum *et al.* (1995) found that prisoners in their sample regarded acceptance of homosexuality in prison to be part of an outdated inmate code. According to one prisoner 'there is an unspoken ridicule of inmates who engage in sex today more than in the '70s and '80s' (p. 413). If Saum *et al.* are right, there may be some potential to utilise social condemnation by other prisoners to increase feelings of shame in perpetrators and so to modify their behaviour.

AIDS/HIV

It is not suggested that AIDS is a control method for rape, but in terms of the opportunity-reduction model, it is relevant to consider the effect of the risk of AIDS on sexual assault. Saum *et al.* (1995) found a perception among many prisoners that there had been a reduction in prison sexual activity (although not necessarily rapes) in recent years and that this reduction could be attributed partly to fear of AIDS. AIDS education or even warning signs about the dangers of AIDS might help to alert potential assailants to the dangers of the sexual assault.

Others have argued the opposite, however. Donaldson (1995) suggested that AIDS in prison had actually made rape more likely. He argued that the risk of AIDS made newly admitted, non-homosexual prisoners even more attractive targets for sexual assault since they were the most unlikely to have AIDS. Accordingly, in addition to strategies aimed at eliminating rape in prison, Donaldson argued for a harm-minimisation approach involving the issue of condoms in prison. Given that some rapes are inevitable, condoms would at least increase the chances of victims physically surviving their ordeal.

RESPONSES OF GUARDS

Numerous researchers have argued that one of the key problems combating sexual assault in prisons is inaction by prison guards (Bartollas *et al.*, 1982; Bowker, 1980: 12; Carroll, 1982: 127; Chonco, 1989; Davis, 1968; Dumond, 1992: 148; Eigenberg, 1994; Nacci and Kane, 1984; Rideau and Sinclair, 1982: 15; Scacco, 1975: 30; Weiss and Friar, 1975: 121; Wooden and Parker, 1982: 212–13). According to Nacci and Kane (1984), officers are more likely to become desensitised to sexual assault than non-sexual assault because they are more inclined to develop the attitude that the victim 'deserved it'.

There are two issues here. First, the acceptance of sexual assault by guards contributes to a general climate of tolerance of the behaviour. Guards are important conveyers of social norms and can assist in strengthening moral condemnation for sexual attacks. Second, if guards do not treat sexual assault seriously then they are less likely to intervene physically to protect victims. There are numerous accounts in the literature of guards ignoring calls for help from a prisoner being sexually assaulted, or failing to respond adequately to complaints from victims (Davis, 1968; Weiss and Friar, 1975: 121). It is even alleged that guards actively encourage sexual exploitation as a way to keep control and to reward powerful prisoners (Scacco, 1975: 30–2).

The importance of staff responsiveness is illustrated in the study by Bartollas *et al.* (1982) of sexual assault in a juvenile institution. The incidence of sexual assault varied considerably among the eight cottages that comprised the institution. Three cottages had no incidents of sexual abuse while abuse was particularly prevalent in one cottage. The crucial factor, according to Bartollas *et al.*, was the closeness of supervision by staff and the extent to which cottages had temporary or inexperienced staff.

Eigenberg (1994) conducted an empirical investigation of guards' willingness to respond to sexual assault in prison. On the basis of a questionnaire, she found that almost all officers (97 per cent) claimed that they would intervene to prevent rape and 93 per cent responded that prisoners should not be placed in cells where they might be raped. However, only 69 per cent of officers believed that prisoners should be placed in protective custody if they were being pressured for sex, and around 50 per cent believed that they should talk to new prisoners about the risk of rape. With regard to attitudes to victims, 46 per cent of guards believed that some prisoners deserved to be raped and around one-third believed that rape victims were weak. Officers with negative beliefs about rape victims were less likely to report that they would intervene in a rape incident, although those with negative views about homosexuality generally were more likely to intervene.

A number of publications suggest that improvement in staff responsiveness might be achieved through better recruitment and staff training as well as the introduction of intervention protocols to guide staff (Cotton and Groth, 1984: 134–5; Dumond, 1992: 151; Eigenberg, 1994; Nacci and Kane, 1984; Wooden and Parker, 1982: 212–13). Wooden and Parker (1982: 212) reported that the California Department of Corrections moved away from the hiring of ex-military personnel and shifted towards hiring personnel who combined 'authoritarian' and 'humanitarian' traits. Pre-service and in-service training should include 'awareness' modules that provide information on the nature of sexual assault in prison (for example, how to recognise signs of sexual assault) and teach appropriate intervention strategies (Eigenberg, 1994; Nacci and Kane, 1984). Others have suggested that staff training needs to be backed by clear institutional protocols for dealing with cases of sexual assault, mandatory reporting policies and criminal prosecution of offenders (Cotton and Groth, 1984: 136; Dumond, 1992: 151).

POLICING OF CONSENSUAL HOMOSEXUAL BEHAVIOUR

One of the most controversial suggestions made to reduce sexual assaults in prison is to clamp down on consensual homosexual activity. Consensual homosexual behaviour is illegal in most prison systems, although the extent to which the rule is enforced varies. Eigenberg (1994) pointed out that it is frequently impossible to distinguish consensual and coercive sexual behaviour in prison and for this reason action should be taken against all homosexual acts. Nacci and Kane (1984) went further and argued that consensual homosexual behaviour in prison was dangerous, since it created the climate that encouraged homosexual attacks. They rejected the alternative notion (e.g. put forward by Scacco, 1975: 107–8) that consensual sex in prison might act as a sexual release and so reduce sexual aggression. Nacci and Kane's conclusions have been criticised as ideologically rather than empirically based (Heilpern, 1998: 204). The debate about the role of consensual homosexual behaviour and the appropriate response to it once again highlights the ongoing tension between permissive and restrictive logics of prison control.

PROGRAMMES FOR VULNERABLE PRISONERS

Research on the characteristics of prison sexual assault victims indicates that they are not selected at random, but on the basis of cues that mark them as suitable targets. The usual advice given to potential victims by guards is to retaliate violently towards any sexual overtures in order to show aggressors that they cannot be pushed around (Bowker, 1980: 6–7; Lockwood, 1980: 53, 129). However, such violent responses may only escalate the problem (Bowker, 1980: 16; Lockwood, 1980: 40–4). Nacci and Kane (1984) suggested that prevention strategies needed to include the offer of advice to vulnerable prisoners on how to send out appropriate cues, such as avoiding feminine gestures and mannerisms (an example of controlling triggers). Lockwood (1980: 150–4) suggested training for likely targets on how to assertively rebuff unwanted sexual advances and so avoid the violence spiral that typically occurs in these situations.

PROTECTING VULNERABLE PRISONERS

If vulnerable prisoners cannot be taught effective strategies for surviving in the general prison population, then segregation of likely sexual assault targets is an obvious alternative. This strategy is frequently recommended by researchers (Cotton and Groth, 1984: 132; Donaldson, 1995; Dumond, 1992: 159; Heilpern, 1998: 209–10; Ibrahim, 1974: 44; Wooden and Parker, 1982: 208–12) and is consistently given a high priority in surveys of prisoners and guards (Lockwood, 1980: 145; Struckman-Johnson *et al.*, 1996). Separating potential victims and predators is clearly a sensible opportunity-reduction strategy (an example of target removal) although there is no empirical evidence to date by which to judge its effectiveness.

Conclusions

On the whole, the evidence on situational control of prison sexual assault is rather more speculative than was the case for other forms of prisoner-prisoner violence covered in chapter 5. While there is a growing body of research on the phenomenon of prison sexual assault, there is little research on the prevention of the behaviour. Most of the prevention strategies found in the literature and outlined in this chapter involve commonsense extrapolations from the epidemiological data. Other strategies suggested in the literature but not discussed here – such as building smaller prisons (Rothenberg, 1983: 81), employing women staff (Ibrahim, 1974: 44; Scacco, 1975: 111–13), permitting erotic literature (Scacco, 1975: 108–9) and increasing work opportunities for prisoners (Ibrahim, 1974: 43; Moss *et al.*, 1979: 827) – are at this stage little more than educated hunches with no empirical foundation (sensible though they may otherwise be).

A summary of promising control strategies is shown in table 6.1. A crucial issue raised in this chapter is the role of sexual deprivation in sexual assault. It has become fashionable in the social sciences to downplay the role of sexual gratification as a motivation for sexual assault and to see the behaviour as a particular form of violence (whether talking about sexual assaults inside prison or in the general community). To the extent that sexual assault can be folded into the more general problem of prisoner-prisoner violence, the need for specific control strategies diminishes. In particular, if sexual gratification plays little role in prison sexual assault then strategies aimed at reducing sexual deprivation – for example, conjugal visits – are unlikely to be effective. However, despite the certitude with which the assertion is made that sexual assaults are primarily acts of violence, this view is largely an expression of a theoretical position rather than an empirically derived conclusion. What is likely, of course, is that sexual assaults involve a mixture of sexual and violent motivations and that the nature of this mixture varies from case to case. For example, brutal inter-gang rapes may be designed to assert dominance and to humiliate the victim. In cases involving the less overtly violent victimisation of effeminate prisoners, on the other hand, sexual gratification is probably an important consideration.

Table 6.1. *Summary of promising strategies for control of sexual assault*

Strategy	Precipitation-control category	Regulation-control category
Single-cell accommodation	Respecting territory Reducing crowding	Target hardening
Functional units	Setting positive expectations Rule setting Personalising victims Controlling environmental irritants	Formal surveillance Natural surveillance
Eliminating blind spots		Formal surveillance Natural surveillance
Age-heterogeneous populations	Reducing inappropriate imitation Reducing inappropriate conformity	
Race-homogeneous or race-balanced populations	Reducing inappropriate imitation Reducing inappropriate conformity	
Gender-mixed populations	Reducing frustrations Setting positive expectations	
Furloughs and conjugal visits	Reducing frustrations	
Changing prisoner values		Increasing social condemnation
AIDS education/signs	Providing reminders	Increasing costs
Staff awareness training	Rule setting Increasing victim worth	Formal surveillance Increasing costs Increasing social condemnation
Institutional protocols		Formal surveillance Increasing costs
Mandatory reporting/ criminal prosecution		Increasing costs
Policing consensual homosexual behaviour		Controlling facilitators Formal surveillance
Teaching strategies to vulnerable prisoners	Controlling triggers Reducing frustration	Target hardening
Segregation of vulnerable prisoners		Target removal

Whether or not sexual assault is sexually motivated, the research supports the distinction between situational precipitators and situational regulators of sexual assault. However, while some suggested interventions are diametrically opposed to one another, direct evidence of counterproductive control is scant. One point of contention is how prisoners should respond to sexual overtures. Conventional correctional wisdom (and the advice typically given to prisoners by guards) holds that an aggressive response is mandatory if the potential victim is to establish a reputation as someone not to be messed with. However, Lockwood (1980: 40–4) found that aggressive responses to a sexual overture were only likely to escalate the conflict and to increase the chance of a violent altercation. Unfortunately, there is no evidence available on how successful the recommended assertive (non-aggressive) responses have proven to be. Another contentious issue is the appropriate institutional response to consensual homosexuality. Some commentators suggest that consensual homosexual behaviour provides sexual release and should be permitted, and others that it encourages sexual assault and should be stamped out. However, again there is insufficient evidence at present to assess which view is correct.

CHAPTER 7

Prisoner-staff violence

Many articles and research papers on prison disorder make no clear distinction between prisoner assaults on staff and assaults on other prisoners, and simply pool assault categories (and often other forms of prisoner misconduct as well) into an overall prison violence or disorder index (e.g. Farrington and Nuttall, 1980; Quinsey and Varney, 1977). This tendency to think about disorder in global terms reflects the prevailing dominance of systemic rather than situational approaches to prison control. That is, researchers interested in situational influences in prison have been generally concerned with diagnosing 'sick' institutions, rather than pinpointing the precise nature of the malady. There is clearly some sense to this logic and in at least one study a moderate correlation (0.57) has been reported between levels of prisoner-prisoner and prisoner-staff assaults (McCorkle *et al.*, 1995). However, there is also good reason for thinking that the dynamics of assaults against staff will be quite different from those of assaults on other prisoners. The very nature of the prison guard's role – the exercise of authority over an involuntary clientele – means that prisoners and guards have a potentially fraught relationship (Hepburn, 1989).

Nature of the problem

Definition and incidence

Prisoner violence towards staff involves intentional physical contact, and includes pushing, spitting, throwing objects, striking and attacking with a weapon. According to Bowker (1980: 129), physical violence by prisoners can be distinguished from a range of other forms of victimisation that a prison officer might suffer. The daily routine of a guard involves constant exposure to threats and manipulation by prisoners. In addition, for officers who do not fit into the traditional prison-officer culture (for example, those considered to be too liberal in their treatment of prisoners) victimisation may occur at the hands of other staff members and prison administrators. Bowker estimated that less than 0.1 per cent of the victimising behaviour endured by guards involved physical assaults by prisoners.

Whether or not being a prison guard is a particularly dangerous occupation depends upon one's perspective. Certainly, the ever-present threat of assault is a major concern of prison guards (Kauffman, 1988: 48). In terms of figures, in 1995 there were 14,165 assaults on prison staff in US prisons, and 14 deaths (Stephan, 1997). In common with prisoner-prisoner assaults, the assault rate against staff has dropped slightly in the past five years (15.5 versus 14.7 per 1,000 prisoners). The assault rate on staff is consistently about half that reported for prisoner-prisoner assaults. Underlining the situational basis of assaults against prison guards, Wees (1996) reported considerable variations in assault rates across US prison systems. In 1995, assaults in California accounted for 19 per cent of the national total, and assaults in three systems (California, Federal Bureau of Prisons and New Jersey) accounted for almost half. Ten states recorded fewer than ten assaults for the year.

Light (1991) argued that despite the apparent dangers of working in prison, an assault on a prison guard is a relatively uncommon event. In a study of assaults in thirty-one New York State prisons, he found less than 2 per cent of inmates had physically assaulted an officer in the previous year. Of this group of assailants, 88 per cent were involved in just one incident for the year, with 8 per cent involved in two incidents, 2 per cent involved in three incidents and 1 per cent involved in four or more incidents. He suggests that the high proportion of one-off offences is evidence that environmental factors have a strong influence. That is, by and large it does not seem to be the case that assaults are carried out by a small band of dedicated repeat offenders who are predisposed to violence. Light (1990) further found that for prisoners involved in assaulting prison officers, individual-level factors – race, age, type of crime, previous prison sentence, number of prior arrests, drug use, time served and sentence length – did not predict severity of assault.

Patterns
Like prisoner-prisoner assaults, the vast majority of assaults against guards are carried out by a lone assailant (Light, 1991; Steinke, 1991). In Light's study, 97 per cent of assaults involved one prisoner, 3 per cent involved two

prisoners, and 0.4 per cent involved three prisoners. A number of studies have reported that around three-quarters of assaults against staff do not involve a weapon (Gaes and McGuire, 1985; Light, 1991). Of the remaining cases, Light (1991) found that in more than half, non-life-threatening objects such as food, paper, faeces and water were used, leaving just over 10 per cent of all cases of assault in which dangerous weapons were employed. The most common dangerous weapon was some form of blunt instrument (7 per cent of all assault cases) followed by a sharpened object (3 per cent of all assault cases).

In terms of the severity of assaults on staff, Light (1991) found that in more than half the cases reported (54 per cent) the officer sustained no physical injury. In 29 per cent of cases the injury was assessed as minor (scratch, slight bruise etc.), 15 per cent moderate (some loss of blood) and 3 per cent serious (significant loss of blood, injuries requiring emergency treatment). Similarly, Kratcoski (1988) looked at assaults against staff in two institutions, one federal and one state. He categorised 57 per cent (federal) and 32 per cent (state) of assaults as minor – pushing, shoving, spitting, throwing liquid, throwing soft objects such as paper – and 43 per cent (federal) and 68 per cent (state) as major – striking forcibly, and causing pain, both of which in some instances might call for medical attention. Kratcoski also found that most assaults on staff occurred without much warning. In the federal facility that he studied, only 19 per cent of assaults on staff were preceded by a verbal threat or heated exchange between prisoner and guard, while in the state facility the figure was as low as 9 per cent.

Motivation

Light (1991) provided a comprehensive breakdown of the various reasons for prisoner-staff assaults. Based on official incident reports, he found that the largest category of assaults (26 per cent) appeared to be unexpected, seemingly unprovoked and essentially random acts of violence against officers as they performed routine custodial activities. Sometimes these assaults had a utilitarian objective, such as providing the means for a prisoner to have himself quickly transferred to another institution. Usually, however, the assaults were examples of expressive violence probably not directed towards the victim in particular but against the system in general. There may have been a specific instigating event that occurred some time prior to the assault and of which the victim is unaware. Alternatively, the assault may have been the result of a culmination of deprivations and frustrations over time.

The next largest category of assaults (13 per cent) occurred in response to an officer's direct command. The most common command to incite assault, accounting for more than half of the cases in this category, was an order to enter or leave an area. Requests for identification (13 per cent of cases) and orders relating to the prisoner's appearance (9 per cent) were also provocative. Light (1991) explained the open defiance of prisoners as reactions to deprivation of autonomy and threats to self-images of masculinity.

A similar theme of prisoner defiance underlies the next category (11 per cent of cases) that Light labelled 'protest'. In these cases, prisoners saw themselves as victims of unfair treatment and trivial, inconsistent or arbitrary rules. A common cause of protest was dissatisfaction with the officer's delivery of goods and services (e.g. having to wait to be taken for medical treatment), an issue that Light sees in terms of wider frustrations about being reliant on staff for the provision of many day-to-day needs. Protest assaults also occurred when prisoners were confronted with routine security procedures, such as the denial of entry into particular areas, the checking of identification or the termination of prisoner visits. A crucial variable, according to Light, was the extent to which the prisoner felt the rule was being directed particularly to him as opposed to being applied generally (even if unfairly) to all.

A similar number of assaults (11 per cent) were precipitated by an officer's search of the prisoner's person, cell or property. This category excluded cases where contraband was actually found. Thus the prisoner's concerns here can be assumed to be related to the violation of personal space rather than fear of detection. The majority (73 per cent) of assaults in this category occurred during 'frisking' or strip searches.

A further 10 per cent of assaults on staff occurred when officers intervened in a fight between prisoners. Often the injury to the officer would seem to be unintentional. On some occasions, however, the fight may have been staged as a trap for the officer, or the assault on the officer was carried out by a spectator of the fight rather than by one of the participants.

Movement-related assaults accounted for 10 per cent of the total. These assaults occurred during the transfer of the prisoner from one section of the prison to another or from one prison to another. Often these assaults involved prisoners who were already on disciplinary charges or who were subject to special security. The movement of the prisoner did not so much provoke the assault as provide an opportunity for him to vent his anger or to make some display of protest.

In 7 per cent of cases the officer was assaulted after finding the prisoner in possession of some prohibited article. The most commonly located contraband were drugs or alcohol (more than half of all cases), unapproved cell furnishings (15 per cent), knives (9 per cent) and food (9 per cent).

None of the remaining categories accounted for more than 5 per cent of assaults. Some assaults occurred after a prisoner had been released from a restraining device (handcuffs etc.). The process of being disciplined by a prison officer for some other offence also provoked a small number of assaults. Only 2 per cent of all assaults were attributed to the emotional instability of the prisoner and in fewer than 1 per cent of cases was the prisoner judged to be under the influence of drugs or alcohol.

In a reduced classification, Bowker (1980: 128–9) distinguished between patterned spontaneous assaults on staff and unexpected attacks. Patterned spontaneous attacks occur while guards are performing high-risk activities such as breaking up fights and escorting prisoners to segregation. Un-expected attacks, on the other hand, are associated with no particular pattern and might be perpetrated by a disgruntled prisoner at any time. Kauffman (1988) proposed four categories of prisoner-staff assault involv-ing two dimensions – spontaneous/calculated and provoked/unprovoked. Spontaneous unprovoked assaults are usually associated with disturbed or drug-affected prisoners; calculated unprovoked assaults are products of expressive anger against guards generally; spontaneous provoked assaults are triggered by guards' deliberate or inadvertent actions; and calculated provoked assaults involve planned retaliation and as such potentially are the most lethal. Kauffman's classification in particular clearly overlaps with the two-stage situational model proposed in this book. The degree of provoca-tion equates with the concept of situational precipitation, while the extent to which an action is calculated is related to the cost-benefit analysis in the situational regulation stage of the model.

Situational context

SEASONAL VARIATIONS

Sylvester *et al.* (1977: 12) found homicides involving staff were more likely to occur in summer months. Other studies, however, have failed to find any relationship between climate and assaults on staff. Steinke (1991) found no difference in levels of assault that might be attributed to outside ambient temperature. Quinsey and Varney (1977) and Harris and Varney (1986) found no seasonal variability.

SECURITY LEVEL

Like prisoner-prisoner assaults, assaults on staff are more common in maximum- and medium-security prisons than in minimum-security pris-ons (Ditchfield and Harries, 1996; Light, 1991; McCorkle *et al.*, 1995), al-though there is no difference in assault severity across prison-security levels

(Light, 1990). In Light's (1991) study, 82 per cent of assaults were in maximum security, 15 per cent in medium security, and 2 per cent in minimum security, although Light did not provide a breakdown of respective prisoner numbers in these locations from which rates might be calculated. Again, the extent to which the high assault level in maximum-security prisons is a function of population or institutional characteristics cannot be determined.

High assault levels have also been recorded in high-security areas within a prison. Kratcoski (1988) found that in one federal institution, 71 per cent of assaults occurred in one cell block, a high-security area housing less than 10 per cent of the inmates. The high proportion of assaults in the high-security area occurred in spite of the extra security that was in place. Although this area had the greatest number of both serious and minor assaults, it was responsible for proportionately more minor assaults (87 per cent) than serious assaults (57 per cent). Kratcoski argued that the disproportionate level of minor assaults reflected the physical restrictions experienced by prisoners in this area. When the opportunity for inflicting serious injury was curtailed, prisoners resorted to attacks such as throwing water.

TIME

There does not seem to be any consistent time of day that assaults on staff are more likely. Where studies have identified clusters of assaults around particular times, the type of activity occurring at that time appears to be the crucial factor. Thus, Atlas (1982) found a decrease in armed attacks during the day when levels of supervision were at their highest. On the other hand, Kratcoski (1988) found most assaults occurred during the day, a fact he attributed to greater levels of activity and interaction in the high-security areas at this time. Dietz and Rada (1983) found assault peaks coincided with the movement of prisoners to the dining-room. Jayewardene and Doherty (1985) found that homicides coincided with release from cells with change of shift.

LOCATION

As for prisoner-prisoner assaults, the location of prisoner-staff assaults varies from institution to institution, but nevertheless several general patterns emerge from the research. Most striking is the relatively large number of assaults that have been recorded in the prisoners' living areas. In most studies this was the single most likely location for the assault to take place and, where comparative data was available, accounted for a greater proportion of the total than is the case for prisoner-prisoner assaults. Sylvester *et al.* (1977: 27) found that 67 per cent of murders of staff took place in cell block or dormitory. Light (1991) found almost half (49 per cent) of the attacks on staff occurred in the cell block. Comparing four prisons Atlas (1982, 1983) found that cells and dorms accounted for between 27 per cent and 58 per cent of cases. The high proportion of assaults on staff in cells and dorms might be explained by a sense of territoriality that prisoners develop for their living areas, and the hostility caused by having territory invaded. The psychological effects of territorial invasion are likely to be most keenly felt if the cell is being searched. The results suggest that staff need to take special precautions when entering prisoners' cells or, where practicable, to avoid trespassing into these areas. One study going against the trend was Harris and Varney (1986). They found that relatively few assaults on staff occurred in patients' rooms (13 per cent) and attributed this low figure to a deliberate policy of restricting the number of times staff enter inmates' rooms.

Assaults on staff have also been found to be relatively common in supervised areas where prisoners are allowed freedom of movement and congregation – hallways, recreation areas and mess halls (Atlas, 1983; Light, 1991; Steinke, 1991; Sylvester *et al.*, 1977: 27). A similar pattern was reported for prisoner-prisoner assaults. However, Atlas (1983) found that differences between prisoner-prisoner assaults and prisoner-staff assaults emerged when assaults were broken down into armed and unarmed. He found that the pattern for armed assaults on staff was roughly the same as that for prisoners, that is, with around 91 per cent occurring in areas of limited supervision. However, the pattern for unarmed assaults differed between the two groups, with around 25 per cent of assaults on guards occurring under direct supervision compared with 12 per cent for prisoners. In other words, there was a greater tendency for unarmed attacks on guards to occur in well-supervised areas. This suggests that armed attacks involve a degree of planning and may be countered by improving surveillance. Unarmed attacks are more likely to be spontaneous and arise in the course of public interaction between prisoners and guards.

Finally, and again paralleling the findings for prisoner-prisoner assaults, few assaults occurred in areas where prisoners were engaged in structured activity (Kratcoski, 1988; Light, 1991; Steinke, 1991; Sylvester *et al.*, 1977: 27). In the latter study there were no murders of staff in workshops or classrooms, and Light (1991) found that workshops and classrooms each accounted for less than 1 per cent of assaults on staff. Quinsey and Varney (1977) also found that few assaults occurred in locations that were considered as privilege areas – visiting and work areas – where access depended upon the display of sustained good behaviour. Kratcoski (1988) made the further point that in the institutions he studied most job sites were supervised by non-custodial staff. It may be that the relatively low assault rates in these areas were partly the result of a less authoritarian relationship between staff and prisoners.

Controlling prisoner-staff violence

The physical environment

FUNCTIONAL UNITS

Unit management places a great deal of emphasis on close interaction between prisoners and staff. While this strategy increases the capacity for direct supervision of prisoners, it also increases the exposure of staff to assaults from prisoners. Countering this is the assumed protection that staff receive working in a less stressful, dehumanising environment.

Research indicates that there are fewer assaults on staff working in unit management than in traditional linear prisons (Farbstein *et al.*, 1996: 21; Farbstein and Wener, 1989: III 5.5–8; King, 1991; Senese *et al.*, 1992; Sigurdson, 1985: vi; 1987a: v; 1987b: i; Wener *et al.*, 1987). For example, in the three audits of podular facilities conducted by Sigurdson (1985: vi; 1987a: v; 1987b: i), there were no reported incidents of assaults on staff. Farbstein and Wener (1989: III 5.5–8) found that prisoners believed that prisoners and staff fought less often and were safer in direct supervision. King (1991), in his comparison of a US new-generation prison (Oak Park Heights) and a British dispersal prison (Gartree), found that Oak Park Heights' prisoners were significantly more likely than Gartree prisoners to rate staff safety as very or quite safe (75 per cent versus 58 per cent). Senese *et al.* (1992) also found that staff in the units were more inclined to use in-house discipline (rather than formal write-up) than staff in the traditional institution, suggesting better prisoner–staff relationships. However, these studies suffer from the same methodological problems as those discussed in earlier chapters, namely the failure to employ adequate comparison groups and the tendency to rely on perceptual data.

Moreover, staff did not always feel safer. Farbstein and Wener (1989: III 5.6) reported that although staff believed that prisoners and guards had better communication in direct supervision facilities than traditional prisons, they also felt in greater danger from attack. Using behavioural tracking, Farbstein and Wener confirmed that the amount and duration of interaction between prisoners and staff was higher in direct than indirect supervision facilities and that prisoners were more likely in direct facilities to initiate communication with staff (p. III 4.2–7). However in both types of institutions, whenever two officers were present, both officers spent most of their time together near the office rather than interacting with prisoners. King (1991: 148–9) found that, despite the perceptions of prisoners that a new-generation prison was safer for staff than a traditional prison, prisoners in the new-generation prison consistently rated their relationship with staff more negatively (staff less fair, less consistent, more racist and less helpful) than did prisoners in the traditional prison. Taken together, these observations highlight the need to conceptualise unit management in both architectural and management terms. The provision of units does not guarantee unit management will occur. If staff in units feel under threat, then, irrespective of the architecture, they are likely to minimise contact with prisoners. As Farbstein and Wener argued, if unit management is to fulfil its potential then it must be supported by the prison administration and staff must be provided with adequate training.

BLIND SPOTS

As with the other forms of violence discussed so far, a significant proportion of assaults on staff occurred in hidden locations and, in particular, in prisoners' rooms. Elimination of blind spots, then, is equally as important for staff safety as it is for prisoner safety. It is noteworthy that one of the design features of functional units is visibility into cells, and this factor may account for the low levels of prisoner-staff violence outlined in the previous section.

Population characteristics

SIZE

There has been generally less interest shown by researchers in the effects of prisoner–population characteristics on assault on staff than on the effect on prisoner-prisoner assaults. Where research does exist no evidence of a relationship between prison size and assaults on staff has been found (Gaes and McGuire, 1985; Light, 1990; McCorkle *et al.*, 1995). McCorkle *et al.* (1995) initially found a positive correlation between prison size and assaults on staff, but this effect disappeared after statistical control for other institutional variables. The failure to find a relationship between prison size and violence against staff is consistent with the findings for prisoner-prisoner violence. Likewise, one explanation for the findings is hyper-vigilance by staff as a compensatory strategy.

CROWDING

The role of crowding remains as contentious for assaults on staff as for assaults on other prisoners. Most studies (Ekland-Olson, 1986; Light, 1990;

McCorkle *et al.*, 1995; Nacci *et al.*, 1977), but not all (Jan, 1980), report no re-lationship between crowding and assaults on staff. Gaes and McGuire (1985) reported mixed findings. They found unarmed assaults on staff increased with crowding, although this trend levelled out at 60–65 per cent over-crowded. On the other hand, armed assaults on staff with weapons decreased with crowding. They speculated that the drop in armed attacks might reflect super-vigilance of staff in crowded conditions. Gaes and McGuire further found that effects of crowding increased with the mean age of prisoners (i.e. crowding was more likely to increase assaults on staff in prisons housing older prisoners), a finding opposite to the reported relationship between crowding and aging in prisoner-prisoner assaults (e.g. Nacci *et al.*, 1977).

AGE COMPOSITION

Apart from the interaction with crowding, assaults against staff have been found to be more frequent (Ditchfield and Harries, 1996; Kratcoski, 1988; Gaes and McGuire, 1985) and more severe (Light, 1990) in institutions where the mean age of prisoners is relatively low. Light found that aggregate institutional characteristics such as low numbers of prisoners with previ-ous arrests, low percentages of recidivists and high numbers of prisoners with drug-use histories were also associated with assault severity, but he interpreted the effects of these variables in terms of their associations with youthfulness. Light also found that the relationship between aggre-gate age and assault severity was over and above the relationship between age and severity at an individual level. That is, the high levels of assault severity recorded for institutions with many young prisoners was not sim-ply the result of the activities of the young prisoners; prisoners of all ages tended to commit more severe assaults in youth-dominated institu-tions. Light's findings suggest the effects of age are mediated by the social environment and so point to the advantages of increasing prisoner-age heterogeneity.

RACIAL COMPOSITION

Contradictory findings have been reported for the role of prisoner racial composition in violence against staff. In a British study Ditchfield and Harries (1996) found that assaults on staff increased with the proportion of black prisoners, a pattern that parallels the findings for prisoner-prisoner violence. However, in a US study, Gaes and McGuire (1985) reported the opposite trend – that the greater the white–black ratio of prisoners, the more numerous the assaults against staff. Gaes and McGuire (1985) argued that the increases in the white prisoner population were associated with an evening-out of the racial composition, that is, that whites and blacks approached equal representation. The authors suggested that the increase in prisoner-staff assaults might have indicated a displacement effect as prisoner-prisoner assaults dropped. Just to add to the confusion Light (1990) found that the racial composition of prisoners had no effect on the severity of assaults.

POPULATION TURNOVER

There is no evidence that prisoner turnover increases the frequency (Gaes and McGuire, 1985) or severity (Light, 1990) of assaults on staff.

The prison regime
PRISONER–STAFF INTERACTIONS

As noted in the introduction to this chapter, the nature of interaction between prisoners and staff is quite different from that among prisoners. Guards have formal power, and their job frequently involves making prisoners do what they do not want to do. The inherent nature of the guards' role makes them targets for assault generally; how individual guards carry out their role may make them particular targets.

Kauffman (1988: 47–71) identified six basic control tactics available to guards. First, guards may exercise control by relying on their authority. Kauffman defines authority as 'a power relationship in which the commands and desires of one individual or group are accepted as legitimate and thus are automatically complied with by another individual or group' (p. 47). Second, guards may attempt to persuade prisoners to comply with directions. Persuasion involves putting rational arguments to the prisoner, pointing out, for example, the advantages of compliance and the likely consequences of disobedience. Third, inducements may be offered to secure compliance. These inducements often fall outside the formal system of rewards and may even contradict official policy. For example, giving small gifts such as cigarettes, doing favours or overlooking other transgressions may be used to buy cooperation. Fourth, cooperation may be obtained through manipulation. Manipulation involves 'conning' prisoners by presenting them with false or misleading information and, while it is morally questionable, manipulation is, according to Kauffman, ubiquitous in prison. Fifth, if the above tactics are unsuccessful in gaining the willing compliance of prisoners, guards may use coercion. Coercion is the application of threats and sanctions. Sanctions may be formal – the instigation of official disciplinary procedures – or informal – harassment and the withholding of goods and services or, more seriously, the use of physical violence. Finally, guards may resort to force to compel prisoners to obey. The use of guns on prisoners who attempt to escape, the physical restraining of rebellious prisoners and the enforced medication of disturbed prisoners are situations where the option of non-compliance is removed from the prisoner. According to Kauffman each of these strategies 'has its failings [and] none by itself is sufficient to overcome all resistance to intrusions into individual autonomy' (p. 71).

The breakdown of assault categories by Light (1991) indicated that the majority of assaults (around 65 per cent) occurred while the victim was engaged in some form of routine interaction with the assailant (issuing commands, enforcing rules and conducting searches). Because Light's categories were derived from official reports of the incidents, the extent to which assaults may have been provoked by the way the officers carried out their duties – the manner in which prisoners were addressed or in which commands were given – is unclear, but it is reasonable to assume that this may well be a factor in some cases. Quinsey and Varney (1977), in a study of a maximum-security psychiatric unit, compared the reasons given by staff with those given by the perpetrators after an assault. Not surprisingly, staff were inclined to see the assault as having no apparent reason (63 per cent), or as occurring in re-action against institutional rules or lawful orders (15 per cent); the perceptions of assaulters were more likely to claim that they were provoked by staff (23 per cent), or staff refused a request (10 per cent). Similarly, Harris and Varney (1986) found that reasons for assaults, as told by staff, were: prisoner given an order (17 per cent); prisoner angry at rules (6 per cent); prisoner's request refused (5 per cent). In comparison, the assaulters said the reasons for their attacks were: provocation by staff (12 per cent); aware of build-up of tension (5 per cent); given an order to do something (5 per cent). Not surprisingly there are marked differences in the respective accounts. When reasons are offered, staff tended to attribute the causes to adverse reactions of inmates to routine rules and orders; inmates saw the incidents in terms of provocation and denial of legitimate requests.

Patrick (1998) conducted an attitudinal study examining the relationship between prisoner–officer behaviour and assaults on staff. He hypothesised that 'the more frequently inmates perceive correctional staff threatening the use of force, the more they will perceive inmate-on-staff altercations' (p. 254). Results confirmed the prediction. Patrick argued that threats by staff are provocative and increase prisoner reactance. The limitation of the study, however, is that it deals only with perceived relationships.

Effective interpersonal strategies for dealing with prisoners is an obvious topic for staff training (Kratcoski, 1988). However, whether such skills can be taught in the classroom, or whether they must be learned through experience, is open to debate.

STAFF EXPERIENCE

Staff experience is relevant at both an individual and an aggregate level. At an individual level it is relevant to examine whether inexperienced staff members are more likely to be victims of assault. At an aggregate level the issue is whether there are more assaults in institutions with a lower overall level of staff experience.

Kratcoski (1988) examined assaults in terms of individual staff experience in both a US federal and a state facility. Staff were grouped into three categories – trainees (<1 year of experience), seniors (1 to 3 years) and seasoned (>3 years). In the federal facility, 35 per cent of assaults were against trainees (15 per cent of total staff), 59 per cent against seniors (76 per cent of staff) and 6 per cent against seasoned (9 per cent of staff). In the state facility, 2 per cent were against trainees (3 per cent of staff), 51 per cent against seniors (3 per cent of staff) and 47 per cent against seasoned (95 per cent of staff). Although patterns are somewhat different, in general it seems that the most experienced staff members are less likely to be assaulted. The age of the officer, as distinct from experience, was not a significant factor. Davies and Burgess (1988) and Ditchfield and Harries (1996) reported similar results in studies of the British prison system. Just what it is about the behaviour of experienced officers that gives them relative protection from attack is unclear, but these findings suggest they have learned more effective and less provocative strategies for dealing with prisoners. Alternatively, it may be that prisoners single out inexperienced officers because they perceive them to be easier targets for assault.

Ekland-Olson (1986) found some suggestion that aggregate assault rates might also be linked to a lack of staff training. He found that assaults on staff increased when there was an influx of new staff. However, McCorkle *et al.* (1995) found assault rates were not related to guard turnover. Light (1990) found assault severity was not affected by officer turnover, percentage of guards with fewer than two years of experience, average number of officer grievances or average level of absenteeism.

STAFF–PRISONER RATIO

Ekland-Olson (1986) found that the higher the staff–prisoner ratio the higher the prisoner–staff assault rate. However, Ekland-Olson argued that this finding needs to be interpreted in reverse – the staff levels were increased precisely because violence was getting out of hand. McCorkle *et al.* (1995)

found assaults were not related to the variations in the staff–prisoner ratio between institutions, or to changes over time in the staff–prisoner ratio. Light (1990) found no effect for staff–prisoner ratio on assault severity.

PRESENCE OF OTHER STAFF

Common sense suggests that there is safety in numbers and no doubt guards feel safer with other staff around them. Kratcoski (1988) examined assaults on staff in terms of the number of staff present. He found that in a federal institution 51 per cent of assaults on staff occurred when the victim was alone, and 49 per cent when the victim was with other officers. In one state facility, 15 per cent of assaults were on lone victims, and 85 per cent on victims who were in the company of other staff. When Kratcoski compared major and minor assaults, he found minor assaults were generally associated with lone victims and serious assault with accompanied victims. This result was accounted for by the policy requiring officers to work in pairs when moving high-security prisoners between cells and other locations. In other words, the officers were accompanied precisely because there was an additional risk of assault. Just the same, the presence of another officer cannot be assumed to provide protection against assault.

STAFF RACIAL COMPOSITION

As with staff experience, there are two questions to be answered concerning the relationship between staff race and prisoner-staff assaults. First, are staff members from certain racial groups more vulnerable to attack? Second, does the overall racial composition of staff in an institution affect aggregate assault rates?

On the first issue, Sylvester *et al.* (1977: 15–16) found that ten of the eleven murder victims in their study were white but that this was roughly in line with proportion of total staff (93 per cent). Of the eleven cases, five (45 per cent) involved victims and assailants of different races, again revealing no significant racial patterns. Sylvester *et al.* caution that the small numbers involved limits the reliability of these findings.

On the second issue McCorkle *et al.* (1995) examined the role of the racial composition of staff. They found assaults on staff increased with the white–black staff ratio. This trend was similar to that recorded for prisoner-prisoner assaults and so further confirms their conclusion that relatively high levels of white staff (when compared with the racial make-up of the prisoner population) are likely to increase racial tensions within an institution. Light (1990) found no effect for the racial composition of guards on assault severity.

STAFF GENDER COMPOSITION

Opinion is divided as to whether women enhance or compromise prison security (Alpert, 1984; Crouch, 1985; Jenne and Kersting, 1996; Kantrowitz, 1996: 3–4; Zimmer, 1987). Those arguing in favour of women guards claim that they introduce a normalising influence into an institution and, more specifically, deal with conflicts in a more 'social', less provocative, manner. Others claim that women are not physically strong enough for the role of prison guard or that their presence may actually escalate tension by arousing sexual desire among prisoners. As with staff experience and race, the role of gender involves both individual-level and institution-level considerations.

Shawver and Dickover (1986) examined assaults on female officers in male prisons in California in 1981–2. They found that women guards were proportionately less likely to be victims of assault than male guards. Kratcoski (1988) found that women staff members were only slightly less likely to be assaulted. In the federal institution, 2 per cent of assaults were on female staff and 8 per cent of staff were women. In the state institution, 8 per cent of assaults were on females and 12 per cent of officers were women. However, Kratcoski notes that there were some restrictions on areas of the institutions where female officers worked, and this might have shielded them from the risk of higher assault levels. Taken together, these findings provide tentative support for the view that women guards may have better interpersonal skills for diffusing tensions, and at the very least do not support the alternative position that women are a 'weak link' in correctional security.

In terms of aggregate assault rates, Rowan (1996) found that as the proportion of female staff increased in an institution, prisoner-staff assaults decreased. However, others found that the presence of female staff had no effect on assault levels (Holeman and Krepps-Hess, 1983; Kratcoski, 1988). There seem to be no empirical studies that show that higher levels of women staff increase assault rates.

STAFF AUTHORITY

The effects on prisoner-prisoner assaults of the end of the building-tender system in Texas were outlined in chapter 5. The building-tender system, it will be recalled, involved using prisoners to control other prisoners, and was abandoned as a result of the Ruiz trial in 1980. Ekland-Olson (1986) also looked at the effects of the Ruiz decision on prisoner-staff assaults. He found that after the trial assaults against staff increased dramatically (91 in 1979 to 1,426 in 1984), despite reductions in crowding and increases in staff–prisoner ratios over this period. He argued that the biggest factor in the increase in assaults on staff after the trial was a perceived shift in power. According to Ekland-Olson the court-mandated changes that limited officers' powers both emboldened prisoners and made staff unsure and hesitant. From the inmates' perspective, assaults became 'a less costly and therefore more viable mechanism for settling disputes or righting perceived injustices' (p. 393). Ekland-Olson showed that clusters of assaults on staff coincided with the key stages of the Ruiz case that highlighted the eroded power of the guards. For example, there was a surge in assaults when the decree was first published and again to coincide with the publication of new disciplinary procedures. The increased violence against staff occurred despite increased staffing levels over this period.

SECURITY CRACKDOWNS

Binda (1975) reported on the introduction of increased security measures that were inaugurated in California prisons in 1973 in response to 'an intolerable violence problem'. Measures included additional gun-coverage, re-arrangement of offices and shops, reduction of inmate assignments, cancellation of evening activities, revision of lock-up times, standardisation of cell furniture and tighter controls on visits. Using a pre-test–post-test design, Binda found an overall reduction in total stabbings of staff, particularly straight after the introduction of the measures, but no reduction in staff deaths or other assaults on staff. However, there were significant changes in the patterns of violence. With respect to the stabbings, there was a shift in the location from general population areas to security areas. This may indicate that as a result of the crackdown, greater numbers of violent prisoners were concentrated in security housing. In terms of weapons used, there was a significant decrease in the use of heavy weapons, but an increase in the number of concealed weapons that were not recovered. This finding suggests a greater concern to avoid detection that was a result of the increased security. There were also changes in stabbing rates among institutions, with three institutions reporting decreases, one an increase, and two no difference, suggesting variations in the degree to which the crackdown was instituted and enforced.

With respect to other forms of assault, while there was no significant difference before and after the security measures, trends indicated an immediate increase in assaults after the introduction of the measures, followed by a drop in assaults. There was a particular reduction in clique-based assaults but a corresponding increase in individual-level assaults. The reduction in gang violence was most likely to be the result of measures specifically aimed at breaking up racial cliques (e.g. transfer of gang members etc.). The increase in individual violence was unexpected. One explanation that is consistent with the model proposed in this book is that while the crackdown reduced instrumental assaults (often associated with gangs) it actually created pressures that increased expressive assaults, especially when the new measures were first introduced. In other words, the tighter security measures were differentially successful depending upon the dynamics of the assault, and in some cases seemed to be counterproductive.

The security crackdown at Marion reported in chapter 5 also resulted in a reduction of assaults against staff (Holt and Phillips, 1991). As a result of the enforcement of strict control over prisoners' movements, the rate of assaults on staff fell from a high of 10.5 per 10,000 to 4.1 per 10,000. There were two members of staff killed by prisoners before the crackdown and none after.

PROGRAMME AVAILABILITY

Consistent with the findings for prisoner-prisoner violence, few assaults on staff occurred in areas where there was structured activity. However, only two studies have examined the aggregate relationship between prisoner-programme involvement and officially recorded assaults on staff, and these produced inconsistent findings. McCorkle *et al.* (1995) found assaults on staff decreased with the level of inmate programme involvement; Light (1990) found that the level of institutional programming was not related to assault severity. An additional study (Frey and Delaney, 1996) used a self-report methodology to compare the effects of prisoner participation in passive and active leisure activities. It was hypothesised that active sports would have a cathartic effect and prisoners who reported high levels of involvement in active sports would also report less trouble with staff. Frey and Delaney found that in fact there was very little participation in active sport reported, and that there was no relationship between participation in either active or passive pastimes and self-reported conflict with staff.

DETERMINATE SENTENCING

Forst and Brady (1985) examined the effects on levels of prisoner-staff violence of the introduction of determinate sentences into the California system in 1976. The purpose of the sentencing reform was to remove discretion of the parole board (thus making release dates more certain) while retaining a remission system as an incentive for good behaviour. Forst and Brady reasoned that reductions in anxiety and frustration associated with a more certain release date would translate into lower violence levels against staff. However, using time-series data they found that violence against staff rose sharply after the introduction of determinate sentencing, although there was a drop in fatal injuries. One problem with interpreting these data is that other possible causes for the change over time are not accounted for. For their part, Forst and Brady do not claim that determinate sentencing was responsible for either the rise or drop in violence, but rather that determinacy and violence are unrelated.

Table 7.1. *Summary of promising strategies for control of prisoner-staff violence*

Strategy	Precipitation-control category	Regulation-control category
Functional units	Setting positive expectations Rule setting Personalising victims Controlling environmental irritants	Formal surveillance Natural surveillance
Elimination of blind spots		Formal surveillance Natural surveillance
Reduced population density Age-heterogeneous populations	Reducing crowding Reducing inappropriate imitation Reducing inappropriate conformity	
Staff training	Encouraging compliance Reducing frustration	
Increasing staff experience	Encouraging compliance Reducing frustration	
Matching prisoner/staff racial composition	Encouraging compliance Reducing frustration	
Increasing women staff	Encouraging compliance Reducing frustration	
Supporting staff authority		Increasing costs
Security crackdowns		Target hardening Controlling facilitators Formal surveillance Increasing costs Removing privileges
Prison programmes/works	Reducing frustrations Clarifying responsibility	Deflecting offenders

Conclusions

Classification of promising strategies is shown in table 7.1. It is apparent that there are a number of strategies – such as reducing crowding, functional units and age heterogeneity – that are generic to all three forms of prison violence (prisoner-prisoner, sexual and prisoner-staff). The strategies specific to prisoner-staff violence relate mainly to the quality of the interpersonal relationship between these two groups. Most assaults on staff occur during routine interaction with prisoners. The evidence suggests that the way that these interactions are conducted can have an important bearing on the likelihood that violence will occur. Notably absent from the literature is any empirical examination of technological aids such as CCTV and personal alarm buttons.

There are some suggestions in the research of counterproductive control, although the evidence is inferential. Patrick (1998) found that prisoners believed that reliance by guards on threats of force increased the probability of prisoner-staff violence. On the other hand, Ekland-Olson's (1986) case study of the unintended consequences of the Ruiz trial is a cautionary tale about the dangers of stripping guards of authority. There was also evidence that functional units, if not properly supported by administrators, can be perceived by staff as intimidating and dangerous places (Farbstein and Wener, 1989). Finally, Binda's (1975) study of a security crackdown leaves open the possibility that tightening controls on prisoners can increase levels of expressive violence against staff.

CHAPTER 8

Self-harm

Perhaps of all the problem behaviours discussed in this book, deliberate self-harm by prisoners is most likely to attract dispositional explanations. This is a behaviour that is easily pathologised. Accordingly, much of the research in this area has been aimed at trying to identify those prisoners most at risk. This research has followed two lines of study. Some researchers have adopted a clinical approach, searching for psychological variables that might be useful in the development of risk-screening devices. Others have taken an actuarial approach, and examined risk in terms of established relationships with type of sentence, length of sentence, stage of sentence, prisoner race, psychiatric history and so forth (Salive *et al.*, 1989).

In keeping with the focus of this book, research on individual-level risk factors is not reviewed in any depth here. This is not to say that many prisoners who engage in self-harm may not have particular psychological deficits and inadequate coping strategies that make them particularly suicide-prone, or that attempts to identify these prisoners are of no value. The situational approach, after all, is based on the assumption of an interaction between environment *and* disposition. However, there are dangers in placing too much faith in screening prisoners. Inevitably, at-risk prisoners will slip through the net. The argument of this chapter is that it is generally safer to assume that all prisoners are at risk and to focus on generic environmental contributors to self-harm.

Nature of the problem

Definition and incidence

Self-harm includes instances of self-inflicted injury that were not intended to be fatal, failed suicide attempts and successful suicide attempts. Self-harm in prison is a serious problem that shows no sign of abating. In the first half of the 1980s in the US the number of deaths of prisoners at the hands of other prisoners was roughly the same as the number of deaths at prisoners' own hands. However, with the drop in prisoner-prisoner violence that has occurred in the last decade, now more than twice as many prisoners kill themselves as are killed by other prisoners (Lillis, 1994). In 1995 in the US prison systems, 169 prisoners committed suicide, up from 134 in 1990 (Stephan, 1997). These figures, however, relate only to prisons. As Hayes (1989: 7) pointed out, the suicide problem in US jails is even more serious. Here suicide is the leading cause of inmate death, accounting for over 400 deaths annually. Similar increases in prison suicides are found in British data. In 1988 there were 37 prison suicides recorded in England and Wales; in 1998 the figure was 82 (HM Chief Inspector of Prisons for England and Wales, 1999: 12).

There is also wide variation in death rates among jurisdictions. Hayes (1995: 440–5), in a comprehensive comparison of suicide rates in all 50 US states between 1984 and 1983 reported a low of 7.1 per 100,000 inmates (New Mexico), a high of 101.7 per 100,000 (North Dakota) and a national rate of 20.6 per 100,000. There are also considerable variations among countries. In a review of international trends, Biles et al. (1992) reported a rate per 100,000 of deaths in custody for England as 14.8, Japan as 17.9, Australia as 29.8 and Canada as 43.9. It should be noted, however, that Biles et al.'s calculations did not distinguish between suicides and death by other means.

A number of studies have compared suicide rates in detention with those in the general community. Hayes (1995: 443) reported that suicide rates in US detention facilities were 50 per cent higher than that of the general population, while Salive et al. (1989) estimated the suicide rate in prison to be three times that of the general community. Ramsay et al. (1987: 295), looking at Canadian figures, put the prison suicide rate at eight times that of the general population. When prison suicide rates are compared with rates in a more closely matched community sample, the difference between the two figures is reduced but is still greater for prisoners (3.5 times the rate). Hayes (1995: 444) further reported that suicide rates in prison did not vary in proportion to suicide rates in the local communities. Comparing prison suicide rates among US states, Hayes found that the highest rates were in states with the smallest prison systems, irrespective of the suicide rates in the general community. Hayes argued that this finding reflected the lack of resources available in smaller systems. If Hayes is correct, then this again points to the crucial role of the prison environment in generating the conditions that promote self-harm.

Patterns

The methods used by prisoners to injure or kill themselves vary among institutions and reflect the availability of instruments within the prison environment. Dooley (1990), in a British study on prison deaths, found 90 per cent of cases involved hanging, 4 per cent drugs or poison, 3 per cent cutting and 1 per cent smoke inhalation or burns. Hayes (1983), in a US study, found 96 per cent of suicides were by hanging, and the rest by cutting or drug ingestion. White and Schimmel (1995: 55) found that 79 per cent of suicide victims hanged themselves and 7 per cent jumped to their deaths, while drug overdose, cutting and shooting each accounted for 5 per cent. In another British study, this time looking at self-injury and attempted suicide, Inch et al. (1995) found that 64 per cent involved cutting, 32 per cent hanging and 4 per cent swallowing a sharp object. Looking specifically at the instrument used, Hayes and Rowan (1988: 31) found that the most common was bedding (48 per cent), followed by clothing (34 per cent), shoelace (5 per cent), towel (4 per cent), belt (2 per cent) and gun (1 per cent). All other instruments (knife, razor blade, glass and drugs) were each involved in less than 1 per cent of cases.

Fleming et al. (1992) also examined self-inflicted harm other than successful suicides and found a difference between patterns in police cells and in prisons. In police cells, 70 per cent of incidents involved hanging, 16 per cent laceration, 9 per cent strangulation and 1 per cent ingestion. Looking further at the instrument used, they found that clothing accounted for half of all reports, bedding was reported in 23 per cent of cases, razors and other sharp instruments (pins, nails, glass) were used in 11 per cent of cases. In prisons, laceration accounted for 68 per cent of self-inflicted harm, hanging 18 per cent, ingestion 7 per cent and fire 2 per cent. A razor or other sharp instrument was used in 49 per cent of cases, bedding 17 per cent and clothing 13 per cent. Hanging was more likely in completed suicides than in non-completed suicides, with 90 per cent of suicides in police cells and 89 per cent of suicides in prison by hanging.

Motivation

As might be expected, there is a relatively high incidence of mental-health problems among prison suicide victims. White and Schimmel (1995: 54) reported that of 43 suicides studied, 23 victims (53 per cent) had received a previous psychiatric diagnosis, including 11 diagnosed with severe psychotic disturbance, 6 with affective disorder and 4 with paranoid ideation. Seventeen victims (40 per cent) had made at least one previous attempt at suicide. At the same time the evidence suggests that the high incidence of suicide and self-injury in prison is directly related to the imprisonment experience. Liebling (1992: 45–6; 1993: 383) reported that a history of psychiatric treatment is less likely for cases of prison suicides than for general population suicides – one-third versus 80–90 per cent – suggesting that situational factors are particularly important in prison suicides.

A common assumption is that a great many suicide attempts are manipulative in nature, designed to achieve some ulterior purpose such as a transfer to another section of the prison or to another institution. However, most researchers caution that there is no reliable way of differentiating between genuine and manipulative suicide attempts. Moreover, Liebling (1992: 232–6; 1993: 400) argued that rather than see attempted suicides/self-injury and completed suicides as separate phenomena, it is more useful to see both behaviours as arising from a similar set of causes. She found a considerable overlap between the two populations, with many prisoners who commit suicide having histories of self-mutilation. It is better, she argued, to regard self-injurious behaviours on a continuum reflecting levels of despair. She challenged the notion that self-injury is usually manipulative, arguing that it is typically reactive and usually impulsive. The common feature in all self-harming behaviour is 'a desperate desire to escape from a situation that had become intolerable and that had overwhelmed the coping mechanisms of the individual concerned' (Inch *et al.*, 1995: 168).

More specifically, Liebling (1993: 396–7) found that 30 per cent of prisoners who had attempted suicide said they did so because of threats or teasing from other inmates, 24 per cent said that they had recently been punished or placed in segregation, 22 per cent said that their sentence was longer than they had expected, 12 per cent had received or were expecting to receive a 'dear John' letter, 8 per cent had received an unwanted transfer and 4 per cent had had their parole refused. Overall, 10 per cent of prisoners cited outside problems, one-third cited prison problems and one-half mentioned a combination of both outside and prison problems.

A similar pattern was reported by Inch *et al.* (1995). They found that the most common reasons for self-harm were being bullied (44 per cent), outside relationship problems (20 per cent), being locked in cells (32 per cent) and being denied a request (4 per cent). White and Schimmel (1995: 56) found the most common precipitating factors were new legal problems (28 per cent), relationship problems (23 per cent) and conflicts with other prisoners (23 per cent). Categorising the causes of prison suicide, Hayes (1995: 433) distinguished between ambient factors conducive to depression – the generally stressful and dehumanising nature of the prison environment – and specific crises faced by prisoners that might trigger suicidal acts.

In terms of the proposed two-stage model, most researchers have focused on the role of the prison experience in generating suicidal behaviour. Relatively little theoretical attention has been paid to the role of opportunity-reduction and, where it has been discussed, it has been generally portrayed as a short-term, emergency, measure. Research outside the prison context suggests that this neglect may be underselling the role of opportunity-reduction in combating suicidal behaviour. For example, Clarke and Mayhew (1988), in a British study, found that suicides in the community fell substantially when non-toxic natural gas was introduced for domestic use. People who would otherwise have committed suicide if lethal coal gas had been available did not necessarily seek out alternative methods of suicide when their preferred method was denied. It seems that the impulse to commit suicide is often transitory and an interruption in the process may be enough to prevent the behaviour.

Situational context
SEASONAL VARIATIONS
Dooley (1990) found that most suicides occurred during summer, but it is uncertain whether this increase was due to climatic stress, or related to a wind-down in prison activity (staff shortages, closing of programmes etc.) over the summer holidays. The failure of Steinke (1991) to find any relationship between temperature and suicide rates suggests the latter explanation might be more plausible. Other researchers have found spring and autumn (Hayes, 1983) and winter (Hayes and Rowan, 1988; 30; Porporino, 1992; White and Schimmel, 1995: 56) to be peak seasons for suicide. Ganjavi *et al.* (1985) found a relationship between suicide rates and geomagnetic disturbances (changes in the earth's magnetic field) although this only occurred during summer.

STAGE OF SENTENCE

One of the most consistent findings with respect to self-injury and suicide in custody is that the greatest risk occurs while prisoners are on remand or in the very early stages of their sentence (Dooley, 1990; Hayes, 1983; 1989; Hayes and Rowan, 1988: 36; HM Chief Inspector of Prisons for England and Wales, 1999: 17; White and Schimmel, 1995: 55). In fact, according to Hayes (1983), most jail suicides (over 50 per cent) occurred within the first twenty-four hours of incarceration, and 26 per cent occurred in the first three hours. In the prison Dooley (1990) found 17 per cent of suicides occurred within the first week of reception and 51 per cent within the first three months. Clearly, the beginning of a sentence is particularly distressing, as the individual deals with the shame of their arrest, the separation from family and friends and the uncertainty of what the future holds.

There is some evidence of a curvilinear relationship between time served and suicide. White and Schimmel (1995: 55), for example, found that in addition to pre-sentence prisoners, the other high-risk group was sentenced prisoners serving more than twenty years. This group accounted for 28 per cent of suicides but only 12 per cent of the prison population. It is reasonable to speculate that for these prisoners suicide was related to the sense of hopelessness that serving a long sentence must engender.

Overall, findings suggest that special care needs to be taken to provide safe environments for prisoners in the initial stages of incarceration. However, most authorities caution against assuming that there are periods during a sentence when any prisoner is safe from suicide risk.

SECURITY LEVEL

A number of studies have reported a higher incidence of suicide and self-injury in maximum security than in medium and minimum security (Correctional Service of Canada, 1981; Hatty and Walker, 1986; Salive *et al.*, 1989; Scott-Denoon, 1984; White and Schimmel, 1995: 55). As with other forms of problem behaviour examined in earlier chapters, the precise role played by maximum-security conditions is unclear. It may be that maximum security is more depressing, or it may be that suicide-risk prisoners are more likely to be kept under maximum-security establishments. The fact that suicide is more likely in the initial stages of a sentence suggests that the second of these alternatives at least plays some role. What can be said is that clearly the additional restrictions on behaviour that occur in maximum security are not sufficient to eliminate the opportunities prisoners have to engage in self-harming behaviours.

TIME

Studies have generally found that most self-harm by prisoners occurred at night (Dooley, 1990; Hayes and Rowan, 1988; 29; Kunzman, 1995; Porporino, 1992; Steinke, 1991). In Dooley's (1990) study, almost half of suicides were found to have occurred between midnight and 8.00 a.m. The remaining 50 per cent of cases were evenly divided between day (8.00 a.m. and 5.00 p.m.) and evening (5.00 p.m. and midnight). The peak period was between midnight and 3.00 a.m. A slightly different pattern was reported by Fleming *et al.* (1992). In a study of self-inflicted harm not resulting in death, they found that 77 per cent of incidents took place between 3.00 p.m. and 2.00 a.m. Because their figures included police lock-ups, the authors speculated that the temporal pattern was related to the high arrest rates over this time. If this interpretation is correct, then Fleming *et al.*'s findings further highlight the crucial role of prevention at the very first stages of detention.

A number of studies have reported a higher incidence of self-harm on weekends than on weekdays (Hayes, 1983; Kunzman, 1995; Porporino, 1992; Scott-Denoon, 1984). However, Fleming *et al.* (1992) found that incidents were spread fairly evenly across the week, although Wednesday and Thursday had the highest and Sunday the lowest. Dooley (1990) and Hayes and Rowan (1988: 30) found no difference for the day of the week.

To the extent that self-harm has been found to cluster around particular times of the day or days of the week, both precipitation and opportunity factors have been offered as an explanation. It is during the night while alone in their cells that prisoners are most likely to dwell on their situation. Similarly, weekends are typically times of low activity when prisoners are most likely to become bored and lonely. At the same time, night-time and weekends are also the times of low staffing levels when there is least direct supervision of prisoners and self-harming behaviour is more likely to go undetected.

LOCATION

Self-harm is a private affair and most frequently occurs when the prisoner is alone. Fleming *et al.* (1992) reported that in cases of non-fatal self-injury, 65 per cent of cases took place in single cells, 9 per cent in special observation areas, 9 per cent in a shared cell, 7 per cent in the yards, 3 per cent in a transport vehicle, 3 per cent in the ablutions block and 2 per cent in the recreation/dining area. In 86 per cent of cases the prisoner was unaccompanied at the time of the attempt. Towl and Crighton (1998) found that for completed suicides 71 per cent occurred in single cells and 23 per cent in shared cells (7 per cent location not recorded). Similarly, Steinke (1991) found that suicides were most likely to occur in the cell or dormitory, and in her sample no incidents occurred at work or education sites, dining-rooms, showers or recreation areas.

A large number of suicides have actually occurred in segregation, hospital and protective-custody areas (Backett, 1987; California Department of Corrections, 1994; Hayes, 1983; Hayes and Rowan, 1988: 33; Home Office, 1984; Scott-Denoon, 1984; Welch and Gunther, 1997; White and Schimmel, 1995: 55). Scott-Denoon (1984) found that 30 per cent of suicides occurred in segregation, observation or protective custody, although only 5.5 per cent of prisoners were housed in these areas. Likewise, a study by the California Department of Corrections (1994) found that 40 per cent of suicides took place in segregation units, while White and Schimmel (1995: 55) reported that 63 per cent of suicides in the US Federal Bureau of Prisons occurred in segregation, administrative detention or a psychiatric seclusion unit. In many cases prisoners were originally placed in these areas precisely because they were regarded as suicide risks. The high incidence of suicides in these areas points to the exacerbating effects of isolation as well as the failure of administrators to institute adequate surveillance and other opportunity-reduction strategies in these locations.

Despite the high prevalence of suicide in locations housing known suicide-risk prisoners, it should be remembered that research has shown that most acts of self-harm occurred in general population areas. Even with well-run suicide prevention units, the identification and segregation of at-risk prisoners is not the solution to prison suicide.

Controlling self-harm

The physical environment
HOUSING TYPE
Research on the effects of housing type on prisoner behaviour have generally highlighted the role of single-cell accommodation in ameliorating harmful effects of crowding on prisoners' health and well-being (e.g. Cox *et al.*, 1984). However, other research suggests that care needs to be exercised extrapolating from these findings with respect to self-harming behaviour. Notwithstanding the negative psychological effects of multiple-occupancy housing, suicides and self-injury overwhelmingly occur in single-cell accommodation (Anno, 1985; Haycock, 1991; Home Office, 1986; Welch and Gunther, 1997; White and Schimmel, 1995: 55). For example, Anno (1985) found that 97 per cent of suicide victims were housed in single cells. Similarly, in the study by White and Schimmel (1995: 55), all but one suicide victim in a sample

of 86 were from single cells. Note, however, that at an aggregate level Lester (1990) reported that there was a greater incidence of suicide in institutions that had multiple occupancy.

The high incidence of self-harm in single cells may be related to both precipitating and opportunity factors. On the one hand, social isolation is likely to exacerbate feelings of shame and despair. Cell-mates may help to psychologically bolster the suicidal prisoner during their personal crisis (e.g. increasing victim worth, reducing frustration). On the other hand, it is simply easier to carry out self-harming behaviour when alone and unobserved. The presence of others in the cell provides natural surveillance.

The finding that single-cell accommodation increases suicide risk poses a dilemma for correctional administrators in that it contradicts the trend found for prisoner-prisoner assaults. The blanket acceptance of single-cell housing as the correctional ideal may need to be rethought. At the very least, there may be particular reasons for preferring multiple-occupancy accommodation in certain cases. For example, an Australian inquiry into deaths in custody (Johnston, 1991: 314–15) found that it was culturally inappropriate to keep indigenous prisoners in single cells, and recommended that they be housed in pairs in order to ease the pain of separation from their kin.

One category of prisoner that certainly should be considered for multiple-occupancy accommodation is known suicide risks (Hayes, 1995: 450). In fact, this group is very likely to be kept in isolation. A typical response to suicide risk is to place the prisoner in administrative segregation. Social isolation, of course, is likely to make the prisoner feel even more alone and depressed and it is unsurprising that administrative segregation is actually the site for a large proportion of suicides. Welch and Gunther (1997), examining causes of jail suicides as identified in subsequent lawsuits, found that in 21 per cent of cases the inappropriate placing of the victim in isolation was cited as a major contributing factor.

According to Liebling (1993: 392), prisoners who had attempted suicide were more likely to prefer sharing a cell than were other prisoners, suggesting that they were particularly affected by solitude, or at least recognised the dangers of it. Suicide-attempters were also found to have spent more time in seclusion or administrative segregation in the past than non-attempters. As Inch *et al.* (1995: 162) observed, if administrative segregation is the reward for self-disclosing suicidal risk, then many depressed prisoners will be dissuaded from seeking help.

Double-bunking does not guarantee that suicides will not take place, however. Kunzman (1995) described a case in which a prisoner stabbed himself to death in a multiple-occupancy cell while his cell-mates slept.

CELL DESIGN

Given that most self-harm occurs when prisoners are alone and unsupervised in their cells, the design of cells can potentially play a crucial role in suicide prevention. While the necessity to have cells that minimise the potential for self-harm would seem to be a matter of common sense, it cannot be assumed that suicide prevention is routinely taken into account by prison architects and administrators. Rowan (1990) conducted a national survey of 175 US jails, prisons and juvenile institutions looking at serious architectural and design 'blunders'. Rowan uncovered a litany of structural deficits. With respect to suicide prevention, problems included windows and doors with bars able to be used as hanging points, the use of commercial-grade removable ventilation covers (providing a hanging point as well as a place to conceal instruments), the use of heavy wire mesh to cover air grills and light fixtures (again providing a hanging point), modesty shields that allowed prisoners to completely conceal themselves, small or poorly positioned viewing windows that did not allow adequate supervision by staff, and the installation of non-breakaway fittings such as clothing hooks and fire sprinklers. Similarly, Welch and Gunther (1997), in their study of 77 jail suicide lawsuits, noted that deficient cell design was cited as a contributing factor in several cases. Examples included an exposed light fixture, a ceiling grate and a shower-curtain rod, all providing the means by which hanging was effected. They noted that some cells had a history of suicides, which suggested that design problems were not remedied even after their role in suicides became apparent.

Atlas (1989) provided a list of twenty-seven suggested design features for safer cells. To eliminate hanging points, Atlas advised replacing metal door bars with polycarbonate glazing, covering light fixtures and ventilation covers with tamperproof screens, eliminating all exposed pipes, hinges, brackets, knobs and so forth, installing solid concrete slab beds, and using ball-and-socket clothing hangers. To guard against other methods of suicide he recommended that there be no electrical outlets in cells, that any padding used in the cell be fire-retardant and that mirrors be made of brushed metal. To improve surveillance, suicide-watch cells should be located as close as possible to the control room and a computer logging system should be introduced to record the time of each cell visit, while the cells should be fitted with smoke-detection equipment, polycarbonate viewing-windows that provide an unobstructed view of the cell and an auditory monitoring intercom. Finally, to minimise the depressing nature of confinement, cells should meet minimum-size standards, have direct access to natural sunlight, have adequate artificial lighting and be painted in pastel rather than institutional colours.

Reser (1992: 175–81) made similar recommendations, although with rather more emphasis than Atlas on the need to deinstitutionalise the environment. His recommendations included the use of natural colours and textures, the provision of radios and use of soft furnishings. Prisoners should have visual access to the outside, for example, through the use of partially open front cell walls, so reducing the sense of confinement experienced by the prisoner and permitting greater levels of monitoring by staff. There should be some facility for individual control over the environment, such as the provision of internal light switches (contradicting Atlas), closable shutters to the outside, access to drinking, washing and toilet facilities, and the choice of single or shared-cell accommodation. Alarm and intercom systems should be available so that distressed individuals can summon help when required.

The issues involved in cell design epitomise those of situational prison control generally. The lists of desirable cell characteristics neatly illustrate the features of the proposed two-stage situational prevention model. In the first place, both Atlas and Reser acknowledge the need to consider both the conditions that reduce suicidal feelings (soft architecture, external visual access, personal control etc.), and those that restrict the ability of the prisoner to act on suicidal feelings (surveillance, elimination of hanging points etc.). Reser was particularly critical of the implication that it was possible to 'suicide-proof' a cell simply by eliminating opportunities for self-harm. This, he asserted, '*is a fatal design error*' (p. 174). Rather:

> Preventative design must alleviate distress as well as reduce opportunity. It must take into account the detainee's *experience* of the situation and the immediate cell environment, and the cumulative and stressful loss of control that has already taken place. An obvious elimination of 'hanging points' and/or the removal of everything that could conceivably be used for self-destructive behaviour, especially in the absence of other measures which provide for a modicum of experienced control, will simply elicit reactance, anger and distress.   (p. 174)

Secondly, and as the above quotation indicates, Reser recognised the possible tension between precipitation-control and opportunity-reduction. Strip and padded cells, for example, might eliminate opportunities for self-harm but they also produce sensory deprivation, increase distress, exacerbate feelings of isolation and may elicit a defiance reaction that leads to a self-fulfilling prophecy. Similarly, there is a delicate balance to be struck between the privacy needs of prisoners and the surveillance needs of staff. Allowing prisoners some control over the visual or physical access others have to them (e.g. privacy screens, closable shutters) simultaneously reduces the ability of staff to monitor prisoners' behaviour. At the same time, the sense of being constantly watched is itself distressing. Clearly, surveillance of prisoners is essential, but the monitoring needs to be as unobtrusive as possible. One way to achieve this, Reser suggested, is to design-in high levels of 'functional proximity', that is, to construct the environment so as to increase the likelihood that individuals will interact with one another in the course of their daily activities. In situational-prevention parlance, this might be thought of as increasing natural surveillance rather than relying on formal surveillance.

In striking the balance between privacy and surveillance, Reser specifically recommended against a reliance on CCTV. As Reser pointed out, CCTV screens need to be constantly monitored and depend upon high levels of staff vigilance. Kunzman (1995) also noted that video surveillance could sometimes fail to show that a suicide is taking place. He recounted a case where a prisoner was able to strangle himself while lying prone on his bed with one wrist and both ankles restrained. The prisoner's actions were not apparent from the video picture. Moreover, CCTV reduces interpersonal contact between staff and prisoners and so contributes to the sense of isolation felt by prisoners. Direct supervision is less alienating for both prisoners and staff. Reser's conclusion is supported by one of the few empirical studies of CCTV in prison. Benton and Obenland (1973) compared the adjustment of prisoners in correctional institutions using CCTV with that of prisoners in institutions that did not. They found that the use of CCTV had a negative 'psychological effect' on inmates, increased their sense of institutional alienation, reduced their levels of interpersonal interaction and resulted in them feeling *less* safe.

FUNCTIONAL UNITS

Theoretically, functional units, with their less depressing architecture, emphasis on communality and high levels of direct supervision, would seem to offer great potential for preventing suicide in prison. Curiously, most formal evaluations of functional units are silent on the issue, with only the occasional incidental reference to reductions in self-harming behaviour. In his audits of new functional units, Sigurdson (1985: vi; 1987a: v; 1987b: i) reported no cases of suicide. However, as noted in previous chapters, there is no comparative data offered to assess the significance of this achievement. Senese *et al.* (1992) found lower suicide rates in a podular-design prison than a traditional linear-designed prison but did not clarify the extent to which the two institutions could be considered comparable. Farbstein *et al.* (1996: 19) found that functional-unit prisoners did not believe that unit living made suicide more difficult.

Population characteristics

CROWDING

The discussion of crowding in earlier chapters has focused on the role of stress in making individuals more susceptible to provocation and prone to expressive bursts of aggression. In the case of self-harming behaviour, the focus is on the presumed effects of crowding on physical and psychological health. Incidence of self-harm is one of a range of symptoms – mortality rates, psychiatric commitments, blood pressure, urine catecholamine, illness reporting – taken to indicate the general level of well-being of a prison population. Overcrowding is generally not seen as a single or direct cause of self-injury and suicide among prisoners, but is thought to exacerbate feelings of depression and hopelessness (Gaes, 1985; Reser, 1992: 156–7). Additionally, overcrowding also potentially increases the suicide risk by reducing the levels of supervision and stretching medical and psychological resources.

A major source of evidence for the deleterious health effects of prison crowding comes from a series of studies by Paulus and his colleagues (Cox *et al.*, 1984; McCain *et al.*, 1980; Paulus, 1988; Paulus and McCain, 1983). Summarising much of this research, Cox *et al.* (1984) described findings from the analysis of more than 175,000 prisoner records across four US state prison systems and field data on more than 2,500 prisoners. Overall, the researchers found evidence of high rates of medical complaints, high stress levels, psychiatric commitments, death rates, attempted suicides and completed suicides in large overcrowded prisons when compared with smaller, uncrowded institutions. Cox *et al.* paid particular attention to the distinction between spatial and social density. They found that the number of prisoners sharing a space (social density) exerted a more powerful influence on behaviour than the amount of space available for each prisoner (spatial density). For example, increasing the physical size of a dormitory while holding the population steady was less effective in reducing health complaints than sub-dividing the dormitory into cubicles, even though the second strategy resulted in greater spatial density than the first.

Against these deleterious health outcomes, it has also been argued that overcrowding may actually help to reduce suicide in prison (Haycock, 1991; Welch and Gunther, 1997). As Haycock (1991: 428) put it, 'the wonder is not that jail inmates contemplate suicide, but rather that they find any space to attempt it'. This tension between crowding as a source of stress on the one hand and as a restriction on behaviour on the other hand was noted earlier in the discussion of prisoner housing.

AGE COMPOSITION

Young prisoners (under 21) are somewhat more prone to suicidal and self-injurious behaviour in prison than are older prisoners (Salive *et al.*, 1989; Towl and Crighton, 1998). Moreover, there are significant differences in the patterns of self-harm between the two groups. Liebling (1993: 401) concluded that self-harming behaviour by young prisoners was more likely to occur in response to immediate situational pressures than was the case for older prisoners. Young prisoners, for example, were far less likely to have received psychiatric treatment prior to their suicide attempts. Part of the explanation for this difference can be attributed to individual developmental factors – young prisoners seem to react to distress more intensely and more impulsively than do older prisoners. Beyond the individual level, there are two ways that a congregation of young prisoners might increase suicide rates. First, suicide rates are related to levels of bullying and victimisation, and these levels are in turn greater in establishments that house large numbers of young prisoners (see chapter 5). Second, contagion effects seem to be more apparent in young-prisoner facilities. Dooley (1990) found that suicides by young prisoners tended to cluster in particular institutions. It appears that the occurrence of one suicide among a young-prisoner population had the effect of prompting other young prisoners to imitate the behaviour.

PRISONER TURNOVER

Towl and Crighton (1998) found that 65 per cent of cases in their study of British suicides took place in local remand prisons. They argued that the high throughput of prisoners in these institutions was a major contributor to the high suicide rate. The transience of the remand prison population creates feelings of uncertainty among prisoners. Moreover, a rapid turnover of prisoners hampers the development of positive staff–prisoner relationships that might otherwise help to prevent suicide attempts.

The prison regime

REACTIONS OF STAFF

A number of studies have noted the crucial role that staff can play in suicide prevention, and the corresponding need to establish protocols and provide training for staff to properly carry out this role (Hayes, 1995: 449; Liebling, 1992: 241; Ramsay *et al.*, 1985: 296–9; Welch and Gunther, 1997). In Welch and Gunther's (1997) study of jail suicide lawsuits, inadequate staff training and supervision was cited as a contributory cause in 52 per cent of cases examined. In many cases attending staff were shown to have received no training in suicide prevention. Staff did not recognise, did not adequately respond to or ignored signs of suicide risk such as intoxication, psychiatric history, previous suicide attempts and expressed intentions of committing suicide.

At a general level, researchers have highlighted low staff morale and poor communication among staff and between staff and prisoners as contributors to prison suicide (Hayes, 1995: 434; Liebling, 1993: 402–3). More specifically, researchers have pointed to the need both to provide staff with necessary information about suicide and suicide prevention, as well as to change staff attitudes that might contribute to the incidence of suicidal behaviour. Information packages need to cover factual data on suicide, recognition of risk signs and protocols for dealing with suicidal prisoners. Inappropriate staff attitudes to be addressed include the belief that suicidal prisoners will always find a way (nothing can be done), and the opposing belief that most prisoners who threaten or attempt suicide are not serious. The second of these attitudes is seen to be particularly prevalent and problematic (Liebling, 1993: 401). If staff believe that an act of self-harm is a manipulative or attention-seeking device then they might be encouraged to ignore or even to punish the behaviour. According to Liebling (1993: 405), 'under no circumstances should the response to a suicide attempt be punitive'. Even well-meaning responses to suicide attempts, such as isolation and strip-cell conditions, might be interpreted by the prisoner as punishment.

Ramsay *et al.* (1987) reported on the introduction of a suicide-prevention staff training programme into the Canadian prison system. The training course comprised fourteen hours of curriculum content presented over two days. There were modules on attitudes, knowledge and skills delivered in a range of media. The study evaluated the effectiveness of the programme after more than 800 correctional staff had been through the course. The researchers claimed that in the areas in which the programme operated, there were increased referrals of at-risk prisoners for professional help, increased levels of intervention by staff in suicidal episodes and an overall reduction in the suicide rate.

SURVEILLANCE PROTOCOLS

Hayes (1995: 446–52) reported on the surveillance regime for a successful suicide prevention unit within Elayn Hunt Correctional Center (EHCC), St Gabriel, Louisiana. As far as possible, all prisoners were double-bunked and each cell contained CCTV. In addition, physical checks were carried out at a minimum of every fifteen minutes and in some cases on a continual basis (with an average of every five minutes), depending upon the assessed level of risk. On top of this, additional random observations were made so that the surveillance pattern did not become predictable to the prisoners and so allow them to plan self-harming behaviour. Hayes reported that over a twelve-year period, 57,000 prisoners were processed though EHCC, with only one reported suicide in this time.

RESTRICTIONS ON DANGEROUS POSSESSIONS

As noted in the introduction, the instruments used to effect suicide in prison come from those things that are readily available to prisoners. Hanging using clothing and bedding is, therefore, the single most common method of suicide. Apart from eliminating hanging points, suicide by hanging might be reduced by the issue of tear-resistant sheets and blankets. Another obvious example of controlling facilitators is the restricting or tracking of the issue of razor blades. However, the definition of what constitutes an instrument for self-harm needs to take into account the ingenuity of prisoners to fashion weapons from otherwise innocuous objects. Kunzman (1995) described how one prisoner sharpened the handle of a plastic disposable razor and stabbed himself in the throat. There are, of course, practical limits to the restrictions that can be placed on prisoner possessions, as well as limits determined by the counterproductive psychological effects (e.g. reactance) excessive restrictions might have.

PROGRAMME AVAILABILITY

Liebling (1993: 393; 1995) found that prisoners who had attempted suicide were generally more idle and solitary than other prisoners. Suicide-attempters reported having fewer friends, were more likely to complain of boredom, were less interested in physical activities, saw fewer opportunities to engage in work and programmes and spent more time alone in their cells. The role played by these factors in the suicide attempt is uncertain. It is likely that to some extent these characteristics are correlates rather than direct causes of suicidal behaviour, that is, they are all symptoms of the same sense of despair and lack of coping skills. Nevertheless, this pattern of institutional existence is also likely to exacerbate suicidal tendencies and to contribute to a downward spiral of depression. The finding by a number of researchers that self-harm increases over the weekend (Hayes, 1983; Kunzman, 1995; Porporino, 1992; Scott-Denoon, 1984) suggests that particular attention might be given to providing activities at this time.

VISITS AND FURLOUGHS

Separation from family and friends, feelings of shame and rejection, and specific outside problems are frequently identified as major precipitators of prison suicide (Liebling, 1993: 395–9; 1995; Reser, 1992: 158–60). A number of researchers have therefore stressed the need to provide adequate visiting arrangements and facilities for prisoners in order to help to maintain family ties and to reduce separation anxieties. Visits in which prisoners are able to make physical contact with loved ones are seen as particularly crucial (Reser, 1992: 177).

Visits may assume special importance for some cultural groups. The inquiry investigating Aboriginal deaths in custody in Australia identified loss of contact with family and tribal support systems as a crucial factor in prison suicide (Johnston, 1991: 308–14; Reser, 1992: 161–2). Similar kinship issues have been reported for Latin-American prisoners in the United States (Johnson, 1976). The Australian inquiry made a number of recommendations regarding the maintenance of Aboriginal kinship ties, including that Aboriginal prisoners be housed as close as was practicable to their family, that financial assistance be given to facilitate visits, that adequate visiting facilities be provided and that recognition be given to the crucial role of extended families in Aboriginal culture when considering applications to attend funerals and other special occasions. Unfortunately, while prison administrators claim that most of these recommendations have been adopted, Aboriginal deaths in custody continue to rise (Dalton *et al.*, 1996).

Conclusions

Suggested situational interventions for self-harm in prison are shown in table 8.1. Again, many of these strategies must be inferred from the data and require a certain leap of faith. It is logical to assume, for example, that prisoners will feel less depressed in physically pleasant surroundings, but whether cell-decoration actually has any measurable impact on levels of self-harm at this stage remains unknown. Notwithstanding these limitations, the available research is consistent with the proposed two-stage situational model. Controlling self-harm requires a combination of strategies that both makes prison a less dehumanising and depressing experience for prisoners and provides for an adequate level of care and supervision.

A number of examples of potential conflict between controlling precipitators and controlling regulators were found. The need to provide

Table 8.1. *Summary of promising strategies for control of self-harm*

Strategy	Precipitation-control category	Regulation-control category
Double-bunking	Reducing frustration	Natural surveillance
Elimination of hanging points		Target-hardening Controlling facilitators
Elimination of other dangerous fittings (e.g. electrical sockets)		Target-hardening Controlling facilitators
Increasing surveillance capabilities		Formal surveillance
Deinstitutionalised cell design	Controlling triggers Reducing frustration Controlling environmental irritants	
Functional units	Reducing frustration Controlling environmental irritants	Formal surveillance Natural surveillance
Reduced population density	Reducing crowding	
Age-heterogeneous populations	Reducing inappropriate imitation Reducing inappropriate conformity	
Slow prisoner turnover	Personalising victims Reducing frustration	
Staff training		Formal surveillance
Surveillance protocols		Formal surveillance
Removal of dangerous possessions		Target-hardening Controlling facilitators
Prison programmes/work	Reducing frustrations	
Visits	Reducing frustrations	

specialised care for suicide-risk prisoners has meant that many prisoners have been isolated in segregation units. The need to restrict access to objects that might facilitate self-harm has led to prisoners being kept in strip-cells under conditions of sensory deprivation. The need to maintain adequate surveillance has meant that prisoners have been subjected to intrusive invasions of privacy. None of these problems are insurmountable. Prisoners need not be isolated in order for them to receive specialised care, they need not be kept in strip-cells in order to restrict their access to dangerous instruments, and they do not need to be kept in fish-bowl conditions in order that their behaviour be adequately monitored. The balance can be struck between controlling precipitators and controlling regulators of self-harm, but to do so it is necessary first to realise that both are important.

CHAPTER 9

Drug use

Drug use in prison has become one of the major control issues facing prison administrators in recent years. The problem of drugs in prison parallels the problem of drugs in the community. That is, the concern is not just that the use of drugs is illegal but that drugs are associated with a range of other crime and health problems. Drugs form the basis of the prisoner economy and are a significant cause of gang conflicts and prisoner violence, as well as staff corruption (Correctional Service of Canada, 1989: 13–14; Fleisher and Rison, 1999: 234–5; Kalinich and Stojkoviv, 1987: 11; MacDonald, 1999; Select Committee on Home Affairs, 1999: 4–6 Section B). In addition, the use of intravenous drugs in prison has implications for the spread of HIV/AIDS (Dolan *et al.*, 1998; Edwards *et al.*, 1999; Ross *et al.*, 1994).

Nature of the problem

Definition and incidence

The drug problem in prison includes the use and trafficking of illegal drugs such as heroin, cocaine and marijuana, prescription drugs and alcohol, as well as the misuse of legal substances such as glues and fruit juices. There is a widespread perception that drug use is endemic in prisons. However, it is difficult to get accurate figures on use, with estimates varying widely across studies. To some extent, of course, such variations reflect true differences in drug-use patterns among institutions. However, two main methods of measuring drug use are employed – chemical analysis of urine, blood, hair or saliva on the one hand, and self-report on the other – and these typically produce different estimates. Chemical procedures in turn employ varying testing criteria that further complicate the picture.

Chemical testing may be either targeted or random. In 1998, 47% of US gaols reported that they employed some form of chemical testing to detect drug use by prisoners (Wilson, 2000). In 69% of gaols that carry out testing, testing only takes place when there is some suspicion of drug use, while 49% of gaols adopt random testing. Around 14% of inmates targeted for testing returned positive results, while the figure was 10% for prisoners randomly selected. For the US federal system, random urine tests on 5% of prisoners found that 2% had used drugs, while testing of all prisoners involved in community activities and of all prisoners suspected of drug use produced positive returns of 1% and 6% respectively (Innes, 1988). In Britain, where 10% of all prisoners are subject to mandatory random testing, 18% tested positive for drugs in 1998–9 (Select Committee on Home Affairs, 1999: 1 Section E). In an Australian study, Incorvaia and Kirby (1997: 236) found that 50% of targeted tests on mainstream prisoners (i.e. those not involved in a drug programme) were positive.

Self-report studies generally indicate higher levels of drug use than testing procedures. In a survey of British medium-security prisoners (both male and female), Johnson and Farren (1996: 32) found 27% admitted using illegal drugs in custody. Korte *et al.* (1998: 175) reported a similar figure (28%) for a sample of Finnish prisoners. Incorvaia and Kirby (1997: 240) found self-report rates of 84% among an Australian mainstream prisoner sample. In a direct comparison of self-report and chemical testing, Edgar and O'Donnell (1998b: 11) found that while 51% of prisoners surveyed admitted using cannabis or opiates, testing of the same prisoners showed a usage rate of 37%. In an exception to this trend, Mieczkowski *et al.* (1998: 1554–8) found that urinalysis and hair-testing showed greater prevalence of drug use among juvenile detainees than did self-report.

There are a number of reasons that self-report rates may be higher than testing rates. In particular, drug tests are generally able to detect drug use in the past three days or so, while self-report studies can specify much wider windows. Tests are also unable to detect certain drugs, or in some cases have high thresholds that increase the return of false negatives (the failure to detect the presence of a substance). Illegal drugs may also be obscured by the presence of other legal drugs or tests may be subverted by prisoners employing tactics such as drinking large quantities of water. Finally, it has been argued that testing is disproportionately carried out during weekdays, whereas the weekend is the peak period of drug use among prisoners (Select Committee on Home Affairs, 1999: 1–4 Section E).

Patterns

Prisoners gain access to drugs in prison from three major sources: some drugs are manufactured in prison (e.g. alcohol); some are diverted from legal sources in prison (prescription drugs such as sedatives, tranquillisers and analgesics, as well as products used as inhalants, such as glues and spray cans); and some are smuggled into the prison from outside (heroin, cocaine and cannabis) (McDonald, 1992).

In terms of the types of drugs used, the results of random testing of US federal prisoners revealed that for those prisoners who tested positive, the most common drug detected was cannabis (60%), followed by opiates (16%), cocaine (13%), amphetamines (5%) and barbiturates (2%) (Innes 1988). Johnson and Farren (1996: 33–4) in their self-report study of British prisoners found that of admitted drug-users in prison, 94% used cannabis, 27% opiates and 16% cocaine. Shewan *et al.* (1994: 205), in a Scottish study, found 73% of prisoners used cannabis, 33% Temgesic, 6% amphetamines, 5% temazepam, 2% heroin and 2% ecstasy. Korte *et al.* (1998: 176–7) found that of drug-users in Finland, 97% used cannabinoids, 58% benzodiazepines, 56% amphetamines, 27% heroin, 22% buprenorphine, 13% cocaine, 12% methamphetamines, 11% morphine, 9% LSD, 8% barbiturates, 6% ecstasy, 6% mushrooms, 5% opium and 5% dextropropoxyphene. Incorvaia and Kirby (1997: 237) found that in a sample of Australian prisoners 45% tested positive for cannabinoids, 15% benzodiazepines, 6% opiates and 1% amphetamines. Self-report data showed a similar pattern but higher levels of use, with 81% admitting to using cannabinoids, 39% benzodiazepines, 36% opiates, 10% amphetamines, 7% barbiturates and 7% cocaine (p. 240).

Van Hoeven *et al.* (1991: 1093–4) compared drug use between male and female prisoners. They found a higher incidence of intravenous drug use among female prisoners. Drug use peaked for both male and female prisoners in the 31-to-35-year age range. Johnson and Farren (1996) found that alcohol use was almost exclusive to male prisoners but there was little overall difference between male and female prisoners in their use of illegal drugs in prison. However, looking at specific drugs the abuse of prescription medication was particularly problematic among female prisoners. Female prisoners were also more likely than male prisoners to use opiates and cocaine (pp. 31–2).

Johnson and Farren also looked at self-reported frequency of drug use (p. 34). Of those prisoners admitting to illegal drug use (27% of prisoners), 13% reported using between four and seven times a week, 38% two to three times a week and 49% once a week. Of those admitting to using alcohol,

82% said they did so less than once a week while 6% said that they used more than four times a week. With respect to prescription drugs, 27% of prisoners reported that they were receiving legal medication, but 5% admitted to storing medication, 4% admitted to trading medication and 9% to using other prisoners' medication. In another British study, Bird *et al.* (1997) reported that the average number of injections over a four-week period among drug-using prisoners (51% of the total) was six.

As for the source of drugs, it is widely believed that the most common method of trafficking involves prisoner visitors and prisoners returning from leave (e.g. Correctional Service of Canada, 1989). However, there are few studies that have empirically addressed this issue. Stevens (1997: 21–4) asked prisoners for their perceptions of how drugs came into the prison. He found that 24% of prisoners believed that civilian staff were most responsible, 19% identified custodial officers, 17% family visitors, 10% incoming mail, 9% transferred prisoners, 6% top brass, 5% official visitors and 2% delivery drivers. Johnson and Farren (1996: 35) found evidence that prisoners were intimidated to take part in drug trafficking, with 9% of prisoners claiming that they had been threatened to keep quiet about drug use, 4% claiming to have been forced to hide drugs, 3% claiming to have been forced to bring drugs into the prison and 3% claiming to have been threatened to carry drugs. Overall levels of intimidation were higher among female prisoners (21%) than male prisoners (10%).

Motivation

Many prisoners, of course, come to prison with existing drug habits and so are already primed to continue that use in prison. A US Department of Justice report (Wilson, 2000) on drug use and testing in jails revealed that in 1998 55% of jail inmates used drugs in the month before their arrest and 36% were using at the time of the offence. In Britain, Bennett and Sibbitt (2000) reported that 69% of arrestees tested positive for at least one drug, with 29% testing positive for opiates and 20% for cocaine. In an Australian study (Dobinson and Ward, 1986), 90% of prisoners convicted of property offences claimed to be heavy or regular heroin-users immediately prior to their arrest. In another Australian study (Indemaur and Upton, 1988), it was found that 74% of prisoners had used cannabis, 27% LSD, 35% barbiturates, 20% heroin, 14% cocaine, 26% amphetamines 6% antidepressants and 9% solvents prior to coming to prison.

On the other hand, it has been argued that just being in prison reduces drug use, with prisoners consistently reporting higher rates of use outside prison than inside (Darke *et al.*, 1998; Edgar and O'Donnell, 1998b: 8–10; Incorvaia and Kirby, 1997: 238–41; Johnson and Farren, 1996: 32; Shewan *et al.*, 1994: 205–6; Strang *et al.*, 1998; Thomas and Cage, 1977; Trace, 1998: 279). For example, Shewan *et al.* (1994: 206) found that 49% of prisoners injected drugs outside prison while 29% injected in prison. Similarly, according to Johnson and Farren (1996: 32), 47% of prisoners used drugs before they came to prison but only 27% used them at any time while in prison and 13% were using currently. Just 2% of the sample said that they used drugs for the first time in prison. Prison also results in lower frequency of drug use. For example, 61% of prisoners who used drugs outside did so between four and seven times a week compared with 13% of prisoners reporting this frequency of use inside prison.

Not all researchers agree that imprisonment necessarily inhibits drug use, however (e.g. Gore *et al.*, 1995; Korte *et al.*, 1998; Swann and James, 1998). Using a questionnaire design, Swann and James (1998) found that 14% of respondents claimed to have used drugs for the first time in prison and only 2% said that they used outside but not inside. Specifically there were increases in the use of heroin, cannabis, barbiturates and alcohol. Korte *et al.* (1998: 175) similarly found 22% of their Finnish sample reported using drugs for the first time in prison. Nelles *et al.* (1999: 137) found that drug use increased with the length of incarceration. The deprivation of prison life is seen as a major reason for the desire to use drugs in prison (Cohen and King, 1987; Incorvaia and Kirby, 1997: 242; Stevens, 1997: 15). Incorvaia and Kirby (1997: 242) found that the most common reasons for drug use offered by prisoners was escapism (58%), boredom (48%), coping (29%), recreation (26%), depression (23%), pressure (10%) and dependence (10%). Support among prisoners for reducing the availability of drugs in prison is mixed. Incorvaia and Kirby (pp. 241–2) found that prisoners distinguished between cannabis and other drugs, with 40% arguing that hard drugs should be eliminated but that cannabis was a positive influence in prison since it helped to relax prisoners and thus reduced aggression. Similarly Edgar and O'Donnell (1998b: 22) found that 70% of prisoners said that testing should apply only to hard drugs and 82% believed that cannabis should be permitted in prison.

In sum, it seems that on the one hand prison can place additional pressure on prisoners to use drugs but on the other hand has the potential to reduce opportunities for drug use. Accordingly, borrowing from community prevention efforts, drug prevention in prison is generally presented as a two-pronged strategy – demand reduction and supply control (McDonald, 1992; Select Committee on Home Affairs, 1999: 1–3 Section A;

van Groningen, 1993: 14). Again, the parallels with the proposed two-stage model are obvious. Demand reduction involves the creation of a climate in which the use of drugs is seen as less desirable – that is, essentially controlling the precipitators of drug use. Supply control involves strategies that further restrict the availability of drugs in prison, or, in other words, reducing opportunities.

Situational context

SECURITY LEVEL

The Select Committee on Home Affairs (1999: 1 Section E) reported the results of random testing in British prisons in terms of prison classification. The highest positive returns were from open prisons and local male prisons. Lowest returns were from high-security male dispersal prisons and category B training prisons. The Select Committee on Home Affairs' results indicate that, over and above any increased levels of deprivation that might be experienced by prisoners in high-security prisons as compared with low-security prisons, the additional security is a significant factor in reducing the opportunities for drug use.

Contradicting this finding, MacDonald (1999) examined the institutional drug violations of 3,995 young male offenders in California. He found that drug violations increased with institutional security level (limited, moderate, medium and close). One possible reason for the discrepancy between MacDonald's findings and those of the Select Committee on Home Affairs is the nature of the respective dependent measures. MacDonald operationalised drug violations as officially recorded institutional misconduct. His findings may reflect the tendency for staff in high security to be more vigilant and/or more likely to officially process incidents of misconduct than staff in low security and so detect and record more drug use.

TIME

Weekend is generally seen to be the main trouble period for drug use in prison (e.g. Grant, 1995: 23, 27; Select Committee on Home Affairs, 1999: 2–3 Section E). Grant (1995: 27), investigating drug use in the South Australian prison system, reported that prison infirmary records showed a sharp increase on Sunday night and Monday in the number of prisoners treated for drug-induced conditions. Custodial staff also reported a higher incidence of drug-related behavioural problems at these times. The majority of family visits occur on weekends, and this undoubtedly coincides with an increased availability of drugs. In addition, staffing levels are lower and there is less structured activity to occupy inmates' time.

Controlling drug use

The physical environment

FUNCTIONAL UNITS

It is argued that functional units enhance dynamic security and so provide the basis for better intelligence about drug use and trafficking (e.g. Correctional Service of Canada, 1989: 45). It can also be argued that, to the extent that functional units provide a less stressful prison environment, pressures to use drugs will be reduced. However, perhaps surprisingly, most evaluations of functional units do not explicitly address the issue of drug use.

PERIMETER SECURITY

Breaches of perimeter security have been cited as a significant avenue for the entry of drugs into prison (Grant, 1995: 24; Select Committee on Home Affairs, 1999: 1 Section D; van Groningen, 1993: 14). Strategies employed by traffickers involve either hiding drugs on the prison boundary or throwing drugs – concealed in cartons, tennis balls or other containers – over the prison wall. The former strategy is used in prisons with low-level perimeter security or in prisons that have outside work gangs; the latter may be used in closed security situations.

Grant (1995: 20) claimed that breaches of perimeter security constituted the second most popular way (after visits) of importing drugs into prison in South Australia. He reported that there were fewer drugs seized in prisons where perimeter security is such that drugs thrown over the wall do not land in areas readily accessed by prisoners (although in interpreting the figures it is difficult to isolate the role of perimeter security from other aspects of the prison regime that might also have contributed to lower drug use). Grant recommended that areas into which drugs might be thrown should be searched daily before prisoners have access to them.

Population characteristics

SIZE

Wilson (2000) reported that the percentage of positive drug tests decreased with prison size. For example, jails with populations in excess of 1,000 inmates returned positive tests in 7 per cent of cases; for jails with populations of 55–100 the rate was 21 per cent and 28 per cent for jails with fewer than 50 inmates. The report does not speculate on reasons for these findings. However, it is possible that the results reflect a confound between prison size and security level. Large prisons are more likely to be higher security than small prisons and, as has already been noted, increased security levels reduces opportunities for drug use.

PRISONER TURNOVER

Johnson and Farren (1996: 31–2) found that prisoner turnover decreased the incidence of alcohol use. They compared alcohol use in two sections of Risley Prison (UK) – one section essentially a classification prison with rapid turnover, the other section for convicted prisoners serving relatively lengthy sentences. In the stable section 8 per cent of prisoners reported using alcohol while only 2 per cent of prisoners in the classification prison reported use. The authors argued that a degree of population stability is necessary in order to arrange manufacture and distribution of the alcohol. No effect of turnover was reported for other types of drugs. However, Grant (1995: 20) found fewer hard drugs in a remand centre than in other institutions, and argued that this was partly due to the rapid turnover of remand prisoners.

Disrupting drug networks may be employed as a deliberate control tactic. The Select Committee on Home Affairs (1999: 2–3 Section D) highlighted the need to distinguish between suppliers and users of drugs in prison. The report stressed the need to use intelligence to identify the drug barons. However, Kalinich and Stojkovic (1987) warn of the counterproductive effects of disrupting prison populations in order to control contraband. They argued that the distribution of contraband was a necessary and legitimate component of the prison economy and ensured a stable prisoner leadership. It is in the interests of prisoner leaders to maintain control in prison. Weakening leadership structures will lead to greater instability.

The prison regime

STAFFING LEVELS

MacDonald (1999) found no relationship between the ratio of staff to prisoners, and reported levels of institutional drug violations. Thus it would seem that variations in levels of supervision alone have a minimal impact on prison drug use.

SCREENING STAFF

Prison staff are undoubtedly responsible for some of the drugs smuggled into prison, although the extent of staff involvement is unclear (Grant, 1995: 24–35; Select Committee on Home Affairs, 1999: 3–4 Section D). Aside from monetary gain, prison staff may become involved in trafficking as a result of pressure and threats of violence to the officer or to his or her family. Staff, too, may be drug-users themselves.

Searching of staff and imposing restrictions on what they may bring into prisons is becoming routine. Practices include the provision of lockers outside the prison for staff to leave bags, the provision of clear plastic bags if staff need to take possessions into the prison, the use of drug-detection screening and the random searching of bags (e.g. Grant, 1995: 7).

Drug testing of staff is also being increasingly employed. The US Department of Justice (1991) recommended testing under the following circumstances – for all applicants seeking employment; when there is reasonable suspicion of drug use; annually for all senior staff, under a random testing programme; and as a follow-up to counselling or rehabilitation. Wilson (2000) found that 49 per cent of institutions drug-tested staff. Of these institutions, 63 per cent employed random testing, 40 per cent tested on indication of use and 20 per cent tested new employees only. The report does not indicate the level of positive tests or the impact of these measures.

DRUG TESTING OF PRISONERS

Drug testing of prisoners is not used only to monitor overall levels of drug use in prison, but is itself a deterrent against drug use by prisoners. Prisoners may be selected for testing for a variety of reasons – to determine their suitability for some specific purpose (screening for release, offender classification, selection for treatment), to support the prosecution of suspected drug-users, as part of a random testing schedule, or as a check on prisoners returning from visits or temporary release (McDonald, 1992; US Department of Justice, 1991). Where testing is not done anonymously, prisoners found to have been using drugs are typically liable to a range of sanctions and loss of privileges.

There is evidence that the introduction of drug testing reduces drug use among prisoners (Correctional Service of Canada, 1989: 41; Government of Victoria, 1993: 89–93; Select Committee on Home Affairs, 1999). For example, the Select Committee on Home Affairs (1999: 1 Section E) reported longitudinal results of random mandatory testing in Britain showing a decreasing trend in drug use over time. In 1996–7 a total of 24 per cent of random tests were positive, in 1997–8 the figure was 21 per cent and in 1998–9 it was 18 per cent. Of course, it is unclear from these figures alone the extent to which other interventions may have contributed to the reduction in drug use. However, a survey of prisoners conducted by Edgar and O'Donnell (1998b: 14) adds weight to the view that testing is responsible for at least some of this reduction. They found that 52 per cent of drug-using prisoners claimed to have altered their drug-use patterns in prison as a specific response to mandatory drug testing. More specifically, 27 per cent of prisoners who had used drugs in prison claimed to have stopped in response to testing, and a further 25 per cent said that they had reduced their usage. Those who changed their drug-use behaviour were more concerned with the prospect of the loss of privileges and incentives than with formal sanctions, such as days added to their sentence. In particular, prisoners were concerned that a positive test would result in the loss of good jobs and open visits, or would reduce their prospects for temporary release, parole or transfer. Prisoners also believed that evidence of non-drug use should positively be rewarded with increased access to home leaves and other privileges. Edgar and O'Donnell concluded that a greater emphasis on incentives in prison would provide a better basis for the effective operation of random testing than a concentration on punishments.

One worrying finding from Edgar and O'Donnell's study (1998b) was the potential for counterproductive effects of testing. In the first place, prisoners perceived random testing to be unfair and claimed that it had adversely affected the prison climate by increasing tension and souring relationships with staff. Moreover, 57 per cent of prisoners surveyed believed that testing encouraged a switch from cannabis to hard drugs because cannabis was more easily detected by drug tests, with 6 per cent claiming to have reduced their cannabis use in favour of heroin.

There has been some debate about the relative advantages of targeted and random testing. Random testing is favoured by many, because uncertainty about who will be tested is seen to increase the deterrent effect. However, others have argued that the number of random tests performed (typically 5 per cent of the prison population) is too small to provide a significant deterrent (e.g. Grant, 1995, 20). Edgar and O'Donnell (1998b: 15–16) found that prisoners believed that their chances of being selected for random testing was low.

Edgar and O'Donnell (1998b: 15) also found that prisoners generally believed that drug-testing procedures were often inaccurate and relatively easy to subvert. In this regard, there have been rapid advances in drug-testing technology in recent years that have reduced error rates (for a comprehensive coverage of drug-testing technology see Mieczkowski, 1999). Traditionally, chemical analyses almost exclusively involved urine testing, and this remains by far the most common testing method. The development in the 1970s of new testing techniques (specifically, immunoassay technology) has increased the specificity and reliability of urinalysis as well as reducing costs (Mieczkowski and Lersch, 1997; US Department of Justice, 1992). However, urinalysis is a relatively invasive procedure and also has specific weaknesses in detecting certain drugs, and so there have also been developments in alternative testing methods. Hair analysis has been advocated as an adjunct to urine testing because it offers a longer window period for drugs such as cocaine, heroine and amphetamines, which are eliminated quickly from the body via urine (Mieczkowski, 1995, 1997; Mieczkowski and Lersch, 1997). Similarly, sweat analysis – with the sweat collected via patches that are worn for an extended period – also provides a longer window period than urinalysis. There is also increasing interest in saliva testing, although Mieczkowski and Lersch warn that this technology is still in its early days. The chief attraction of saliva testing is the ease with which samples may be collected, making it an ideal procedure in field-testing situations.

DRUG SEARCHES

The strategies discussed above involved the direct testing of prisoners' body fluids to detect drug use. In addition, attempts are also made to detect the presence of drugs secreted on prisoners or in hiding places around the prison. Particular targets for a search are prisoners returning from visits, outside leave or court. Returning prisoners may be initially placed in a holding cell, then strip-searched in a second cell (Grant 1995: 24). In addition, prisoners are liable for frisk searches in the course of serving their sentence. The Correctional Service of Canada (1989) recommends that frisk searches should not be routine but conducted on an irregular basis to increase the deterrent effect. Prisoners' mail may also be routinely searched for drugs (Grant, 1995: 8). Cell searches are also conducted, although one difficulty is the tendency for many suspected drug-dealers to bribe or intimidate other prisoners into hiding the drugs (Select Committee on Home Affairs 1999: 2 Section D).

Devices that can detect the presence of drugs are increasingly being used as the technology develops. Trace-detection equipment is designed to detect microscopic quantities of drugs in the form of vapour or solid particles (Parmeter *et al.*, 2000: 5–20). The two primary methods of collecting trace material are vacuuming and swiping. Vacuuming collects vapour and airborne particles; swiping is used to collect residues on surfaces. The chief difficulty with vapour techniques is the small amount of vapour that is emitted from most drugs at room temperature. In the case of heroin, for example, this may be as little as one part per trillion molecules, although some current technologies are capable of this sensitivity. The problem with particle analysis, on the other hand, is the high level of contamination as particles transfer from one surface to another, giving rise to potentially high rates of false positive testing. In the prison context, prisoners may be required to pass a drug-detection check-point or may be examined with a mobile hand-held detector. Trace-detection equipment is also used to search prisoners' cells and incoming mail. However, concern has been expressed by some jurisdictions about the reliability and cost of drug-detection equipment (Select Committee on Home Affairs, 1999: 5–6 Section D).

The use of drug dogs is also popular (Grant, 1995: 32–5; Parmeter *et al.*, 2000: 21–4; Select Committee on Home Affairs, 1999: 5–7 Section D). A distinction is made between active drug dogs, used to seek out substances, and passive drug dogs, used to detect the presence of drugs hidden on the person. A chief advantage of dogs is their mobility, which makes them particularly suited to on-site searches. Grant (1995: 32–3) argued that the use of dogs in random searches is inefficient and that searches should be carried out based on intelligence reports. He reported that the amount of drugs seized in South Australian prisons correlated with the frequency of dog searches, and that in periods when dog searches were suspended drug seizures fell significantly.

PRISONER–STAFF RELATIONS

As noted earlier, one potential problem with employing rigorous testing and screening procedures is that there may be a negative impact on prisoner–staff relations. Prisoners do not necessarily see the advantages of reducing the availability of drugs in prison and may interpret a focus on this goal as punitiveness (Edgar and O'Donnell, 1998b: 20–3). A climate of punitiveness may in turn encourage a demand for drugs. Some evidence of the counterproductive effects of harsh regimes is provided in a study by Stevens (1997). Stevens compared prisoner perceptions of drug use in two US (North Carolina) prisons. He found that reported levels of drug use were inversely related to perceived levels of punitiveness, that is, the prison with fewer restrictions, more informal approaches to resolving grievances and better inmate–guard relationships had less drug use and fewer rule violations in general. Unfortunately, no independent measures of drug use were provided.

THE CONDUCT OF VISITS

Visits are frequently identified as a major source of drugs entering the prison. For example, Grant (1995: 23–4) reported Australian statistics indicating that approximately one-third of all drug seizures are from visitors, with 90 per cent of these from female visitors. Abru (1999: 19) reported that in one year 43,450 visitor searches in an Australian prison system resulted in 202 cases where drugs were detected. Numerous ingenious methods of trafficking by visitors have been reported. Drugs can be passed during kissing, spat into a beverage purchased during the visit or secreted in food or gifts brought for the prisoner. They may be wrapped in plastic or balloons and swallowed by the prisoner, hidden in the mouth or body cavities or consumed during the visit (Fleisher and Rison, 1999: 235; Grant, 1995: 23; Inciardi *et al.*, 1993: 121–2; Wilkinson and Unwin, 1999: 285). Hence considerable attention has been given to addressing the supply of drugs in prison by altering the nature of visits. Tightening of visiting procedures may include screening and searching of both prisoners and visitors (e.g. body searches, the wearing by prisoners of special clothes, provision of lockers for visitors' bags, the use of dogs, electronic portals and X-rays), tightening of ID checks on visitors (e.g. requiring visitors to book ahead, requiring finger-print or photographic identification, the compilation of a data base of visit rule violators), special visiting rules (e.g. the banning of visits to the toilet, the banning of gifts), restricting physical contact between visitors and prisoners (e.g. non-contact visits, altering the layout of furniture to restrict the passing of contraband), greater surveillance of visits (e.g. the use of CCTV, more staff assigned to visits, reduction of crowding in visitor areas), providing explicit warnings of the consequences of drug trafficking to prisoners and visitors (e.g. pamphlets, signs) and increasing sanctions for visiting rule violations (e.g. visits as a privilege not a right, laying of formal charges against traffickers) (Abru, 1999: 19; Grant, 1995: 27–32; McDonald, 1992; Select Committee on Home Affairs, 1999: 4–8 Section D).

There is evidence that tightening visiting procedures can reduce the flow of drugs into prison, although the relative success of the various initiatives is difficult to gauge. Holt and Phillips (1991: 35) claimed that drug trafficking at a US Penitentiary at Marion fell virtually to nil after the introduction of non-contact visits and close control of prisoner movements. A report to the Government of Victoria (Australia) (1993; 91–2) found that positive drugs tests in four maximum-security prisons fell from 14 per cent to 6 per cent in the six months following the introduction of more rigorous visiting rules. Similarly, the Report of the Select Committee on Home Affairs (1999: 2 Section D) found that in Britain the number of drug finds fell from 8,561 in 1995 to 5,086 in 1998, a result attributed largely to stricter visiting rules. The report estimated that current methods of screening detected around 20 per cent of drugs entering prisons and argued that attacking drug supply in this way was more successful than attempts to reduce demand. However, the report also noted that reductions in overall drug finds masked an increase in heroin finds, which rose from 678 in 1995 to 1,079 in 1998. The report speculated that tighter screening methods make it particularly difficult to smuggle cannabis because it is relatively bulky. Heroin is more easily concealed.

A specific recommendation of the Select Committee on Home Affairs (1999: 4 Section D) report is the establishment of separate areas where visitors prepare for visits. These visitor centres should provide information and education to visitors about drug abuse and the dangers of smuggling. In one such centre, there is a free phone number that provides advice and allows anonymous reporting of smuggling activity.

METHADONE PROGRAMMES

Methadone is a synthetic opiate that can be taken orally and, because of its relatively long-term effect, needs only to be administered daily. Methadone provides a legal and controlled alternative to illicit drug use. During the 1970s the preferred treatment model was the prescription of large doses of methadone that blocked the euphoric effects of other opiates. The aim was to maintain the addicts while they received other forms of treatment that directly tackled their drug problem. By the late 1970s the popularity of methadone waned as many treatment programmes moved away from maintenance approaches and sought instead to achieve abstinence from all opiates including methadone. In recent years methadone has regained some popularity as drug policies have shifted towards harm minimisation, a goal that has been given impetus by the HIV/AIDS epidemic. However, doses now are typically half that of the original blockage doses (Hall *et al.*, 1993).

Relatively few prison systems routinely prescribe methadone to prisoners, but there is some evidence that methadone programmes can be successful in reducing other drug use in prison. In an Australian study, Wale and Gorta (1987) found that self-reported levels of drug use in prison decreased among prisoners taking part in a methadone programme. A follow up study involving urinalysis (Bertam and Gorta, 1990) confirmed that prisoners on the methadone programme had high compliance rates of methadone use and low rates of illicit drug use. Similarly, Dolan *et al.* (1998: 154–5) found lower self-reported levels of injecting among methadone-maintenance prisoners than prisoners who received standard drug treatment (counselling) or time-limited methadone treatment. Vambucca (1999: 7–8) found that staff involved in a heroin and/or methadone prescription programme in a Swiss prison reported a reduction in overall drug use as well as in associated violence and prostitution in the prison.

It might be objected that methadone is a therapeutic, rather than a situational, strategy. However, as Hall *et al.* (1993) stress, the goal of prison methadone programmes is not the treatment of drug abuse *per se* but the reduction of harm associated with drug use. Methadone treatment provides a behavioural alternative to illicit drug use by making illicit drugs relatively less attractive. In terms of the two-stage model, methadone treatment can be considered a version of encouraging compliance.

NEEDLE DISTRIBUTION

Needle-exchange programmes are operated in some prisons as part of a harm-reduction strategy to reduce the prevalence of viral infections such as hepatitis and HIV/AIDS. However, a major concern with such programmes is that they will increase levels of intravenous drug use among prisoners. Needle exchange is discussed here, then, not because it is seen as a strategy for reducing drug use, but in order to examine possible counterproductive effects of providing prisoners with needles. To examine this issue, Nelles *et al.* (1999) conducted a longitudinal study to examine the introduction of a needle-exchange programme in a Swiss prison. They found that drug use did not increase as a result of the programme. Rather, the frequency of drug use was related to the availability of drugs.

SUBSTANCE-FREE ZONES

One popular approach to controlling drug use is to create within a prison a substance-free zone (SFZ) (sometimes called drug-free units – DFUs – or voluntary testing units – VTUs) (Incorvaia and Kirby, 1997; Johnson and Farren, 1996; Schippers *et al.*, 1998; Trace, 1998: 281; Vambucca, 1999: 8). Typically, SFZs are separate sections or wings where prisoners commit not to use drugs, agree to regular searches and urine tests, and undertake to report rule violators. Johnson and Farren (1996: 35–6) found strong support among prisoners for the creation of SFZs, with 85 per cent of prisoners surveyed believing that they were a good idea. Incorvaia and Kirby (1997) reported on the formation of a drug-free unit in an Australian prison. They conducted urinalysis to compare unit prisoners (n=272) with mainstream prisoners (n=455). No significant demographic differences between the groups were found. However, 50 per cent of mainstream prisoners tested positive for drugs but only 6 per cent of unit prisoners. Looking at results over time, the researchers found that over an eighteen-month period positive test results in the unit (carried out 'on suspicion') fell from 8 per cent to 1 per cent. Self-report data showed higher levels of use but a similar difference between unit and mainstream prisoners. Overall, 32 per cent of prisoners in the unit admitted currently using drugs compared with 84 per cent in mainstream prisons. The most common drug used was cannabis (42 per cent v. 81 per cent), followed by opiates (13 per cent v. 36 per cent) and benzodiazepines (10 per cent v. 39 per cent). These results are reflected in the respective attitudes to drug use in prison, with 84 per cent of unit prisoners claiming they wanted to be drug-free compared with 52 per cent of mainstream prisoners.

Not all findings are as positive as those of Incorvaia and Kirby. Schippers *et al.* (1998) found no difference in drug-use patterns between a drug-free unit and other prisoners, although there was a greater acceptance among unit prisoners of searching and drug treatment.

MONITORING PRISONER ACCOUNTS

Drugs are a commodity that have to be paid for. One method of reducing drug use is to restrict the methods by which prisoners pay for drugs by exercising stricter control over prisoners' accounts (Grant, 1995: 36–7; van Groningen, 1993: 15). Often prisoner accounts are held within the prison and can be monitored for unusual transactions. However, access to telephones facilitates the establishment of external accounts. Grant (1995) reported the experience in South Australia where drug transactions were being conducted via phone betting accounts. It was discovered that there were more than a hundred betting accounts used by prisoners that showed little betting use, but that were accessed up to ten times a day to monitor balances. The clear implication is that prisoners were checking that money had been transferred into the accounts before a drug transaction was completed. Grant recommended tighter restrictions on the use of telephones to prevent prisoners from establishing such accounts.

TRACKING PRESCRIBED MEDICATION USE

An often-overlooked component of drug abuse in prison is the misuse of prescription drugs obtained through the prison pharmacy. Pilant (1998) outlined a pilot study examining the use of smart cards to track prescribed medicine use. The cards have a computer chip that stores a prisoner's photograph, prisoner number and details of medication use, including whether the prisoner has previously been refused medication.

Conclusions

Despite the significance of the problem, drug use in prison has been the subject of relatively little academic research. As with other behaviours examined in this book, much of the available social science research on drug use by prisoners has a therapeutic rather than a preventative focus. In contrast to this lack of academic interest, preventing drug use in prison is clearly a major concern of prison administrators, and the issue has been the subject of numerous official inquiries. In fact, a great deal has been

Table 9.1. *Summary of promising strategies for control of drug use*

Strategy	Precipitation-control category	Regulation-control category
Functional units	Reducing frustration Controlling environmental irritants	Formal surveillance Natural surveillance
Tightening perimeter security		Target hardening Formal surveillance
Rapid prisoner turnover		Deflecting offenders
Drug testing of staff		Formal surveillance
Restrictions on items taken into prison by staff		Entry/exit screening
Drug testing of prisoners		Formal surveillance
Searching prisoners		Formal surveillance Entry/exit screening
Use of drug-detection technology		Entry/exit screening Formal surveillance
Use of drug dogs		Formal surveillance Entry/exit screening
Improved prisoner–staff relations	Reducing frustration	
Searching visitors		Entry/exit screening
ID checks on visitors		Entry/exit screening
Banning gifts from visitors		Entry/exit screening
Restricting physical contact between visitors and prisoners		Entry/exit screening
Greater surveillance of visits		Formal surveillance Entry/exit screening
Warnings of the consequences of drug trafficking	Providing reminders Rule setting	Increasing costs Making an example
Increasing sanctions for visiting rule violations		Increasing costs
Methadone programmes	Encouraging compliance	
Substance free zones	Rule setting Reducing inappropriate conformity Encouraging compliance	Formal surveillance
Monitoring prisoners' accounts		Controlling facilitators Formal surveillance
Smart cards		Formal surveillance

done in an attempt to reduce the use of drugs in prison, but there has been little formal evaluation of the success of these endeavours. Where drug use has been monitored over time, it is usually impossible to say with any certainty just which particular interventions are responsible for any changes in drug-use patterns, since typically a combination of strategies are introduced at the same time. For example, the Pennsylvannia Department of Corrections (1999) claimed an 80 per cent reduction in prisoner drug use in two years – down to 1 per cent – through a combination of initiatives including urine and hair-testing, electronic drug-detection devices, monitoring inmate telephone calls, searching staff, increased cell searches using dogs and increased punishments for prisoners and visitors convicted of trafficking.

A summary of promising strategies that have been employed to control prison drug use is shown in table 9.1. One thing that is evident from this list is the bias in favour of attempts to reduce supply (regulation-control) rather than reduce demand (precipitation-control). The most common strategies involve stemming the flow of drugs into prison by increasing restrictions on people who come into contact with prisoners, especially visitors. On the demand-reduction side, perhaps the most promising strategies are the introduction of methadone programmes and the establishment of drug-free zones.

There is some evidence of counterproductive control effects. In particular, it seems that some attempts to control supply have the unintended consequence of encouraging a shift from cannabis to opiates because the latter are less likely to be detected in drug testing and are also easier to hide. Some researchers have also argued more generally that heavy-handed attempts to stamp out drugs in prison can sour prisoner–staff relations and create an oppressive prison climate that fuels the demand for drugs. However, this issue remains to be more fully researched.

CHAPTER 10

Escapes

As was the case for prison suicide and self-injury, so too there is a particular tendency for researchers and administrators to conceptualise prison escapes largely in terms of risky prisoners. The propensity to escape is considered a critical factor in the determination of a prisoner's security rating and so there have been a number of attempts to develop clinical and actuarial tools that might assist in the classification task (e.g. Farley and Farley, 1972; Scott *et al.*, 1977; Shaffer *et al.*, 1985; Thornton and Spiers, 1985). However, just like the research on prisoner suicide risk, research on prisoner escape risk has produced little of practical value. Studies have generally failed to find any personality factors that distinguish escapees from non-escapees (Brown *et al.*, 1978; Clarke, 1980; Laycock, 1977: 17–34; Proteus and McLoughlin, 1974). While there has been more success in identifying some consistent socio-demographic trends related to escaping (most common offence categories of escapees, most likely stage of sentence escape takes place, etc.) (Gorta and Sillavan, 1991; Laycock, 1977: 34) there simply is no reliable way of determining with any certainty at an individual level just who is and who is not likely to escape.

Nature of the problem

Definition and incidence

A major problem in establishing the incidence of escapes from prison is the differing definitions of escape used from one jurisdiction to another. In many cases, the term 'escape' is used to describe any unlawful absence from custody (e.g. Centre for Research, Evaluation and Social Assessment, 1996: 6). However, some jurisdictions make a distinction between escapes from secure institutions (not necessarily maximum security) and walkaways from open institutions (Laycock, 1977: 47; Michael, 1992; Wees, 1996). Other jurisdictions distinguish between escapes from any institution and non-returns from some form of prison furlough (Gorta and Sillavan, 1991: 207; Wees, 1996). Often in the reporting of figures, however, these distinctions are not made clear, making comparisons between jurisdictions problematic.

Keeping these definitional problems in mind, Wees (1996) reported that in 1994 there were 2,287 escapes and 5,311 walkaways or non-returns from leave from US prisons, from a total daily average population of 882,073 prisoners (data were missing for six states). California accounted for 46 per cent of escapes and Florida for 14 per cent, while the District of Columbia had the highest walkaway/non-return rate with 26 per cent of the total. To put these figures into perspective, on average (disregarding institutional security levels) a prison holding 100 prisoners could expect 8.6 escapes by any method (escapes plus walkaways/non-returns) in the course of a year. Obviously, the escape rate as a percentage of admissions over the year would show an even lower incidence. As these figures show, escape is a relatively rare event.

Patterns

Most prisoners who escape do so alone. Gorta and Sillavan (1991: 211) found that about two-thirds of escapes were carried out by single escapees. Michael (1992) found that 62% escape alone, 22% in pairs and 9% in threes. Mass escapes are rare but do occur. In one incident in Michael's study there were eight escapees. The incidence of multiple escapes is somewhat higher for juvenile institutions than for adult institutions, presumably because younger prisoners are more group-dependent, and for open rather than closed institutions. Laycock (1977: 41–2) found that for young prisoners only 43% escaped alone from open institutions, although the figure for closed institutions (62%) was similar to that usually reported for adults. Laycock argued that group escapes were more likely from open institutions, since minimal planning was required and it was easy for last-minute joiners to tag along. Escape from a closed institution required more planning and secrecy.

Escapees are generally recaptured soon after their escape. In an Australian study, Gorta and Sillavan (1991: 213–14) found 28% of New South Wales escapees were caught the same day or the day following their escape, and over half within eight days. Fewer that 10% remained at large after six months. In another Australian study, Michael (1992) found 65% of Queensland escapees were captured within four days, and 98% within a year. Lyons

(1997) found that for New York State, 79% of escapees were apprehended within seventy-two hours. Similarly, escapees commit relatively few crimes while free (Banks *et al.*, 1975; Centre for Research, Evaluation and Social Assessment, 1996: 55; Gorta and Sillavan, 1991: 213–14). Gorta and Sillavan found that about three-quarters of escapees were charged with no other crimes when they were recaptured, about 20% were charged with property offences and 5% with violent offences. As Gorta and Sillavan concluded, the 'idea that still exists within the community that all escapees are "determined desperados" is ill-founded' (p. 216).

Motivation

The evidence suggests that most escapes are impulsive. In a New Zealand study the Centre for Research, Evaluation and Social Assessment (1996: 54) found that of thirty-four escapees interviewed, only eight had formulated a specific plan to escape. In an Australian study, Thompson (1992: 14) found that 64% of escapees had been planning their escape for less than a day, a further 20% for less than a week and only 17% for more than a week. In 87% of cases, respondents indicated that they had not thought about escaping on any previous occasion.

   At the same time, given that relatively few prisoners who are in a position to escape actually do escape, escapes are not just the result of prisoners capitalising on opportunity – they occur for a reason. Duncan and Ellis (1973) reported that only 20% of escapes involved prisoners taking advantage of an exceptional opportunity that was presented to them. Thompson (1992: 5–8) found that the most common reason for escape offered by recaptured prisoners was outside family/relationship problems, either of a chronic nature or involving some specific incident of which the prisoner had recently become aware. This category accounted for 52% of all escapes. Threats and pressure from other prisoners accounted for a further 21% of cases; being under the influence of drugs or alcohol 7%; general prison stress 9%; impending transfer or extradition 6%; pressure to follow companions 4%; to obtain drugs or alcohol 4%; conflict with staff 3%; parole uncertainty 2%. Laycock (1977: 32–3) found for young British detainees, 36% identified family or relationship problems as the prime reason for their escape, 29% identified general frustrations and boredom, with the remainder offering a mixture of reasons. Gorta and Nguyen Da Huong (1988), in an Australian study, found that bad news from outside and chronic family problems were the major reasons given for escape (68%), followed by threats from other prisoners (21%), inability to cope (11%), conflict with staff (8%), and parole uncertainty (6%).

The Centre for Research, Evaluation and Social Assessment (1996: 10–15) made a broad distinction between internal (prison) and external pressures to escape. Internal pressures included problems accepting the sentence, being fed up with prison life, threats and inducements from other prisoners, conflicts with staff, uncertainty about the future, uncertainty about parole or release, drug or alcohol intoxication and desire to obtain drugs or alcohol. External pressures included family and relationship problems, concern about the security of personal property and intention to wreak vengeance of some sort. In addition, there was a range of reasons for escape related to personal risk-taking. These included the desire for excitement, wanting to accompany a friend, copying the exploits of others, wanting an extension to a sentence, wanting a change of prison or classification, wanting infamy through escaping, wanting to punish an unpopular officer (by having him blamed for the escape), unintentional escape (such as returning late from leave) and simple unplanned opportunism.

In their study, Duncan and Ellis (1973) calculated that up to 43 per cent of escapes might have been prevented if administrators had responded appropriately to inmate needs. Thompson (1992: 12–13) asked recaptured escapees what authorities could have done to prevent their escape. More than half (53 per cent) of respondents believed that their escape could have been prevented. Of this group, 42 per cent said that they would not have escaped if their request for transfer had been enacted, 17 per cent said that they should have been granted extra leave to deal with family problems, a further 17 per cent cited the importance of improved prison conditions and 14 per cent wanted to receive more counselling. A similar list is provided by the Centre for Research, Evaluation and Social Assessment (1996: 52). They too found that more than half of the escapees interviewed believed that their escape was preventable, with suggested interventions including improvements to the prison environment, treating prisoners like human beings, providing more recreational and educational programmes, providing more counselling, improving visiting conditions, reacting more quickly to grievances and complaints, transferring prisoners closer to home and improving security.

Interestingly, it was Ron Clarke's inability to find consistent personality or demographic profiles of juvenile escapees that encouraged him to develop rational choice perspective and to seek solutions to crime problems through situational crime prevention (Clarke, 1980, 1987; Sinclair and Clarke, 1982). Looking for patterns in absconding from juvenile detention facilities, he concluded that differences between high-escape institutions and low-escape institutions were more important than differences between absconders and non-absconders (Clarke, 1980). It was the way an institution was run that either encouraged or inhibited escapes. In other words, situational variables were better predictors of escaping than dispositional variables.

Even more interestingly, Clarke (1980) proposed a model of escaping that gave equal consideration to institutional variables that make it either easy or hard for prisoners to escape, and those factors that might increase or decrease the desire of prisoners to escape in the first place. Summarising his own and colleagues' research in the area he wrote: 'we found many environmental variables to be related to absconding – either, it seemed, because they mediated opportunities to abscond or because they were the source of feelings of unhappiness or anxiety which fuelled the behaviour' (p. 123). That is, in terms of the language used in this book, the model acknowledged both regulators and precipitators of escaping. While Clarke has since gone on to develop a model of situational prevention that emphasises the primary role of opportunity-reduction, the distinction between precipitators and regulators still appears useful.

Situational context
STAGE OF SENTENCE
There appears to be no particular stage of a sentence during which escapes are most likely to occur, and many escapes are carried out towards the end of the prisoner's sentence. Gorta and Sillavan (1991: 210) found that 50 per cent of escapees in their sample of 812 had served at least four months of their sentence when they escaped, 50 per cent escaped in the last five months of their sentence. In terms of proportions, over 10 per cent of escapees had served 80 per cent of their sentence.

Of course, there is a potential confound between stage of sentence and the relative constraints on escaping. That is, the spread of escapes across the sentence might simply reflect the changing opportunities available to prisoners as they progress through the security levels. An alternative approach is to examine the relationship between escaping and the time spent at a specific institution. Examined in this way, there appears to be a tendency for prisoners to escape relatively soon after arrival at an institution. Clarke (1980) suggested that coming to a new institution was a particularly unsettling time emotionally for prisoners – a problem he referred to as 'admission crisis' – as they tried to adapt to unfamiliar surroundings. Advancing a more cognitive explanation, Laycock (1977) argued that escape at the earliest opportunity involved fewer costs (e.g. there are fewer earned privileges to be forfeited) and provided the greatest pay-off (e.g. there is less time spent at the institution) for prisoners than escape later in the sentence. Whichever the reason, Gorta and Sillavan (1991: 210) found that 19 per cent of prison escapes took place in the first week of the prisoner's arrival at an institution, and 50 per cent within thirty-eight days of arrival. Laycock (1977: 37) found that the tendency to escape soon after arrival applied only to open institutions. She found that 32 per cent of escapes from open juvenile institutions took place within two weeks of arrival, compared with 6 per cent for closed institutions.

There are two points to be taken from the research described in this section. First, there is clearly an opportunity factor evident in the pattern of escapes. Admission crisis is a bigger problem at open institutions than closed institutions because it is much easier to escape from the former than the latter. Some opportunity-reduction strategies for dealing with admission crisis are suggested later in the chapter. Second, despite the problem of admission crisis, not all – not even most – escapes occur at the earliest opportunity. Gorta and Sillavan (1991: 210–11) found that nearly 10 per cent of escapees had spent more than six months at the institution before they escaped. Further, prisoners who escaped from lightly supervised work parties had spent an average of twelve weeks on the work party before their escape and those on completely unsupervised education leave took six months before they decided to escape. Presumably in these cases something happened to the prisoners in the course of their sentence that persuaded them to take advantage of the opportunities for escape that were available.

SEASONAL VARIATIONS

Hilderbrand (1969) found that most escapes occurred in July, September, January, May and June, and fewest in February, March and April. As a general trend, there were more escapes in summer than in winter. The higher-than-expected rate for January might be related to post-Christmas depression.

A somewhat different pattern was found by Clarke (1980). He found that escapes were least frequent in summer, gradually increased as winter approached, dropped during mid-winter (there seemed no particular pressure to escape around Christmas), then rose again before gradually decreasing as summer returned. Temperature and rainfall were not directly related to absconding rates, but more escapes occurred on particularly sunny or particularly dull days. Clarke suggested a number of ways that the weather might have directly affected the decision to escape. For example, mid-winter weather would have made freedom a rather unattractive proposition, while sunny days would make the outside world particularly inviting and dull days make the institution seem more depressing.

SECURITY LEVEL

Unsurprisingly, escapes overwhelmingly take place from low-security institutions and by low-security-rated prisoners. Lyons (1997) found that in New York State, 92 per cent of escapes took place from minimum- or medium-security facilities. Herrick (1989), reporting 1988 data for all US prison systems, found that only 6 per cent of escapes were from maximum- or medium-security prisons. Gorta and Sillavan (1991: 208) found that only 2 per cent escapes in an Australian sample took place from maximum security. Of the remaining cases, 83 per cent occurred from minimum security, including 12 per cent who were non-returns from some form of leave programme. The Centre for Research, Evaluation and Social Assessment (1996: 27) found that of 117 escapes from the New Zealand prison system only two took place from maximum security.

Despite the apparently high levels of escape from minimum-security conditions, the proportion of minimum-security prisoners who escape is remarkably small, given the ease with which escape under such conditions might be effected. For example, Smith and Sabatino (1990) examined non-returns from furlough for forty-seven US state systems and the Federal Bureau of Prisons. For the 67,736 furloughs examined (those issued in the first half of 1988) the rate of absconding was less than 1 per cent. These figures emphasise once again the point that opportunity alone is not sufficient to explain escapes. The majority of prisoners do not require physical constraints to make them remain in custody.

TIME

Hildebrand (1969) found that Saturday was the most common day for escapes and Wednesday the least common. Saturday was said to have fewest programmes for prisoners while Wednesday had the most programmes. The fact that Sunday was visiting day probably accounts for it having fewer escapes than Saturday. However, in the absence of other research addressing day of the week it remains unclear whether this finding is generalisable.

Several researchers agree that the most frequent time for escaping is early evening, usually after 6.00 p.m. and up until 9.00 p.m. (Clarke, 1980; Hildebrand, 1969). These authors suggest two reasons for the peak at this time. First, this is generally a period of unstructured activity when prisoners have free time before lock-up. There is greater potential for boredom at this time and there are often also reduced staffing levels. Second, as night closes in there is a cover of darkness which increases the chance that the escape will not be detected.

Clarke (1980) also noted a link between the seasonal and temporal patterns of escape that perhaps provides a more persuasive explanation for the effects of climate than those offered earlier. He pointed out that the frequency of escapes increased as days grew shorter. The increase in escapes was shown to have occurred primarily between 6.00 p.m. and 9.00 p.m., that is, the period most affected by changing sunsets. Escapes were 2.5 times more likely on a winter evening than on a summer evening. Winter evenings, Clarke concluded, provided more opportunities to escape. A similar pattern was reported by Hildebrand (1969).

LOCATION

Escape is by definition an ambulatory behaviour and so it is not possible to fix a precise location for it as it is for other forms of misbehaviour. One way to consider location is to look at where within the prison the escapee was housed prior to the escape. A number of studies have found that escapees consistently come from particular units or dormitories, although what distinguishes those locations varies. For example, Clarke (1980) found a relationship between crowded dormitories and escapes; Hildebrand (1969) found there were more escapes from dormitories that were less secure or had more liberal regimes (despite the fact that these units also had the most trusted prisoners). An alternative approach to location is to examine whether the prisoner escaped from inside or outside of the prison. Research in this area is sketchy but it seems that a significant proportion of escapes are by 'trusted' prisoners who are under minimal or no supervision and are already outside the prison walls when the escape takes place. Gorta and Sillavan (1991: 208) found that 12 per cent of all escapes in an Australian sample were non-returns from outside education programmes or from home visits. Duncan and Ellis (1973) found that 22 per cent of escapes occurred while the prisoner was on an outside work-detail.

Controlling escapes

The physical environment

FUNCTIONAL UNITS

Reductions in escape are yet another benefit claimed for functional units, although again the supporting empirical evidence is rather sparse. In his description of the introduction of unit management in various institutions, Sigurdson (1985: vi; 1987a: v; 1987b: i) reported no instances of escape. Likewise, King (1991: 150) noted that there had never been a serious escape attempt from the new-generation prison Oak Park Heights (Minneapolis) in its nine years of operation. Senese *et al.* (1992) found fewer escapes from a podular prison than from a traditional prison, but provided no other data about the nature of the two institutions.

While unit management comprises numerous elements, as has been noted, we may speculate that an important factor for escape prevention is the improved staff–inmate relations and the greater opportunity afforded to prisoners to have their concerns dealt with. The issue of the availability of counselling and welfare services is taken up on p. 186.

PERIMETER SECURITY

Perhaps the most obvious way to reduce escapes from secure institutions is to strengthen the barrier dividing the prisoners from the outside world. No discussion of escape prevention, therefore, would be complete without some mention of perimeter security. However, probably because perimeter security is such an obvious strategy for reducing escapes, there is little empirical research that examines its effectiveness. Hildebrand (1969) reported that escapes from a juvenile institution were mainly from dormitories that were located outside the main compound, which was surrounded by a fourteen-foot-high cyclone fence. He also reported that the erection of an observation tower resulted in a drop from twenty-six escapes in the year prior to its installation to two escapes the following year. Apart from this research, the very fact that the vast majority of escapes take place from minimum security indicates that physical constraints on escaping are a very effective strategy.

There is no empirical research that examines the relative effectiveness of different types of perimeter security. According to McManus and Conner (1994: 142), effective perimeter security should possess three features. First, it should appear so daunting that most prisoners will not even consider the possibility that it can be breached. Second, it should in fact be difficult and time-consuming to penetrate. Third, it should allow staff to monitor activity within the precincts of the perimeter. There are numerous articles in the correction's literature dealing with methods and techniques for meeting these conditions and improving prison perimeter security (American Society for Industrial Security, 1979; Buchanan *et al.*, 1988; Camp and Camp, 1987; Czerniak and Upchurch, 1996; McManus and Conner, 1994; Travis *et al.*, 1989). These articles describe both hardware options – such as multi-barrier configurations, new fencing materials and designs, advances in barbed wire, and new technological aids such as fence-mounted sensors, underground seismic systems, micro-wave and infrared detection devices and CCTV coverage – and procedural considerations – such as ID checks, search practices and key control. The relative merits of these strategies are typically discussed from a technical point of view and assessed on the basis of the expert opinion of the particular author. Since the empirical data demonstrating their effectiveness in preventing escapes is not presented, these strategies will not be discussed further here. This is not to say that the claims made for these suggested improvements to perimeter security are unfounded – undoubtedly many of these advances make good sense from a situational-prevention point of view – but only that technical evaluations of this sort fall outside the scope of this book.

Population characteristics

CROWDING

The effect of crowding on escape rates is as ambiguous as the effect of crowding on the other forms of prison disorder discussed so far. Clarke (1980) found that escapes from juvenile institutions increased if youths were admitted during particularly busy periods or were accommodated in units that were unusually full. He argued that in busy times staff were less able to help new arrivals settle in and he suggested staggering admissions as a way of overcoming the problem.

Against these findings, other researchers have found no effects for crowding, or negative effects. Jan (1980) tracked escapes in four Florida state prisons over a four-year period. Escapes were found to be unrelated to population size for institutions housing male young offenders and female offenders. For the institution housing adult male prisoners there was an unexpected negative correlation between escapes and population increases in this period, that is, escapes decreased as the prison population grew. Further, the negative relationship became stronger when an overcrowding index (over-capacity level) was correlated with changes in escape rates. This finding was interpreted as indicating that the escape rate was affected by crowding over and above population size. Jan was at a loss to explain these findings, except to suggest that they may be related to the fact that the adult male institution was a high-security facility. One possibility consistent with this observation is that high-security staff may become hyper-vigilant in overcrowded conditions.

The prison regime

GRADUATED REDUCTIONS IN SECURITY LEVEL

It has been noted that escapes occur most frequently soon after a prisoner's arrival at an open institution, either because the prisoner is emotionally unsettled at this time, or because escape at the earliest opportunity max-imises the benefits of the behaviour. The obvious strategy suggested by these findings is to delay the entry into general discipline of new arrivals until admission crisis has passed.

The importance of the progressive security ratings is shown in a study by Laycock (1977: 39–41). Laycock suggested that delaying the release of prisoners into an open institution until later in their sentence (after they had earned various privileges and so had more to lose) might decrease the absconding rate by increasing the costs of absconding. She compared two open juvenile institutions, one that had a secure induction unit where new arrivals were held before their progressive release into normal discipline, the other in which new arrivals went straight to normal discipline. As expected, the number of escapes taking place in the first month after admission was greatly reduced in the institution with the induction unit. Moreover, there were relatively fewer escapes overall from this institution. That is, there was no evidence that escapes had merely been delayed (displaced) until release into normal discipline. Laycock was able to replicate this general finding in a longitudinal study of an institution that introduced an induction unit.

PRISON DISCIPLINE

If escaping is a prisoner's way of dealing with an unpleasant situation, it might be supposed that the stricter the institutional regime then the greater the likelihood that escapes would occur. In fact the available research (albeit, most of it conducted on juveniles) suggests that escapes are often less frequent in institutions that have relatively strict (though not draconian) disciplinary regimes (Cornish and Clarke, 1975; Martin, 1977; Millham *et al.*, 1977; Sinclair, 1971).

Cornish and Clarke (1975) examined behavioural outcomes, including escape rates, for two juvenile detention units run along traditional lines and a unit run in accordance with a therapeutic regime. The therapeutic regime was based on four principles – democratisation, communalism, permissiveness and reality confrontation. One of the traditional units was a control, in that boys considered suitable for the therapeutic community were randomly assigned either to it or to the therapeutic unit; the other traditional unit housed boys deemed unsuitable for the therapeutic regime. Cornish and Clarke found that there were more escapes from the therapeutic unit than the traditional units. According to Cornish and Clarke, the stricter regimes provided necessary structure for the boys as well as reducing their opportunities to escape.

However, most researchers agree that the disciplinary regime needs to be balanced. For example, Millham *et al.* (1977) found fewer escapes by juveniles in institutions that imposed restrictions on 'individual choice, movement, privacy and relationships'. At the same time, these authors emphasised the need for good pastoral care to go along with the restrictive regime. A similar co-dependency between discipline and care was found by Sinclair (1971). He examined absconding by juveniles from probation hostels. He found great variations in absconding rates among hostels that could not be explained by individual difference in the absconders. Instead he found that the lowest absconding rates occurred in hostels in which the warden was judged (using a questionnaire) to be both low on permissiveness and high on emotional warmth. The other three permutations (e.g. high on permissiveness and high on warmth) were equally unsuccessful with respect to the prevention of absconding. The ideal institutional regime, then, seems to be one that combines structure and discipline with a caring social climate or, as Clarke (1980) put it, adopts an approach to inmates that is 'kind but strict' (p. 118).

GENERAL DETERRENCE

While most escapes are carried out by lone escapees, a number of researchers have reported what Clarke (1980) calls an infectious element in the behaviour. Escapees may induce others to accompany them, or may trigger a subsequent rash of the behaviour. In behavioural terminology, an escapee models a behaviour that others emulate. Clarke found an increase in escapes among juveniles admitted into an institution at the same time as other juveniles with a history of escape. The presence of known escapees, Clarke surmised, influenced other residents to perform the behaviour. Also focusing on juveniles, Laycock (1977: 41–3) asked recaptured absconders whether they had asked others to join them. She found that 23 per cent of escapees from open institutions and 19 per cent from closed institutions had actively recruited accomplices. Thompson (1992: 11), however, found that only 4 per cent of adult escapees said that they were strongly influenced by a companion to escape.

While the process by which followers are induced to emulate other escapees might be conceptualised in terms of situational precipitation, the proposed remedies fit very much into a deterrence model. Laycock (1977: 43) asked escapees whether or not they thought they would get caught. She found many escapees grossly underestimated the likelihood of recapture, with 55 per cent estimating that they would not get caught. (As indicated earlier, the recapture rate for escapees is almost 100 per cent within a year.) The underestimation of risk was particularly evident among 'joiners' compared to lone escapees and group leaders. Laycock recommended a publicity campaign to alert prisoners to the actual risks of escape.

The Centre for Research, Evaluation and Social Assessment (1996: 54) also found that there was some ambiguity in prisoners' minds about the penalties for escape. While most escapees (twenty-nine of the thirty-four interviewed) understood that they would receive extra time, five prisoners thought that they would suffer only a loss of privileges or were unsure what would happen to them.

An explicit example of general deterrence is provided by Clarke (1980). He found that escapes from juvenile institutions dropped if it was known by the other inmates that a recaptured escapee had been caned as punishment (when compared with cases where the recaptured escapee was not caned). Without necessarily advocating caning, Clarke cited this finding as evidence that escaping was a rational decision that could be affected by the application of suitable deterrents and, more generally, that the nature of the institutional regime is a crucial determinant of the escape rate. The implication is that escapes may be reduced if prisoners are made more aware of the consequences of the behaviour. In behavioural jargon, this is an example of vicarious punishment and is included in the two-stage model under making an example.

PROTECTION AND TRANSFERS

Threats and pressure from other prisoners is consistently identified as a major cause of prison escapes, usually given as the second most important factor after outside problems (Centre for Research, Evaluation and Social Assessment, 1996: 49–50; Gorta and Nguyen Da Huong, 1988; Thompson, 1992: 8). Thompson (1992: 8) found that 59 per cent of prisoners in this category escaped because they feared physical attack, 30 per cent because they feared sexual assault, 10 per cent because they were subject to other kinds of threats (e.g. to set up the prisoner with illegal possessions) and 2 per cent because they were being pressured to carry drugs or other contraband.

Gorta and Sillavan (1991: 217) noted the presence on the files of a significant number of the escapees' requests (usually denied) for protection. For these prisoners, often their intention in escaping was not to gain freedom, but to force a transfer to another institution. The prisoners knew that when they were recaptured they would be returned to a secure institution away from their tormentors. Thompson (1992: 12) found that nearly one-half of all escapees who nominated preventative action that could be taken by authorities claimed that they would not have escaped if they had been transferred as requested.

Clearly, there is an inter-relatedness between the issue of escapes and the issues of prisoner-prisoner violence and sexual assaults, as outlined in chapters 5 and 6. Strategies aimed at reducing prison violence may have the auxiliary effect of reducing prison escapes.

PROGRAMME AVAILABILITY

Many prisoners claim that they escape because of boredom and a lack of programming (e.g. Centre for Research, Evaluation and Social Assessment, 1996: 47, 53; Laycock, 1977: 32; Thompson, 1992: 9) and there is some evidence to substantiate a link between programme availability and escape rates. Carter (1963) found that juvenile absconders were less likely to be involved in trade training, and, at an aggregate level, Dunlop (1974) found overall lower absconding rates in juvenile institutions that had trade training.

COUNSELLING

Generally, counselling has not been suggested as an intervention in this book because the object of counselling is often to effect some dispositional change in the potential offender. The term 'counselling' is used broadly here to refer to any significant communication between the prisoner and staff on matters concerning the reasons for the possible escape. In this sense, counselling can be considered a situational intervention in that the aim is to resolve immediate pressures acting on the prisoner.

The reasons for escape given by recaptured escapees – family problems, bad news, fear of other prisoners – suggest that many escapes are preventable through the provision of basic pastoral care and welfare services. Several studies of juveniles have found that absconding rates were lower in institutions where boys felt able to discuss personal problems with staff (Cornish and Clarke, 1975; Johnson *et al.*, 1978; Millham *et al.*, 1977; Sinclair, 1971). Laycock (1977: 42) asked recaptured juvenile absconders if they had talked over their problems with staff prior to their escape. Only 31 per cent of escapees had done so. Lone escapees and leaders of groups of escapees were less likely to have talked to staff than followers were. Thompson (1992: 12–13) found that of recaptured adult escapees who believed that their escape was preventable (more than half the sample), 14 per cent claimed that they would not have escaped if they had received more staff counselling. The Centre for Research, Evaluation and Social Research (1996: 52) also found that many escapees interviewed thought that counselling could have prevented their escape. However, while more than half had discussed the pressures to escape with other prisoners, they expressed reservations about the interest or ability of staff to assist them. Only seven of the thirty-four escapees interviewed had discussed the pressure on them to escape with staff. Of the other non-impulsive escapees, eleven respondents did not believe that staff would be helpful and a further five believed that staff would only be interested in preventing the escape rather than helping with the problem. These findings suggest that staff may need training in order to fulfil an effective counselling role.

In addition to any tension-relieving effects that counselling might have, it is only through approaching staff that more practical solutions to prisoners' problems – compassionate home visits, transfer to alternative institutions, protection from other prisoners – might be arranged.

VISITS AND FURLOUGHS

As has been noted, escapes often involve non-returns from home visits. The question addressed here, however, is what impact the availability of such outside contact has on escapes more generally (i.e. from the institution)?

Because many escapes are motivated by loss of outside contact, then increasing that contact may reduce the risk of escape. Family and relationship pressures from outside have been consistently found to be a major reason for prison escapes, in some studies accounting for more than two-thirds of all cases (e.g. Centre for Research, Evaluation and Social Assessment, 1996: 49–50; Gorta and Nguyen Da Huong, 1988). Moreover, Duncan and Ellis (1973) cite insensitivity or inaction by prison authorities for failing to help resolve these outside pressures. In 18 per cent of cases in their sample, escapes occurred after requests to visit a sick relative, to attend a funeral or to make a special phone call had been denied.

Thompson (1992: 7) found somewhat different patterns for prisoners who escaped because of chronic family problems, and those who escaped because of some specific bad news from home. Prisoners who escape because of chronic family troubles were more likely to have thought about escaping for a long period of time. In many cases there was no specific trigger for the escape. Those prisoners who escaped due to bad news from home were less likely to have thought about escaping on previous occasions. That is, their escapes represent rational (if muddle-headed) attempts to solve particular problems. In Thompson's study, 17 per cent of recaptured escapees who believed that their escape was preventable nominated extra leave as the action that would have stopped them escaping.

At the same time, Clarke and Martin (1975) found that escapes from juvenile institutions increased after the juvenile returned from a home visit. They argued that the process of going home only to be removed again and returned to the institution was unsettling and intensified the juveniles' unhappiness. Staff may need to be especially attentive to prisoners' moods after visits and furloughs.

Conclusions

Situational prevention strategies for escape are summarised in table 10.1. Of all the prison-control problems covered in this book, escapes have received the least attention from a situational perspective. Much of the research that is available has been conducted on juveniles rather than adult prisoners, and much of that is now rather dated. There is a particular dearth of published US studies (compared with British and Australian studies) and that which is available tends to be 'in-house' research or reports of official inquiries into specific escape incidents.

One reason for this lack of empirical interest may be that for many academics the solution to escapes is very obvious. Almost all escapes take place from minimum-security establishments or from some form of outside

Table 10.1. *Summary of promising strategies for control of escapes*

Intervention	Precipitation-control category	Regulation-control category
Functional unit management	Setting positive expectations Controlling environmental irritants	Formal surveillance Natural surveillance
Improved perimeter security		Target hardening
Reduced population density	Reducing crowding	
Graduated reductions in security level		Target hardening Increasing costs
'Strict' discipline, structured regime		Deflecting offenders Formal surveillance Increasing costs
Publicise risks		Increasing costs
Publicise punishments		Making an example
Responding to requests for protection/transfer	Reducing frustration	Deflecting offenders Target hardening
Programmes/work opportunities	Reducing frustration	Deflecting offenders
Counselling and pastoral care	Reducing frustrations	
Compassionate visits/phone calls	Reducing frustration	

leave. Escapes could be almost totally eliminated if all prisoners were kept in maximum-security conditions. Of course, such a policy would be both socially objectionable and financially crippling and no one seriously suggests it. But the corresponding view to this position is that escapes from minimum security are inevitable and unavoidable. As long as a progressive system of security is retained then, it is argued, the best that can be done is try as far as possible to ensure that escape-prone prisoners are not classified to minimum security. The primary prevention strategy, according to this rationale, involves the development of better instruments for assessing individual escape risk.

There is a seductive logic to this view. As van den Haag (1980) argued, there is a certain absurdity to increasing security in minimum-security institutions. If prisoners are intent on escaping, he argued, then extra security at a minimum-security institution is unlikely to discourage them, and if they are not intent upon escaping then the security precautions are a waste of effort and money. Moreover, at what point does the enhanced security redefine the institution as no longer 'minimum'? For van der Haag, minimum-security institutions should become no-security institutions, and escapes should be simply accepted as a necessary by-product of a no-security policy. The question is not how to eliminate escapes but how to strike the balance between having cheap and humane methods of confining prisoners on the one hand and keeping escapes to an acceptable level through judicious classification of prisoners on the other.

But this assessment of escape prevention in minimum security as futile is unduly pessimistic on two counts. First, the characterisation of the intention to escape as either absent or present is simplistic. Potential escapees may possess gradations of intent ranging from single-minded determination to ambivalence. Consequently, there does not need to be a choice between maximum security and no security. The lesson from crime prevention in the community is that opportunity-reduction strategies need not necessarily involve setting up impenetrable barriers to crime – often inconvenience is enough to deter the casual offender. There is potential to employ meaningful opportunity-reduction in a minimum-security institution without sacrificing its minimum-security status. Second, the strength of an individual's intention is not fixed but changes depending upon circumstances. Most escapees are not inherently escape-prone – more often than not their escape is a response to a specific situation. The primary escape-prevention strategy in a minimum-security institution (and an important strategy in a maximum-security institution) is not to reduce the opportunities to escape but to reduce the pressures on prisoners that prompt their escapes.

CHAPTER 11

Collective disorder

Potentially the most serious form of prison disorder is a riot. The two most notorious riots in American history – Attica in 1971 and New Mexico in 1980 – are evidence of the brutality and destructiveness that can be unleashed when prison control disintegrates. These two riots alone cost seventy-six lives and caused tens of millions of dollars worth of damage. As with other forms of prison disorder there are many who readily attribute the causes of riots to the inherently violent nature of prisoners. Explaining the cause of the Attica riot, the warden observed; 'You are dealing with a highly selected individual who has been a failure from all society' (Mahan, 1994: 257). However, as the official inquiry into the Attica riot (the McKay Commission) concluded, the causes of the riot can be traced to the physical and social conditions that existed in the prison (New York State Special Commission on Attica, 1972: 31–102). At the same time, Attica was far from unique. Every prison, McKay warned, is a potential Attica (p. xii).

Nature of the problem

Definition and incidence

Like escapes, the incidence of collective disorder is dependent upon the definition employed. According to Wees (1996: 17) 'an inmate is engaged in a riot when he, with two or more persons, participates in conduct that creates danger or damage or injury to property or persons and obstructs the performance of facility functions'. On this basis, Wees reported 186, 277 and 402 riots for 1993, 1994 and 1995 respectively for US prison systems (data from seven states were missing). Looking more closely at the 1995 figures, Texas was found to account for 55 per cent of all disturbances. The most serious incident (in the District of Columbia) involved more than 1,000 prisoners.

Using a more restrictive criterion for participant numbers, Stephan (1997: 13) defined riots as 'incidents that had 5 or more inmates participating, that required the intervention of additional or outside assistance, and that resulted in serious injury or significant property damage'. He reported that for 1995 there were 317 riots in the US, down from 814 in 1990. It may be noted that the downward trend over five years reported by Stephan is at variance with the upward trend within that time-span reported by Wees.

More restrictive still, Montgomery (1994: 227) defined riots as 'incidents involving 15 or more inmates and resulting in property damage or personal injury'. Citing research conducted by the South Carolina Department of Corrections in 1973, Montgomery reported that between 1900 and 1970 there were 200 such incidents in the US. Citing follow-up research for 1971 to 1983 conducted by Montgomery and MacDougal in 1984, he reported that there were a further 260 riots, with California (80) and Florida (34) accounting for the largest number.

Of course, the US is not the only country to have experienced prison riots. The US riots of the early 1970s heralded and perhaps sparked disturbances in prison systems around the world. In 1972 in Britain there was a series of disturbances at Brixton, Albany, Parkhurst, Camphill, Chelmsford and Gartree (Woolf and Tumin, 1991: 225). Prison disturbances continued in Britain throughout the 1970s, 1980s and into the 1990s, including the notorious spate of rooftop demonstrations (Adams and Campling, 1992: 159). Similarly, France had major riots throughout the 1970s and 1980s, beginning with Toul in 1971, and including disturbances in 89 prisons in 1974 (Vaag, 1994: 246). In Australia, there was major rioting at Bathurst Gaol in 1974 leaving the prison uninhabitable and foreshadowing further instability in the prison system around the country (Nagle, 1978: 43–105).

Patterns

Montgomery (1994: 227–35) provided a comprehensive breakdown of the characteristics of the 260 riots that occurred in the US between 1971 and 1983. Overall, the analysis presented by Montgomery revealed that the vast majority of riots were relatively minor, with a small number of very serious disturbances accounting for most of the injuries, deaths and property damage. The chief patterns were:

- 38 per cent of riots involved fewer than 100 prisoners, while 8 per cent involved 400 or more prisoners.

- 88 per cent of riots involved the taking of no hostages, 8 per cent between 1 and 5 hostages and 4 per cent more than 5 hostages. The largest number of hostages was 50.
- A total of 748 prisoners were injured and 89 killed. In 59 per cent of cases there were no injuries or deaths involving prisoners, while in the two most serious riots a total of 175 prisoners were injured (85 and 90) and 65 were killed (32 and 33).
- A total of 81 members of staff were injured and 7 killed. In 73 per cent of cases there were no injuries or deaths involving staff, while 37 were injured in the four most serious riots. (Since the period of Montgomery's analysis includes the 1971 Attica riot, in which 11 officers were killed by guards retaking the institution, it is assumed that these figures refer only to staff killed by prisoners.)
- 56 per cent of cases involved property damage of less than $500, while for eight riots the damage bill in each case exceeded $1 million.
- 16 per cent of riots lasted less than an hour, and 77 per cent were over in less than 9 hours. In 15 per cent of cases the riot lasted more than 24 hours.

Motivation

Montgomery (1994: 239), again reporting the analysis of US riots between 1971 and 1983, indicated that by far the major cause was racial tension, accounting for 34 per cent of cases. The next most common causes were demonstrations (7 per cent), dissatisfaction with rules or privileges (7 per cent), living conditions (i.e. overcrowding, heat and food) (4 per cent) and a combination of these last two factors (4 per cent). Numerous other causes were reported but each individually accounted for less than 2 per cent of cases. These included gang-related and alcohol-related protests over discipline, power outage, escape attempts, inmates attacking staff, rumours, insufficient supervision or discipline and lockdowns or shakedowns.

Montgomery also reported a survey of prisoners (n=904) and guards (n=704) on perceived causes of riots. Reasons given by prisoners were: the behaviour of guards (17%), racial conflict (12%), lack of communication (10%), deficiencies in administration (10%), general frustrations (8%), prison conditions (8%), unjust treatment (5%), boredom (4%), prejudice or favouritism (4%), aggressive inmates (3%), power struggles (3%), prisoner instigators (3%), food (2%), suppression (2%) and the parole system (2%). Reasons by guards were: lack of communication (14%), militants (12%), poor conditions (11%) outside influences (10%), boredom and frustration (10%), racial conflict (8%), food (6%), poor discipline (5%), incompetent officers (4%), leniency towards prisoners (4%), agitators (3%), overcrowding (3%), aggressive prisoner leaders (3%), publicity and media reports (2%) and lack of programmes (2%). There is a surprising level of agreement between the two groups, with both prisoners and guards inclined to view boredom, frustration and generally poor prison conditions as prime causes of rioting. One unsurprising difference between the groups is the tendency for prisoners to believe that riots are caused by excessive or unfair discipline and for officers to believe that too little discipline is more likely to be the problem.

The distinction between chronic and acute situational factors noted in previous chapters is particularly evident in situational explanations of prison rioting. A popular analogy is to compare prisons with timebombs waiting to explode and requiring only some trigger to set them off (e.g. Boin and Van Duin, 1995: 360; Fox, 1971: 9–12; Mahan, 1994: 254; Martin and Zimmerman, 1990: 714). In this analysis, a history of sub-standard conditions and repressive treatment predisposes a prison to rioting. The riot, when it eventually occurs, may be spontaneous and involve little planning. The psychological processes by which a triggering incident, perhaps involving just one or two prisoners, progresses to collective action have been described in chapters 2 and 4. Group cohesion and a sense of intra-group righteousness are intensified by perceptions of external threat from other groups. Against a background of chronic intergroup hostility, the witnessing of a perceived injustice inflicted upon a fellow prisoner, or the explicit urgings of prisoner leaders, can induce deindividuation and galvanise prisoners to a united response.

Cutting across the chronic/acute dimension is the familiar precipitation/regulation distinction. The time-bomb view of prison riots fits neatly within the deprivation-model tradition, and so leads logically to the conclusion that riots arise largely through oppressive prison conditions – that is, when control is too hard. More recently, however, management-oriented perspective in corrections has suggested that riots occur because of a breakdown in prison administration (DiIulio, 1987, 1991a, 1991b). According to this perspective, riots occur in institutions in which security procedures have broken down – that is, when control is too soft. The strength of the disagreement among researchers on this issue is evident in DiIulio's (1991a) savage portrayal of the too-hard proponents:

> For years, leading sociologists have argued that the more prison officials do to crack down on inmate predators, to maintain tight security procedures, and to run things strictly by the book, the more likely it is that prison riots will occur. This theory has been based on selective interpretations of a few prison riots, and,

as both common sense and existing evidence make clear, it is demonstrably false. But its radically counterintuitive appeal has enshrined it for the last three decades as a piece of conventional sociological wisdom. Aunt Tessie would guess that a maximum security prison where inmates are frisked, cells are searched, crowds are dispersed, and contraband is controlled is far less likely to have a riot than one where security-conscious procedures are not followed on a routine basis; and, empirically she would be right. And Aunt Tessie has lived long enough to reckon that a prison run by a warden who is 'wet behind the ears' is more likely to be troubled than one with an experienced, no-nonsense administrator; and, again, the empirical record, so far as anyone can reconstruct it, would bear her out. (pp. 219–20)

However, the too-hard and too-soft positions are not necessarily irreconcilable. As DiIulio (1991a: 12) made clear, poor prison management does not just result in weak control, but also leads to poor prison conditions. Following DiIulio's analysis, Boin and Van Duin (1995: 363) made an important distinction between prison conditions and prison security. They proposed a 2×2 matrix for combining these two dimensions. Riot-safe institutions have good living conditions and high levels of institutional security, riot-prone institutions have poor living conditions and low levels of institutional security, while riot-vulnerable institutions are high on one dimension and low on the other. There are obvious parallels between Boin and Van Duin's two dimensions of prison control and the concepts of situational precipitators and regulators.

Riots differ from other forms of misbehaviour covered in this book in that they may span an extended period of time. Some consideration is warranted, therefore, of the behaviour of prisoners during a riot. Whether the actions of rioting prisoners are haphazard, expressive outpourings or 'rational' and instrumental responses to an intolerable situation is a matter of some debate (e.g. see Unseem and Kimball, 1989: 201–4). At first glance, once a riot is under way the behaviour of rioters might be seen as motiveless. The collapse of order and period of 'unrestrained violence and destruction' (Davies, 1991: 120) that follows the initial collective response can be understood as an example of deindividuated behaviour. The harrowing descriptions of prisoner behaviour in the New Mexico riot, for example, suggest a fundamental breakdown of internal control mechanisms. In that riot, prisoners engaged in horrific acts of brutality that included torturing other prisoners with blow-torches, mutilating corpses and in one case carrying around the severed head of a victim (Unseem and Kimball, 1989: 105–6). However, even in this extreme example there was a degree of purpose amongst the chaos. By and large attacks were restricted to specific inmates – those identified as 'snitches' – and the treatment of staff hostages varied according to their reputation among prisoners. Similarly, the damage to property was selective. For example, the office of the psychologist, who prisoners believed passed on confidential information to authorities, was one of the first areas to be destroyed, while the library, chapel and hobby shop were left untouched. The capacity for self-control may have been impaired but the behaviour seemed designed to prove a point. The behaviour of rioters gives some clue to the tensions that helped to produce the riot in the first place.

Situational context

SEASONAL VARIATIONS

Montgomery (1994: 230) reported that summer is the most likely time for riots, with 27 per cent taking place in July and August. March (4 per cent) and February (6 per cent) had the lowest incidence of rioting. Apart from effects of climate suggested in these figures, seasonal patterns might also reflect changes in institutional regime. For example, the riot at West Virginia Penitentiary on New Year's Day, 1986, is said to have been precipitated in part by the high level of staff absenteeism on that day (Unseem and Kimball, 1989: 178–9).

SECURITY LEVEL

Riots are more likely to occur in maximum or medium security than in minimum security (McCorkle *et al.*, 1995; Montgomery, 1994: 227). Montgomery reported that 56 per cent of riots were in maximum-security institutions. There were also more riots in institutions that have administrative segregation units. Montgomery argued that the existence of administrative segregation encouraged the overuse of punishment.

TIME AND LOCATION

Woolf and Tumin (1991: 349) found that the disturbances in British prisons during 1990 all occurred on weekends, and attributed this fact mainly to lower staffing levels and reduction in prisoner activities at this time. Beyond this observation, there seems to be no published research that provides a systematic breakdown of when and where riots are most likely to start. However, some flavour of the geography of riots may be gleaned from the collection of case studies presented by Unseem and Kimball (1989). The riot at Attica in 1971 began at 8.45 a.m., as a group of prisoners were being escorted from the dining area to an exercise yard (pp. 29–30). A fight with officers started in a passageway when the procession was stopped so that one of the prisoners could be taken back to the cells for an earlier infringement.

Trouble had been brewing for several days prior to the riot. A somewhat similar set of circumstances preceded the 1975 riot at Joliet (pp. 72–3). The disturbance at Joliet started at 12.30 p.m., again as prisoners were leaving the dining area, and when officers tried to remove a prisoner for transfer. Rumours about the impending transfer of this and several other prisoners had been circulating all that morning and followed a period of increasing unrest in the prison. The New Mexico riot in 1980 began at 1.30 a.m., when prisoners, acting on a plan hatched the previous evening during a home-made beer party, overpowered guards during a routine inspection of a dormitory (p. 101). The riot at the State Prison of Southern Michigan in 1981 was sparked by an unauthorised morning lock-down of prisoners, an action backed by the union but in defiance of orders issued by the administration (p. 133). Just before noon, a group of prisoners (kitchen crew) who had been left in one of the yards entered a cell block to find out why the prisoners had not been released for lunch. They took the keys from some guards (or in some accounts were given the keys in an act of industrial sabotage) and released the other prisoners. Finally, the 1986 riot at West Virginia Penitentiary began at 5.30 p.m. in the packed dining-room when about twenty inmates initiated a pre-planned attack, urging the others to join them (pp. 178–9).

Caution should be exercised, of course, in extrapolating from such a limited sample. Nevertheless, some trends are suggested. Only one riot started at night (New Mexico). In that case, there was a degree of planning and the selected time maximised the advantage of the prisoners. Three of the other cases occurred when large groups of prisoners were congregating (West Virginia) or moving from one location to another (Attica and Joliet). It may be no more than coincidence, but four of the riots occurred immediately before (Southern Michigan), during (West Virginia) or immediately after (Attica and Joliet) mealtimes.

Controlling collective disorder

The physical environment
PRISON AGE
Montgomery (1994: 228) reported that the frequency of prison riots increased with the age of the facility. Similarly, a number of case studies have identified prison age as a predisposing condition for rioting (Unseem and Kimball, 1989: 59–60, 163–4). Older prisons are associated both with substandard and depressing living conditions that might predispose prisoners to riot, as well as with antiquated designs and security systems that make it more difficult to monitor and regulate prisoners' behaviour.

Whether simply building new prisons will reduce riots, however, is debatable. DiIulio (1987: 84–6), while conceding that the 'physical structure may be a great ally or a great adversary in any attempt to establish and maintain orderly institutions' (p. 85), argued that architecture alone cannot account for differences in disturbance rates between institutions. Many old prisons do not have riots and many new ones do. DiIulio illustrated this point by comparing the records of major disturbance levels in three prison systems – Texas, California and Michigan. He argued that of the three systems Texas had the oldest institutions but traditionally the lowest rates of collective disturbance. Huntsville unit in Texas, for example, 'is the oldest prison in the system, one simply teeming with unsafe physical features', but also 'one of the system's most orderly higher-custody institutions' (p. 85). On the other hand, Michigan's Huron Valley Men's Facility has been plagued with major disturbances since its opening in 1981. DiIulio's point was that factors other than architecture – namely efficient administration and security-conscious staff – are the keys to controlling prison disturbances.

DiIulio may be right about the importance of prison management, but there are problems with his analysis of the role of prison architecture (and with his similar analyses of other prison features described in following sections). In the first place, identifying exceptions to a rule does not invalidate a general trend. The role of prison age is not determined by examining disturbance rates at the oldest or newest prison, but by examining the overall relationship between prison age and disturbance levels. Furthermore, examining any factor in isolation from other factors is problematic. The question is whether prison age has an effect over and above (i.e. adjusted for) other correlates of prison disturbance. For example, if all other things were equal, would the older Huntsville institution still have a better riot record than the newer Huron Valley facility?

FUNCTIONAL UNITS

Whether new-generation prisons (as distinct from new prisons) have fewer riots is a separate question. Unfortunately, evaluations of new-generation facilities have not specifically reported comparative data on collective disorder. However, the implication that new-generation prisons experience fewer riots can be inferred from more general research showing overall reductions in disorder in new-generation facilities (Farbstein and Wener, 1989; Wener *et al.*, 1987).

But things can go wrong. Nelson and Davis (1995) described at least one instance – at Rensselar County (New York) – where a riot occurred in a new-generation prison. In 1993, just two months after opening, the institution experienced serious disturbances in two general-population pods resulting in significant damage. According to Nelson and Davis, the problem was not so much a failure of unit management, but a failure to properly implement the principles of unit management. Pressure to open the institution early meant that preparations were inadequate. In particular, Nelson and Davis highlighted the lack of training in unit management received by all levels of staff, and the failure to assign permanent staff as unit officers.

PHYSICAL DESIGN DEFECTS

Some riots have occurred with the assistance of inherent design flaws or the failure to maintain security equipment. Unseem *et al.* (1996: 151–2) described a number of structural deficiencies that contributed to the riots they analysed: a prisoner was able to jimmy an electric lock with a screwdriver; the location of a transformer provided a hiding place for two prisoners; a control console's plateglass was not sufficiently reinforced to withstand an attack by prisoners; the interior walls of a high-security unit were made from non-reinforced blocks; and a large unsecured table in a security unit provided prisoners with a battering ram to gain access to the control centre. Montgomery (1997) provided a similar list. The Attica riot is reported to have spread because of a defective gate. The New Mexico riot took hold when prisoners gained access to the control centre by breaking the security glass. Woolf and Tumin (1991: 231–2) noted that the rooftop occupations at Bristol and Strangeways prisons in 1990 were accomplished because prisoners were able to bypass the roof-security measures. They also highlighted the fact that disturbances were able to spread more quickly because the same keys operated several sections of the prison (pp. 269–70). Woolf and Tumin recommended the use of electronic doors, and failing this that different keys be used for different units.

SECURITY FIREBREAKS

Woolf and Tumin (1991: 230–1) argued that there should be security firebreaks for staff in the initial stages of the riot. Provision needs to be made for staff to withdraw to a safe place at the first sign that control has been lost. Woolf and Tumin suggested that secure areas be created at the entrance to each unit and in areas where prisoners congregate. The firebreaks should have electronically controlled doors and should be strong enough to withstand prisoner attacks until support arrives.

PRISON LAYOUT

The physical layout of the prison can have significant implications for the subsequent shape of the riot and the options that authorities have in retaking the institution. Unseem and Kimball (1989: 213) contrasted the layouts of several riot-affected institutions and their role in the progress of the disturbance. The telegraph-pole design of New Mexico was blamed for helping to produce the disorganised nature of that riot. With no central meeting-place, there was little chance for prisoner unity and centralised control. In contrast, Attica prisoners congregated in one of the yards and were able to coordinate their actions. The prison layout also determined how well the actions of rioters could be monitored by authorities. The rioters at Southern Michigan were easily observed and so deterred from perpetrating violence, while at New Mexico rioting prisoners could not be seen and so had greater licence to engage in acts of barbarity.

Population characteristics

SIZE

Montgomery (1994: 228) reported that riot frequency increased with prison capacity. Of the riots examined in this study (1971–83), 82 per cent occurred in institutions with rated capacities of 300 prisoners or more. Examining the US Department of Justice census data between 1984 and 1990, McCorkle *et al.* (1995) found a significant positive correlation between institution size and frequency of riots, but this finding disappeared when size was adjusted for other institutional variables. That is to say, it seemed that other factors associated with prison size actually accounted for the effect.

CROWDING

Crowding is almost universally advanced as a crucial predisposing condition for riots (Adams and Campling, 1992: 199; Barak-Glantz, 1985: 53, 61; Lombardo, 1982: 79–80; Woolf and Tumin, 1991: 281–4). Direct empirical support for the role of crowding in rioting is less abundant. It is certainly true that many of the notorious riots – both Attica and New Mexico for example – have occurred in overcrowded institutions (Unseem and Kimball, 1989: 22, 86). But as the McKay Commission observed, these institutions were not distinguished in that regard – there were many equally overcrowded institutions that did not riot (New York State Special Commission on Attica, 1972).

DiIulio (1987: 74–6) compared crowding and riot levels for the Texas, California and Michigan prison systems between 1978 and 1984. Two indices of crowding were employed – population compared to capacity, and average living area (square feet per inmate). Over this time he found that Texas was invariably the most overcrowded of the three systems but had the lowest disorder rates. In addition, disorder within the Texas system increased at the same time that crowding levels decreased. Again, however, DiIulio's conclusions are limited by the methodological problems described earlier.

At a micro-level, a number of major riots have started in areas where prisoners have been congregating (Unseem and Kimball, 1989: 27–30, 101, 113, 179). In these cases, triggering incidents assumed greater importance than they otherwise might have. The immediate presence of a crowd greatly increased the likelihood of a collective response.

RACIAL COMPOSITION

Racial tensions have consistently been identified as a major cause of collective violence. Montgomery (1994: 231) claimed that 34 per cent of riots were racially motivated and case studies of riots have frequently identified racial tensions and gang activity as key causes. At Attica, the population breakdown was 55 per cent black, 36 per cent white, 9 per cent Puerto Rican and 5 per cent American Indian; at New Mexico the breakdown was 58 per cent Chicano, 30 per cent white, 10 per cent black and 2 per cent American Indian (Mahan, 1994: 256). Strategies for dealing generally with racial and gang tensions have been described in previous chapters. There is no specific empirical research that shows the effectiveness of these measures in stopping riots.

The prison regime

STAFF TRAINING

It might be expected that an educated and well-trained staff would be less likely to provoke prison disturbances and would be better prepared to deal with trouble should it begin (e.g. Woolf and Tumin, 1991: 351–6). Counterintuitively, the only available empirical research suggests that rioting increases with the educational levels and amount of training of staff (DiIulio, 1987: 76–84; Montgomery, 1994: 228). In explaining this finding, DiIulio drew the distinction between the amount of training that an officer receives and the content of that training. DiIulio examined the training offered by Texas, Michigan and California prison systems. He found that the level of training of prison guards was lowest in the Texas system that at the same time had the lowest disturbance levels. Texas had the lowest entry qualifications for staff, with a high-school diploma not required. In addition, Texas officers received only 80 hours of pre-service training, while Californian officers received 400 hours, and Michigan officers 640 hours. However,

DiIulio distinguished between formal pre-service training and on-the-job training. The Texas officers, he argued, learned their craft as 'apprentices' to more experienced operational officers. Their training was simple and security-oriented. Much of the training given to Michigan officers, in contrast, 'focused on topics such as race relations, human relations, working with people, due process, and theories of criminal justice' (p. 77). Again, DiIulio's agenda is clear – hands-on security is the key to maintaining order.

STAFF EXPERIENCE

An issue related to staff training is level of experience. Staff turnover is one way of inferring levels of experience. Using macro-level data, McCorkle *et al.* (1995) found that guard turnover was unrelated to rioting. Case studies of particular riots, however, have frequently identified staff inexperience as a contributory factor. In the case of New Mexico, annual staff turnover reached 80 per cent for the two years before the riot (Unseem and Kimball, 1989: 92). In addition, Unseem *et al.* (1996: 150–1) found that in several major riots staff inexperience or high absenteeism of regular staff were contributory causes.

STAFF–PRISONER RATIO

The supposed security advantages of high staff–inmate ratios have not been borne out in empirical research. McCorkle *et al.* (1995) found that staff–inmate ratios and increases in staff–inmate ratios were unrelated to rioting. DiIulio (1987: 76), comparing the Texas, California and Michigan prison systems found that levels of rioting *decreased* as staff–inmate ratios decreased – that fewer staff were associated with a lower incidence of rioting. Furthermore, within each system rioting levels over time decreased as staff–inmate ratios decreased. Of course, DiIulio's point in highlighting these findings was not that security does not matter, but that simply increasing the staff–inmate ratio does not guarantee better security. It is more important to look at what staff members actually do than simply how many there are.

STAFF RACIAL COMPOSITION

DiIulio (1987: 93–4) found little evidence that the racial composition of staff contributed to racial tensions within institutions that might precipitate rioting. The staff racial composition in California, Texas and Michigan were all overwhelmingly white. However, through affirmative-action policies the discrepancy between prisoner and staff racial composition is less in California and Michigan than in Texas. As has been already described, however, Texas had the lowest level of prisoner disturbance.

INMATE–STAFF RELATIONS

The relations between inmates and staff prior to a riot appear to fall into one of two categories. Either there is a history of repressive treatment of prisoners and great hostility towards staff, or the authority of staff has disintegrated and they are treated with contempt by the prisoners.

The New Mexico riot is an example of the first category. Based on interviews with prisoners, Unseem and Kimball (1989: 90–8) describe the brutal treatment of prisoners by guards prior to the riot. Prisoners complained that the guards 'talk to you like you're a dog' (p. 96). In one incident after a non-violent work strike (protesting over cuts to programmes) prisoners were stripped and forced to run a gauntlet of axe-handle wielding guards. Particularly hated by prisoners was the 'snitch system'. This was a method of control that involved coercing prisoners to inform on one another. Providing information was rewarded with better housing and work assignments and favourable parole reports. However, prisoners who refused to cooperate with the system might be punished or be maliciously labelled a snitch. The snitches, of course, were the primary targets of prisoner violence when the riot ultimately occurred.

On the other hand, the conditions conducive to rioting may be caused by a lack of guard authority (DiIulio, 1987; Ekland-Olson, 1986; Unseem and Kimball, 1989). Unseem and Kimball (1989: 66–71) put prisoner–staff relations at Joliet in this category. It has been argued that the weakening of guard authority is one of the unintended consequences of prison reform. Ekland-Olson (1986) illustrated this point by analysing the riots that coincided with the implementation of decisions of the Ruiz trial that ended the building-tender system in Texas prisons (outlined in chapters 5 and 7). As a result of the Ruiz trial a special master was appointed to oversee the court-mandated changes (changes to disciplinary procedures, increased staff–prisoner ratios and a cessation of the use of prisoners in administrative/control capacities). Ekland-Olson contended that the presence in the prisons of the powerful outsiders in the form of monitors from the special master's office resulted in a redistribution of institutional power. According to Ekland-Olson, guards felt that their authority was compromised and prisoners were emboldened by what they perceived as official support for their actions. The effect of implementing the court-mandated changes on individual-level attacks on staff has been described in chapter 7. However, there was also a significant rise in levels of collective violence. In the five years prior to the trial collective disturbances occurred on average every 568 days; after the appointment of the special master there were disturbances every sixteen days.

The key to staff–prisoner relations, a number of authors have contended (Bottoms *et al.*, 1995; Sparks *et al.*, 1996; Unseem and Kimball, 1989: 227–31), is legitimacy. Legitimacy refers to the acknowledgement by prisoners that authorities have a right to exercise control. In order to establish legitimacy authorities must themselves demonstrate an adherence to rules, procedures and externally validated standards of behaviour (Unseem and Kimball, 1989: 231). Prisoners must feel that they are treated fairly, equally and consistently (New York State Special Commission on Attica, 1972: xix). The belief that guards are exercising illegitimate control is likely to incite frustration and defiance.

SECURITY PROTOCOLS

In many cases inquiries after major riots identify breakdowns in security procedures that contributed to the riot. The precise nature of these lapses, of course, varies from case to case. Unseem *et al.* (1996: 151) highlighted the failure to provide staff with written updated post orders. In the riots they analysed, new staff typically learned the specialised routine in the high-security unit through observing or asking existing staff. A specific example described by Unseem *et al.* was the failure to specify to staff which keys should and should not be carried in the high-security area. As a consequence, an officer carrying keys to cell doors was taken hostage and prisoners could be released to join the riot. Woolf and Tumin (1991: 230) also commented on the stealing of keys from officers in the series of British riots they examined, and recommended that the practice of officers carrying keys attached to their uniform be reviewed. Montgomery (1997) claimed that the New Mexico riot spread because a practice had developed among officers not to lock security grills during the night.

CONTROLLING CONTRABAND

Stolen, smuggled and homemade weapons used in riots obviously increases the likelihood that prisoners and guards will be injured or killed. Woolf and Tumin (1991: 231), for example, noted that prisoners at Bristol and Pucklechurch used stolen Works Department tools to bypass security systems. In addition, a number of riots seemed to have been sparked by prisoners gaining access to drugs or alcohol. According to Unseem and Kimball (1989: 101), plans for the New Mexico riot were formulated when a group of prisoners were drinking homemade alcohol. Montgomery (1997) described a riot in a juvenile institution for females that began after inmates sniffed nail-polish remover. Regular drug testing, increased searches, the use of metal detectors and restrictions on the ingredients for home-brews were common methods of clamping down on contraband (see chapter 9). In opportunity-reduction terms these strategies may be labelled as controlling facilitators.

GENERAL PRISON CONDITIONS

Prisoner demands issued during riots and evidence given at inquiries after riots almost always highlight poor prison conditions as a contributing cause of riots (Adams and Campling, 1992: 117–29; Mahan, 1994: 261; Nagle, 1978: 44–8; New York State Special Commission on Attica, 1972: 31–102; Unseem and Kimball, 1989: 242–4, 248–9; Woolf and Tumin, 1991: 391–401). The list of complaints typically include poor food, inadequate pay, institutional-quality clothing, too few or badly run visits and censorship of correspondence. Accordingly, most inquiries into prison disturbances have recommended that attention be given to improving prison conditions and that relevant standards of treatment of prisoners be strictly enforced.

PROGRAMME AVAILABILITY

Idleness is frequently argued to be a foundation cause of rioting (Mahan, 1994: 259; Montgomery, 1994: 228; Woolf and Tumin, 1991: 382–91). There is some empirical support for the proposed ameliorating effects of programming. Montgomery reported that there were 10 per cent fewer riots in medium- and minimum-security institutions that provided meaningful work compared with medium- and minimum-security institutions that did not. Similarly, there is a further 10 per cent reduction in rioting in institutions in which inmates feel they have active recreational programmes. However, McCorkle *et al.* (1995) did not find a relationship between inmate programme participation and level of collective disorder.

DiIulio (1987: 88–93) argued that the type of programme offered to prisoners was important. Again comparing Texas, California and Michigan prison systems, he highlighted the advantages of the Texan emphasis on productive industries, basic education and vocational training (as opposed to mere time-filling activities). He also criticised the policy in California and Michigan that allowed treatment and educational programmes to substitute for prison employment rather than requiring prisoners to fulfil work obligations in the first instance.

PRISONER TRANSFERS

In their report on the series of prison disturbances in Britain during 1990, Woolf and Tumin (1991: 227) noted that in all cases the precipitating incidents involved recently transferred prisoners. They argued that transfers are stressful events for prisoners, and that a rapid turnover of prisoners works against the creation of a stable and predictable environment. Moreover, when prisoners are repeatedly transferred against their will, and are given no satisfactory explanation for the transfer, they become resentful at the perceived unfairness of their treatment. Vaag (1994: 252) further noted that using the transfer of the ringleaders of a disturbance in one institution in an attempt to regain control can also backfire. These individuals can act as carriers of discontent and have been known to incite unrest in their new institution. Woolf and Tumin (1991: 319) recommended that transfers be used sparingly and that transfers should not be used as a form of punishment. Where transfers are essential the prisoner should be told the reasons for the transfer as soon as possible.

GRIEVANCE MECHANISMS

To the extent that riots are expressions of political protest by prisoners, the discontent and sense of injustice that motivates rioting prisoners may be reduced by the provision of formal avenues of complaint (Adams and Campling, 1992; 232; Davies, 1991: 122; Dillingham and Montgomery, 1985: 37). It is difficult to show empirically that grievance mechanisms will reduce collective disorder. However, some support for the benefits of improved communication between prisoners and authorities was presented by Montgomery (1994: 228). He found that riots increased as the amount of contact time between the warden and inmates decreased. There was a 15 per cent lower incidence of rioting in institutions in which the warden spent twenty-five hours or more per month in direct contact with inmates.

MEDIA MANAGEMENT

Though the media are not strictly part of the prison regime, the way that prison administrators handle the media is an important consideration once a riot has begun. Mahan and Lawrence (1996) examined the news reporting of three major riots – Attica (in 1971), New Mexico (in 1980) and Lucasville (in 1993). In each case the media were shown to be active participants in the unfolding drama, not just passive observers. The prisoners were able to monitor media coverage, which meant that the reporting of the riot itself affected the way that the riot proceeded.

There were a number of ways that the media influenced the behaviour of the prisoners in the course of the riots. First, observing themselves in the media 'gave the inmates a sense of importance, dignity and power'. Suddenly, the rioters found themselves thrust into the limelight. Media coverage provided the prisoners with social rewards in the form of recognition and enhanced status. One implication of this is that it quickly became in the interests of rioters to prolong the disturbance and keep the issue in the news. It was also claimed that the presence of television cameras encouraged prisoners to engage in rhetorical displays rather than serious negotiation.

Second, the media provided a forum for presenting the rioters' demands. The rioters saw the media coverage as a crucial way to expose prison conditions. Moreover, media coverage was welcomed because of the scrutiny it placed on the official response to the riot, and for the degree of immunity from reprisal it was likely to provide. In the Lucasville riot prisoners displayed banners proclaiming 'We want the media.' In the case of the New Mexico riot, reporters actually became involved in negotiations with prisoners. At one point a hostage was released in return for television coverage of prisoners voicing their demands. Thus, not only did prisoners receive social reinforcement from seeing their behaviour reported, they also recognised the prospect of tangible benefits that the media presence offered.

Third, the media have provided prisoners with information and misinformation about the progress of the riot and the thoughts and tactics of the authorities. In several cases this was shown to have escalated the trouble. For example, in the Attica riot a false media report that a hostage had been thrown from a window inflamed hostilities towards the authorities, who were perceived by the rioters to be using the media to discredit them. In the Lucasville riot, the media reported that a prison official dismissed rioters' threats to kill hostages. The rioters observed this report and it is claimed that as a result a hostage was killed to prove that the rioters were serious.

Based on these analyses, Mahan and Lawrence listed several recommendations concerning the role of the media during riots:

- By naming individuals, the media give credit and strength to what they are doing. By making their methods public, the media may be encouraging imitation. By publicising what rioters say, the media help them accomplish what they want.
- If media coverage is part of the demands, it should be done in as limited a manner as possible, involving as few people as possible.
- Rioters should not be portrayed as heroes.
- The point should be made that no hostage situation has been successful.
- Direct calls to the rioters should be avoided because they tend to draw out the process.
- Site coverage should be limited because it gives away intelligence information to the rioters.

- Keep airtime in proportion to the objective news value of the act.
- Give documentaries and analyses on the problems facing the system and even access to the media for the voices of reason among dissident groups, thereby reducing the likelihood of their resorting to violence to have their grievances heard. (1996: 435–6)

USE OF FORCE

One of the most contentious questions once a riot is under way is if and when to use force to regain control. Montgomery (1994: 235) indicated that around three-quarters of riots were ended by force or a show of force. Debate about the advisability of using force has often taken place in the context of a post-riot autopsy and has been set within a broader question about the preparedness of authorities for the riot. In many cases prisons have been found not to have a riot plan and/or an appropriately trained riot-response team. The response of authorities to riots have often been found to be *ad hoc*, inadequate and in some case to have escalated the disturbance (Boin and Van Duin, 1995: 365–8; Unseem and Kimball, 1989: 210–11; Unseem *et al.*, 1996: 158–61).

The use of overwhelming force is most likely to be recommended in the very early stages of a riot when prisoners are poorly organised and the disturbance is contained (Davies, 1991: 122; Unseem *et al.*, 1996: 170–4). The corrections' literature contains numerous testimonials to the role played by the swift and decisive actions of staff 'nipping in the bud' potential riots (Brown, 1994; Karacki, 1989; Ogborn, 1993; Spertzel, 1993; Stahl, 1993). Similarly there are other cases where it has been argued that the failure to take immediate decisive action permitted a riot to develop (although it is a matter of conjecture, of course, just how successful such action would have been). Unseem and Kimball (1989: 29) claimed that a lockdown at Attica at the first sign of trouble might have at least 'forestalled the explosion'.

Less certain is the role of force at later stages in the riot. While an assault on the institution has the capacity to bring a riot to a quick end, it is a risky alternative. There is a danger that the assault team may be overpowered and have their weapons seized. If there are hostages, prisoners may become enraged and begin killing. There are many examples of successful interventions by trained riot squads retaking riot-torn institutions (Unseem *et al.* 1996: 170–3). Equally, however, there are examples where the assault has gone wrong. For example, Attica was the bloodiest riot in US history, and most of the deaths, including those of the hostages, were caused by the assault force retaking the institution (Unseem and Kimball, 1989: 54–8). As Unseem *et al.* (1996: 170) also pointed out, the use of force at Attica did not appear to act as a deterrent to future rioting and hostage-taking. The following year (1972) had more prison riots than any previous year.

Conclusions

Riots may vary from the collective defiance of three prisoners who cause minimal injuries and property damage to the wholesale rebellion of an entire prison population which results in hundreds of injuries, many deaths and the destruction of the institution. Not unnaturally, most research attention has been paid to the relatively few riots at the serious end of the scale. This has meant that the information about the causes and prevention of riots has come principally from retrospective case studies and official inquiries. The small number of serious cases generally precludes correlational analyses and certainly rules out pre-test/post-test experimental designs. The problem with a case-study approach, of course, is hindsight bias. In reconstructing events it is easy to impose cause and effect relationships in the process of fashioning a plausible narrative. For example, if a riot occurs in an institution that has notoriously bad food it is tempting to conclude that these events must be linked. Moreover, even if it could be firmly established that poor food was indeed a causative factor in a particular case, it remains uncertain how generalisable the finding would be. How many institutions that have bad food did not have riots? Perhaps even more than other categories of misbehaviour that have been discussed, much of the analysis of prison riots relies on interpretation and many of the prevention strategies suggested in the literature fall into the category of informed opinion. The best of these strategies are summarised in table 11.1.

The division between hard and soft positions on control has become particularly entrenched in the case of collective disorder. The advent of the management perspective in corrections (DiIulio, 1987, 1991a, 1991b) has challenged the dominant social science wisdom that prison riots occur in institutions that are overcontrolled. In fact, this chapter has revealed examples both of riots under draconian regimes (e.g. New Mexico) and riots under lackadaisical regimes (e.g. Joliet). Clearly, neither extreme is desirable. Moreover, hard and soft control ought not to be treated as unidimensional constructs. While there is a tendency to think of hard and soft control in polar terms, elements of each are able to – must – coexist in the same institution. As Unseem and Kimball (1989) warned:

Table 11.1. *Summary of promising strategies for control of collective disorder*

Strategy	Precipitation-control category	Regulation-control category
New facilities	Reducing frustration Controlling environmental irritants	Target hardening Formal surveillance
Functional units	Setting positive expectations Rule setting Personalising victims Controlling environmental irritants	Formal surveillance Natural surveillance
Equipment maintenance		Target hardening
Security firebreaks		Target hardening
Open lay-out		Formal surveillance Natural surveillance
Small prison size	Reducing anonymity Personalising victims	
Reduced population density	Reducing crowding	
Reduced prisoner congregation	Reducing anonymity Reducing crowding	Deflecting offenders
Race-homogeneous or race-balanced populations	Reducing inappropriate imitation Reducing inappropriate conformity	
Increased staff experience	Encouraging compliance	Formal surveillance Increasing costs
Improving staff–prisoner relations	Reducing frustration	
Supporting staff authority		Increasing costs
Security protocols		Target hardening Formal surveillance
Controlling contraband		Controlling facilitators
Humane prison conditions	Increasing victim-worth Reducing frustration	
Prison programmes/work	Reducing frustrations Clarifying responsibility	Deflecting offenders
'Fair' prisoner transfers	Encouraging compliance Reducing frustration	
Grievance mechanisms	Encouraging compliance Reducing frustrations	
Media management	Reducing inappropriate imitation	Denying benefits
Use of force		Increasing costs

It must be stressed that 'good administration' means much more here than military discipline. It also refers to the provision of programming, work, cell space, and the amenities of life, to a reasonably legitimate standard. Any administrator who takes our finding as warrant for the belief that firm enough discipline in a given prison can prevent a riot, regardless of how flagrantly unconstitutional the conditions are, is taking a chance.   (pp. 227–8)

CHAPTER 12

Conclusions: hard and soft situational prison control

The analysis of situational prison control undertaken in this book has been based on the following assumptions:

1 A great deal of prison disorder is a function of characteristics of the prison environment
2 The environmental forces acting upon prisoners can both generate misbehaviour and provide the opportunities that allow misbehaviour to occur
3 Prison disorder can be prevented by changing the prison environment in ways that reduce the propensity of prisoners to misbehave and make misbehaviour more difficult to perform
4 Prevention attempts that fail to address adequately the environmental factors that both generate and allow misbehaviour are likely to be ineffective and may even increase disorder.

These assumptions were formulated into a two-stage model of prison control. The model was tested against the available situational research on seven specific kinds of prison misbehaviour – prisoner-prisoner violence, sexual assaults, prisoner-staff violence, self-harm, drug use, escapes and collective disorder. The purpose of this concluding chapter is to assess the contributions that a situational perspective can bring to an understanding of prison disorder and its control and, more specifically, to consider the overall utility of the proposed model in accounting for the data.

Is situational prison control necessary?

The point has been made that prison control necessarily involves situational elements. Both hard and soft prison control have existed long before the articulation of situational crime prevention as a criminological model. The question might be asked, then, how does a situational approach differ from existing conceptions of control? More pointedly, is a situational approach really necessary?

Situational control versus traditional approaches

Traditional approaches to prison control – strategies evident in first- and second-generation prisons and in the control model of prison management – bear many similarities to the opportunity-reduction model (the basis of the controlling regulators stage in the present model). The basic approach in both cases is to make misbehaviour more difficult, risky or costly by tightening security, improving surveillance and enforcing rules and regulations. However, despite the similarities in the respective approaches, there are important differences in the conceptualisation and implementation of control strategies.

At a conceptual level, a crucial difference between traditional prison control and situational control based on opportunity-reduction is the assumption each makes about the essential malleability of behaviour. Prison regimes have typically been based on an importation model that holds that prison misbehaviour is an expression of the inherent antisocial disposition of prisoners. As a consequence of this view, the control tactics employed in traditional prison regimes are generally at the heavy-handed, target-hardening end of the opportunity-reduction spectrum. The control task is conceived simply in terms of physically restraining determinedly violent and uncooperative individuals from carrying out their intended transgressions.

On the other hand, the opportunity-reduction approach is located within the situational tradition. Notwithstanding the fact that opportunity-reduction may involve physically constraining potential offenders, the rational choice perspective upon which the logic of opportunity-reduction is based offers a much wider range of interventions. According to rational choice perspective, misbehaviour is not an inherent and fixed response pattern confined to a select group of antisocial individuals. The potential to perform illegal acts is widely distributed. Whether or not an individual engages in any behaviour is governed by the ongoing assessment he/she makes of the perceived costs and benefits. Manipulating situational costs and benefits does not necessarily require physically constraining behaviour but may simply involve making that behaviour a less attractive option. Sometimes simply making a behaviour inconvenient will be enough to deter potential offenders.

A second important feature of the opportunity-reduction approach is its problem-solving nature. Despite the apparent obsession in prisons with opportunity-reduction, closer inspection reveals that often the approach to control is a broad, scattergun affair that takes little account of the various motivations for misbehaviour. Typically, prison disorder is seen in fairly global terms and as an institution-wide problem. Against this, opportunity-reduction is at its best when it adopts a behaviour-specific, micro-level focus. Just as in the general community there are hot spots of crime, so too in the prison problem events are not uniformly distributed but tend to concentrate around particular points in time and space. Moreover, opportunity-reduction interventions depend upon an understanding of what it is the prisoner is hoping to gain from his/her misbehaviour, since altering the perceived costs and benefits of behaviour is the key to prevention. By taking a systematic approach to prison control in this way, opportunity-reduction need not involve particularly draconian measures.

Only a handful of studies reviewed in this book have analysed prison control explicitly within an opportunity-reduction framework (e.g. Atlas, 1982, 1983; Bottoms *et al.*, 1995; Clarke, 1980, 1987; La Vigne, 1994; O'Donnell and Edgar, 1996; Sparks *et al.*, 1996). These studies, however, give some indication of the possibilities for more effective prison control that a problem-based approach can yield. La Vigne's (1994) report on the introduction of a computerised phone system on Rikers Island is a good example. Before the introduction of the computerised system, Rikers Island experienced high levels of illicit phone calls by prisoners that created security concerns and resulted in significant financial costs. In addition, fights and even murders occurred as prisoners battled for control over this lucrative commodity. The new telephone system required PIN access and automatically cut off calls after six minutes. There was an immediate reduction in telephone abuse and a 50 per cent reduction in inmate violence associated with phone use, with little evidence of displacement to other forms of violence. There are a number of things to note from this study. In the first place, the intervention tackled a very precise problem. The target of the intervention (albeit a secondary target) was not prisoner violence in general, or even prisoner-prisoner assaults in general, but prisoner-prisoner assaults specifically associated with phone use. Second, the intervention itself involved relatively small-scale changes to a particular aspect of the prison environment. The implementation of the new system was relatively inexpensive and in fact proved to be less costly than retaining the previous system. Third, the intervention could not be considered draconian, and it ultimately benefited most prisoners. The success of the intervention in reducing prisoner-prisoner assaults depended upon manipulating the motivations for violence. The solution to the problem turned out not to involve an increase in security to detect and punish assaulters, but simply neutralising the benefits of violence. Finally, unlike security crackdowns, the intervention provided a permanent solution to the problem, one that did not require ongoing staff commitment and vigilance.

Situational control versus the deprivation model

If controlling regulators has parallels with traditional hard methods of control, then controlling precipitators may be seen as overlapping attempts to gain control by normalising the prison environments. The theoretical rationale for normalcy was in turn provided by the deprivation model.

Following the work of Sykes and his contemporaries in the 1950s and 1960s, social-scientific analysis of prison disorder focused on the role of the prison social structure and the deprivations or pains of imprisonment. Sykes (1958: 63–83), in his classic work *Society of Captives*, listed five deprivations of imprisonment – deprivations of liberty, goods and services, heterosexual relationships, autonomy and security. Superficially these deprivations can be described in physical terms, but far more important were the psychological and social consequences attending on each deprivation. Thus, deprivation of liberty refers not only to the physical separation of the prisoner from society but also to the sense of isolation and alienation caused by a loss of social acceptance. Deprivation of goods and services is not just inconvenient but, in a culture where assessments of worth are bound up in material possession, challenges the prisoner's concept of personal adequacy. Likewise, deprivation of heterosexual relationships involves both frustrations associated with the physiological aspects of sexual abstinence as well as the psychological effects that separation from the opposite sex has on prisoners' sense of their masculinity (Sykes did not speculate on the effects on female prisoners) and feelings of sexual adequacy. Deprivation of autonomy refers to the requirement to conform to institutional rules and restrictions, and to the indignity and sense of powerlessness felt at having to depend upon guards for basic needs. Finally, deprivation of security refers to the anxiety caused by the ever-presence of danger from other prisoners but, more so, to the prisoners' nagging self-doubt whether they possess the necessary courage and inner resources if an attack did come.

In a similar vein, Goffman (1961: 23–72) described the techniques of control and the process of institutionalisation in total institutions such as prisons. The process typically begins with admission procedures that mark the inmates' departure from civil life and entry into the institutional world. These procedures may include washing, shaving, confiscation of personal belongings and the issue of inferior replacements, the compilation of a personal dossier and so on. The effect is a symbolic loss of identity – the mortification of the self. The mortification process is reinforced by the on-going institutional regimen. Staff and inmates use non-mutual forms of address that emphasise the subservience of the latter to the former. Privacy – both physical and psychological – is routinely violated. The inmate must endure constant contaminate exposure – literally by having to live in an enclosed and unsanitary environment and metaphorically by being forced into close interpersonal contact with strangers. There is the humiliation of being seen in degrading circumstances by visiting friends and family: the list goes on. The point that both Goffman and Sykes make is that the psychological indignities and assault on the self that institutional life nec-essarily entails are far more profound than the superficial lack of physical comfort.

According to the deprivation model, the harshness of the prison regime forces prisoners to band together for psychological self-preservation. A prisoner subculture is formed with its own code of conduct and social organisation. Prisoner society is characterised by its direct repudiation of conventional values and its demands on members to maintain solidarity against institutional authority. The interpretation of the effects of depriva-tion offered by Sykes, Goffman and other theorists of the era places the analysis very much within a sociological-cum-psychodynamic (rather than situational) framework. They viewed prison disorder as the product of a deviant subculture, which in turn was created to resolve the deep psychic trauma associated with the pains of imprisonment. Thus, the prison envi-ronment and prison disorder were seen as twice removed. Disorder is not a direct product of the prison environment but the result of the fundamental changes to the prisoner's personality and the negativistic subculture that the environment has created.

The solution to prison disorder that is suggested by this analysis is to fundamentally change the coercive nature of the prison regime. Sykes (1958: 78–83) cautioned that simply softening and humanising the prison environment would not of itself eliminate the behaviour problems of pris-oners. Reforms must specifically address the deep psychological pain caused by the deprivations of imprisonment and through this alter the social or-ganisation of prisoners from which the disorder emanates.

Bottoms *et al.* (1995) were explicit in drawing the distinction between the cultural-mediational approach to tackling prison disorder and situa-tional control. They linked subcultural interventions in prison with social crime prevention. Social crime prevention, they argued, seeks to prevent crime through social policies and community action (improved education, housing, recreation facilities and so forth) that help to change the values and social relationships of potential offenders. Bottoms *et al.* illustrated the difference between this and situational prevention (or, more specifically, opportunity-reduction) by contrasting parents who prevent their children from stealing by not leaving loose change lying about (situational prevention) on the one hand, with parents who prevent their children from stealing by teaching them that stealing is wrong (social prevention) on the other. A clear difference between social prevention and situational prevention, then, is that the former is assumed to effect permanent changes in the individual that will militate against him or her committing crime in locations away from the place of intervention.

According to Bottoms *et al.* prison regimes that minimise the deprivations of imprisonment – supply the necessities of life, foster links with family and friends outside the prison, allow a degree of autonomy, involve fair and consistent application of rules – are more likely to receive legitimisation from prisoners. This increased legitimisation in turn results in a more cooperative relationship between prisoners and staff and through this a reduction in social disorder. A more specific example of these changed social relationships occurs in therapeutic units. One of the key features of unit living is the development of community. In the unit community prisoners learn strategies of cooperation, ways of coping with frustration, improved verbal fluency and new non-criminal values. The improvement in their behaviour is the result of this new repertoire of social skills.

However, the necessity to resort to the concept of social crime prevention to explain these effects is debatable. The changes that Bottoms *et al.* describe can also be explained in situational terms. The sorts of interventions that they advocate involve the modification of immediate environmental forces acting upon the prisoner. In this analysis, there is a direct (rather than pschodynamically or culturally mediated) causal relationship between the pains of imprisonment and prisoner misbehaviour. Disorder is viewed as a more-or-less immediate reaction to the psychological pressures of prison life. The process by which these pressures manifest in disorder may be explained by situational concepts such as expectancy, frustration-aggression, cognitive disengagement, deindividuation and environmental stress. Functional-unit living, for example, reduces the incidence of aberrant behaviour because prisoners have more satisfying levels of autonomy, are better able to meet privacy needs, live in more physically pleasant surroundings, know those around them on personal terms and are treated with the expectation that they will not misbehave.

Even Bottoms *et al.* conceded that at least some of the control benefits of a less coercive environment might be attributed to situational factors. Their preference for an interpretation in terms of social prevention is based on the contention that changes to the prison regime have long-term effects on the values and behaviours of prisoners over and above an immediate situational impact. Graduates of therapeutic units, they argue, take away newly acquired social skills that they can apply in their future interpersonal dealings. A situational analysis depends upon no such claim. It is simply enough that the behaviour of prisoners is modified while they are exposed to the normalised prison conditions. Given the notorious lack of evidence for the long-term therapeutic efficacy of any prison intervention (e.g. Martinson, 1974), the situational alternative would seem the more parsimonious of the two interpretations.

The utility of the two-stage model

The two-stage model was proposed as a way of integrating the opposing arguments that disorder is generated by prison conditions on the one hand, and that it is simply permitted by prison conditions on the other. Precipitating and regulating forces are linked in the model in a temporal chain. According to the model, behaviour is first initiated by situational conditions, and only then does the consideration of opportunity come into play. In the case of self-harm, for example, prison conditions may contribute to the feelings of despair that then motivates prisoners to seek out methods of carrying out the behaviour. Similarly, the opportunity to escape from prison often is not acted upon unless other situational factors first make escape a desirable option. In some cases the sequencing of situational influences was found to be less obvious, giving the appearance of two distinct patterns of behaviour. For example, some prisoner-prisoner assaults seemed to be largely expressive in nature while others seemed largely instrumental. Prisoners engaging in expressive assaults showed little concern for whether they were being observed while those carrying out instrumental attacks did not seem to be responding to any particular situational provocation. These cases are still consistent with the model, however. There is no requirement that the relative contributions of precipitating and regulating influences need to be constant for all behaviours.

In general, the two-stage model provided a useful basis from which to examine situational prison control. Three aspects of the model are reviewed here – the categorisation of interventions, the integration of hard and soft methods of control and possible tensions between hard and soft control.

Labelling interventions

As with any classification system, the distinctions among categories are not always clear-cut and in some cases when applying the model it was a matter of debate where particular interventions most appropriately belonged. In the first place, it is acknowledged that there is some degree of conceptual overlap among categories in the model. Because the model was constructed by combining diverse theoretical perspectives, in some cases similar processes are described in different terms. For example, the idea that individuals minimise self-disapproval for actions carried out while a member of a group is covered by the concept of deindividuation and the corresponding strategy to reduce anonymity (emphasising the social elements), and by the concept of cognitive disengagement and the strategy to clarify responsibility (emphasising the cognitive elements).

A second problem occurred when there was more than one plausible explanation for the efficacy of a particular intervention. For example, while the effects of crowding are usually explained in terms of the environmental-stress model (categorised under reducing provocations), it could also be argued that crowded environments increase feelings of anonymity (reducing anonymity) and add to the depersonalisation of other prisoners (personalising victims).

A third difficulty arose when a single intervention involved multiple facets and so combined several rationales. Unit management is the best example of this. Typically, unit management is understood to include a softer physical environment (setting positive expectations and controlling environmental irritants), intimate prisoner groups (reducing anonymity), clear, strictly enforced rules (rule setting and removing privileges) and direct supervision by staff (formal surveillance). It is generally not possible and perhaps not even valid to isolate individual elements.

Similarly, in other cases a cluster of distinct interventions was introduced in an omnibus fashion. A security crackdown, for example, might simultaneously involve increasing patrols (formal surveillance), increasing time in cells (target hardening) and transferring trouble-makers (reducing inappropriate conformity). Again, to the extent that such an approach is successful, it is not possible to determine the relative importance of the contributing measures.

Finally, there were cases where the nature of an intervention varied depending upon the behaviour in question. For example, the provision of single-cell accommodation may reduce assaults because of the reductions in social density (reducing crowding). In the case of sexual assault, single cells are best conceptualised as providing the opportunity for potential victims to protect themselves (target hardening). In the case of preventing self-harm single cells are contra-indicated since they reduce the capacity for natural surveillance.

Hard and soft control

The problem associated with labelling interventions occurred mainly at the fine-grained levels of the model. The broad distinction made between precipitating and regulating situational forces was rather more robust. For all seven behaviours examined there was evidence that the prison environment variously promoted and permitted disorder. Similarly, there were examples of successful interventions aimed at alleviating pressures on prisoners to misbehave and at reducing opportunities for prisoners to misbehave.

This distinction between the precipitation and regulation of prison disorder, of course, is far from new (although the terminology has varied). Indeed, debate about prison control (at least for the past forty years) has largely revolved around the question of whether prisoner misbehaviour is reactive or purposive, and whether, therefore, control requires the easing or tightening of prison conditions. Too often, however, the debate has involved proponents for each side taking polarised positions. Two separate views of prison disorder have been presented and a choice has been required between two very different control solutions. The assumption made in the present model is that both views of prison disorder are valid and both approaches to control are necessary. The relationship between hard and soft control is shown in figure 12.1.

As figure 12.1 shows, there is no implication that one form of intervention is necessarily superior to the other. Whether precipitation-control or opportunity-reduction is appropriate will depend upon an analysis of the particular circumstances. Undoubtedly there are predatory prisoners who enter situations already determined to misbehave and ready to exploit any perceived security weakness. In these cases, the control emphasis will be on opportunity-reduction strategies. By the same token, some precipitating events may be so powerful as to override any meaningful cost-benefit analysis by the prisoner. Extremely frustrated individuals, for example, may lash out with little regard to the immediate consequences of their behaviour. In these cases, frustration-reduction strategies are likely to be more important than attempts to constrain behaviour. The issue for prison control is not a choice between precipitation-control and opportunity-reduction. Rather, the task is to find the appropriate balance between these interventions.

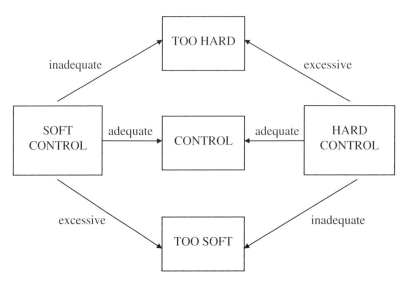

Figure 12.1 Balance between hard and soft control

How then are the control of precipitators and the control of regulators to be simultaneously effected in a prison environment? In fact, these two approaches to prison control are not as contradictory as they might at first appear. In the first place, while the terms 'hard' and 'soft' prison control have been used as a convenient way to broadly characterise the nature of the respective interventions, these labels oversimplify the case. Not all attempts to control precipitators involve softening or liberalising the prison environment. Age-heterogeneous institutions, for example, can reduce prison violence by providing young prisoners with mature models. Similarly, many efforts to control regulators do not involve hardening the prison environment or tightening the regime. For example, the double bunking of depressed prisoners is designed to reduce their opportunities to inflict self-harm.

Moreover, even when hard and soft seem appropriate labels for the methods of control, often the respective interventions are directed at different situational domains. Principal targets for soft control have been the physical and social characteristics of the prison. Pleasant physical surroundings, the provision of good food, the division of prisoners into small social groups and uncrowded institutions were all found at various points in the previous chapters to be related to low levels of disorder. A major focus of hard control, on the other hand, has been the prison regime. Increased surveillance, security crackdowns, highly trained staff and consistent discipline were also found to be effective methods of prison control. Looked at in this way, hard and soft control need not be incompatible. Good prison conditions and effective prison security are largely separate institutional dimensions (Boin and Van Duin, 1995). DiIulio (1991a: 12) has gone even further, arguing that good prison conditions can only be guaranteed through strong, effective security.

A number of authors have taken up this theme of marrying hard and soft approaches to control. Clarke (1980) advocated an approach to prisoners that was 'kind but strict' (p. 118). Similarly, Wooden and Parker (1982) talked about the ideal correctional officer as one who was 'kindly authoritarian' (p. 212). In practice, all prisons employ a combination of precipitation-control and opportunity-reduction techniques. Most administrators of traditional prisons, for example, recognise the dangers of deliberately provoking tensions through employing excessively repressive measures and neglecting basic prisoner needs. Similarly, even the most liberal prisons necessarily restrict prisoners in various ways, including the most basic restriction of not letting prisoners leave whenever they please. Unit management is a good example of the explicit reliance on both precipitation-control and opportunity-reduction. Functional units not only provide a less stressful living environment for prisoners, they also afford an increased-level surveillance for staff through the architectural layout and the close prisoner–guard interaction. Similarly, many units have strict and rigidly applied rules of behaviour and non-compliant prisoners are liable to be quickly expelled.

Hard or soft control

Nevertheless, there are certainly instances when controlling precipitators and controlling regulators involve contradictory logics and the possibility of counterproductive control needs to be considered. Throughout the reviews in the previous chapters, quite divergent approaches to the same problem were frequently encountered. For example:

- Is vandalism best controlled by using domestic-quality furnishings or vandal-proof furnishings?
- Should suicide-risk prisoners be under constant surveillance or should they be allowed a degree of privacy?
- Are prison officers safer when they have direct contact with prisoners or when they are separated from them?
- Are riots less likely in institutions that allow some degree of inmate self-government or in institutions that are firmly controlled by staff?

- Does permitting consensual homosexuality in prison reduce the likelihood of rape or does it encourage it?
- Do women correctional officers reduce tension in an institution or are they weak links in the institution's security?

Plausible arguments could be made in support of most of the strategies listed above. Unfortunately, the available research is not much help trying to decide between the hard and soft alternatives. While there is plenty of evidence of contradictory approaches to the same behaviour problem, there is far less direct evidence that particular interventions are counterproductive. In fact, where there is research, findings sometimes support both alternatives. For example, vandalism does seem to reduce in new-generation prisons (Wener *et al.*, 1987), but so too can it be reduced by opportunity-reduction methods (Graham, 1981).

Just because two strategies are contradictory, then, does not necessarily mean that one must be counterproductive. It does not even mean that one strategy must be wrong – both may be effective. Within limits, a degree of dualism is quite consistent with the proposed model. The model holds that most behaviours are subject to both precipitating and regulating forces. For any given behaviour, intervention may be successful at either stage, even if the interventions are contradictory. The issue of counterproductive control arises when administrators err too far in either direction – when control is *too* hard or *too* soft.

There were some examples in the literature where the limits of precipitation-control and regulation-control were clearly exceeded. The breakdown of control in some functional units illustrates the dangers of ceding too much unconditional liberty to prisoners (Nelson and Davis, 1994). The problem in these cases was a failure to properly resource the units. Staff was given inadequate training and support. In the absence of strong and consistent leadership by the guards, prisoners exploited the freedoms they were given to take control. On the other hand, the New Mexico riot is a classic example of the explosive consequences of brutal treatment and a crushing regime (Unseem and Kimball, 1989: 86–98).

How, then, is the balance between hard and soft control to be determined? While there is no easy answer to this question, a number of general principles for the exercise of control were discussed. Control methods that are perceived as unnecessarily manipulative, those that incite frustration and anger and those that do not show respect for human dignity run the risk of encouraging disorder rather than controlling it. At the same time, restrictions on freedom of choice do not always lead to reactance, the blocking of goal-directed behaviour is not always frustrating and physical deprivations are not necessarily dehumanising. Prisoners are more likely to accept prison controls if they perceive those controls to be fair, consistent, equitable and justifiable.

Some authors have used legitimacy as an overarching term to describe these features of prison control (Bottoms *et al.* 1995; Sparks *et al.*, 1996; Unseem and Kimball, 1989). Bottoms *et al.* (1995) talked about legitimacy as a component of social prevention. They used the term in a global sense, referring to the legitimacy given to the prison regime as a whole by prisoners. However, legitimacy can also be used in a situational sense to refer to authority of a particular person or to the appropriateness of a particular intervention. Through their individual behaviour, guards earn personal legitimacy. Similarly, the enforcement of some rules might be seen as legitimate while the enforcement of others may not.

Legitimacy is a guide to both soft and hard control. On the one hand, Bottoms *et al.* (1995) argued that legitimate controls allow administrators to use less restrictive practices. Prisoners adhere to legitimate prison rules because they accept the lawfulness and fairness of those rules, not because they are compelled to do so. On the other hand, prisoners will also accept a greater level of control if that control is perceived as legitimate. The enforcement of rules, the issuing of punishments and the loss of physical comforts are not of themselves counterproductive control measures. Prison by its very nature involves a loss of personal freedom and physical comfort. It is not possible or perhaps even desirable to eliminate stresses and frustrations from the prison environment. All human beings as they go about their daily lives face and must learn to cope with situations that are not as they would wish. Likewise, prisoners should – and for the most part do – tolerate legitimate controls over their behaviour.

Conclusions: 'more research needed'

It has become something of a cliché to end academic works with the cry that 'more research is needed'. Be that as it may, such a call is warranted in the present case. Overall, empirical research on situational-related prison control is of indifferent quality and often conflicting in its conclusions. While there is a great deal written on the topic of prison control, much of this comprises informed opinion, theoretical speculation and mere assertion. The empirical studies that have been conducted have generally involved correlational data. Very few studies have employed pre- and post-test designs, used comparison groups or adequately controlled for extraneous influences.

Almost none of the research was conceived with a situational perspective in mind and issues important for situational control have generally been ignored. There is a particular paucity of microanalyses of disorder and the prison environment.

In some cases the lack of research is especially surprising. For example, hard empirical support for the supposed control advantages of new-generation prisons – often touted as the single most important advance in prison management of the twentieth century – is relatively rare. Almost all of the studies conducted on new-generation prisons have examined perceptions of levels of violence, feelings of safety, patterns of social inter-action and so forth. The few studies that have looked at actual behaviours of inmates and staff have either not provided a basis for comparison (e.g. Wener *et al.*, 1987) or have not shown that comparison of institutions are otherwise equivalent (e.g. Senese *et al.*, 1992). Claims made about the stress-reducing effects of soft architecture (pastel colours, noise-absorbing surfaces, subdued lighting and so on) continue to be justified with reference to (dated) laboratory research (Farbstein *et al.*, 1979).

The other noteworthy gap in the research concerns recent technological advances in corrections. Modern prisons are being transformed by the use of new construction materials and electronic aids such as centralised control centres, electronic doors, CCTV and infra-red sensors. Yet this headlong rush to embrace technology is taking place in the absence of any real evidence concerning the impact of these innovations on prisoner misbehaviour. With the exception of La Vigne's (1994) study on the computerised telephone system at Rikers Island, the literature search conducted for this book did not locate a single empirical study that examined the behavioural outcomes of the introduction of new technology. The only available information on the subject is in the form of technical reports by security experts and surveys of how extensively various technologies are used (Atkinson *et al.* 1999; Rowan, 1990; Travis *et al.*, 1989; US Department of Justice, 1995, 1999). The use of CCTV in corrections' literature illustrates the point. According to Travis *et al.* (1989) over half of recently opened correctional institutions had CCTV installed, and a survey by the US Department of Justice indicated that most administrators (86 per cent) are satisfied or very satisfied with their per-formance. Yet there is no available evidence to show whether or not CCTV achieves the outcomes intended for it. Even the most basic information – whether or not the introduction of CCTV in an institution reduces assault rates – is unavailable.

The problem for situational prison control, as with situational crime pre-vention, is that it is too easily dismissed as involving no more than common sense. Basic research on prison control has probably been ignored precisely because it is considered too basic. However, there is enough research on prison control to show that nothing should be taken for granted. In some cases, well-established articles of faith have turned out to have little empirical support (assumptions about the detrimental effects of large prisons, for example). Because of the gaps in the research, a number of the propositions contained in the two-stage model remain for the time being at least plausible but untested hypotheses. This book cannot claim to be the definitive word on situational prison control but hopefully may encourage further research in the area.

References

Abru, E. 1999, 'Drugs behind bars', *NSW Police News* 79: 18–19.

Adams, K., Bennett, K.L., Flanagan, T.J., Marquart, J.W., Cuvelier, S.J., Fritsch, E., Gerber, J., Longmire, D.R. and Burton, V.S. 1994, 'A large-scale multidimensional test of the effect of prison educational programs on offenders' behavior', *Prison Journal* 74: 433–49.

Adams, R. and Campling, J. 1992, *Prison Riots in Britain and the USA*, London, Macmillan.

Adams, V. 1981, 'How to keep 'em honest: Honesty as an organizational policy can help prevent employee theft', *Psychology Today* November: 50, 53.

Akers, R.L., Krohn, M.D., Lanza-Kaduce, L. and Radosevich, M. 1979, 'Social learning and deviant behavior: A specific test of a general theory', *American Sociological Review* 44: 636–55.

Almy, L., Bravo, V., Burd, L., Chin, P., Cohan, L., Gallo, F., Giorgianni, A., Gold, J., Jose, M. and Noyes, J. 1980, 'A study of a coeducational correctional facility', in J.O. Smykla (ed.), *Coed Prison*, New York, Human Sciences Press, pp. 120–49.

Alpert, G.P. 1984, 'The needs of the judiciary and misapplication of social research', *Criminology: An Interdisciplinary Journal* 22: 441–56.

Altheide, K.K., Adler, P.A., Adler, P. and Altheide, D. A. 1978, 'The social meaning of employee theft', in J.M. Johnson and J.D. Douglas (eds.), *Crime at the Top: Deviance in Business and the Professions*, Philadelphia PA, J.B. Lippincott, pp. 90–124.

Altman, I. 1975, *The Environment and Social Behavior*, Monterey CA, Brooks/Cole.

American Correctional Association 1981, *Standards for Adult. Correctional Institutions*, College Park MD, American Correctional Association.

American Society for Industrial Security 1979, 'A low profile jail', *Security Management* 23: 46.

Anderson, C.A. 1987, 'Temperature and aggression: Effects on quarterly, yearly and city rates of violent and non-violent crime', *Journal of Personality and Social Psychology* 52: 1161–73.

Anno, B.J. 1985, 'Patterns of suicide in the Texas Department of Corrections, 1980–1985', *Journal of Prison and Jail Health* 5: 82–93.

Asch, S.E. 1955, 'Opinions and social pressure', *Scientific American* November: 31–5.

Atkinson, D.J., Pietrasiewicz, V.J. and Junker, K.E. 1999, *Video Surveillance Equipment Selection and Application Guide* (NIJ Guide 201–99), Washington DC, National Institute of Justice.

Atlas, R. 1982, 'Violence in Prison: Architectural Determinism', Unpublished doctoral thesis, School of Criminology, Florida State University.

1983, 'Crime site selection for assaults in four Florida prisons', *Prison Journal* 63: 59–72.

1984, 'Violence in prison. Environmental influences', *Environment and Behavior* 16: 275–306.

1989, 'Reducing the opportunity for inmate suicide: A design guide', *Psychiatric Quarterly* 60: 161–71.

Atlas, R.I. and Dunham, R.G. 1990, 'Changes in prison facilities as a function of correctional philosophy', in J.W. Murphy and J.E. Dison (eds.), *Are Prisons Any Better? Twenty Years of Correctional Reform*, Newbury Park CA, Sage, pp. 43–59.

Backett, S.A. 1987, 'Suicides in Scottish prisons', *British Journal of Psychiatry* 151: 218–21.

Bandura, A. 1965, 'Influence of models' reinforcement contingencies on the acquisition of imitative responses', *Journal of Personality and Social Psychology* 1: 589–95.

1976, 'Social learning analysis of aggression', in E. Ribes-Inesta and A. Bandura (eds.), *Analysis of Delinquency and Aggression*, Hillsdale NJ, Erlbaum, pp. 203–32.

1977, *Social-Learning Theory*, Englewood Cliffs NJ, Prentice-Hall.

Bandura, A., Barbaranelli, C., Capara, G.V. and Pastorelli, C. 1996, 'Mechanisms of moral disengagement in the exercise of moral agency', *Journal of Personality and Social Psychology* 71: 364–74.

Bandura, A., Underwood, B. and Fromson, M.E. 1975, 'Disinhibition of aggression through diffusion of responsibility and dehumanization of victims', *Journal of Research in Personality* 9: 253–69.

Banks, C., Mayhew, P. and Sapford, R.J. 1975, *Absconding from Open Prisons*, London, HMSO.

Banzinger, G. and Owens, K. 1978, 'Geophysical variables and behavior: Weather factors as predictors of local social indicators of maladaptation in two non-urban areas', *Psychological Reports* 43: 427–34.

Barak-Glantz, I.L. 1985, 'The anatomy of another prison riot', in M. Braswell, S. Dillingham and R. Montgomery (eds.), *Prison Violence in America*, Cincinnati OH, Anderson, pp. 47–71.

Baron, R.A. and Bell, P.A. 1975, 'Aggression and heat: Mediating effects of prior provocation and exposure to an aggressive model', *Journal of Personality and Social Psychology* 31: 825–32.

Bartollas, C., Miller, S.J. and Dinitz, S. 1982, 'The "booty bandit": A social role in a juvenile institution', in A.M. Scacco (ed.), *Male Rape: A Casebook of Sexual Aggression*, New York, AMS Press, pp. 153–62.

Baum, A., Singer, J.E. and Baum, C.S. 1981, 'Stress and the environment', *Journal of Social Issues* 37: 4–35.

Baum, A. and Valins, S. 1977, *Architecture and Social Behavior: Psychological Studies of Social Density*, Hillsdale NJ, Erlbaum.

Bayens, G.J., Williams, J.J. and Smykla, J.O. 1997, 'Jail type and inmate behavior: A longitudinal analysis', *Federal Probation* 61: 54–62.

Bell, P.A. and Barron, R.A. 1977, 'Aggression and ambient temperature: The facilitating and inhibiting effects of hot and cold environments', *Bulletin for the Psychonomic Society* 9: 443–5.

Bell, P.A., Baum, A., Fisher, J.D. and Greene, T.E. 1990, *Environmental Psychology* (3rd edn), Fort Worth TX, Holt, Rinehart and Winston.

Bennett, T. and Sibbitt, R. 2000, *Drug Use Among Arrestees* (Research Findings No. 119), London, Home Office Research, Development and Statistics Directorate.

Benton, F.W. and Obenland, R. 1973, *Prison and Jail Security*, Washington DC, National Clearinghouse for Criminal Justice Planning and Architecture.

Berkowitz, L. 1983, 'The experience of anger as a parallel process in the display of impulsive, "angry" aggression', in R.G. Green and E.I. Donnerstein (eds.), *Aggression: Theoretical and Empirical Reviews* (Vol. 1), New York, Academic Press, pp. 103–33.

——— 1989, 'The frustration aggression response: Examination and reformulation', *Psychological Bulletin* 106: 59–73.

Bertam, S. and Gorta, A. 1990, *Inmates' Perceptions of the Role of the New South Wales Methadone Programme in Preventing the Spread of Immumo-Deficiency Virus. Evaluation of the NSW Prison Methadone Programme: Study 9*, Sydney, NSW Department of Corrective Services.

Biles, D., McDonald, D. and Fleming, J. 1992, 'Australian deaths in prison 1980–88: An analysis of Aboriginal and non-Aboriginal deaths', in D. Biles and D. McDonald (eds.), *Deaths in Custody Australia, 1980–1989*, Canberra, Australian Institute of Criminology, pp. 107–36.

Binda, H. 1975, 'Effects of increased security on prison violence', *Journal of Criminal Justice* 3: 33–45.

Bird, A.G., Gore, S.M., Hutchinson, S.J., Lewis, S.C., Cameron, S. and Burns, S. 1997, 'Harm reduction measures and injecting inside prison versus mandatory drug testing: Results of a cross sectional anonymous questionnaire survey', *British Medical Journal* 314: 21–24.

Bloomberg, S.A. 1977, 'Participatory management: Towards a science of correctional management', *Criminology* 15: 149–63.

Boin, R.A. and Van Duin, M.J. 1995, 'Prison riots as organizational failures: A managerial perspective', *Prison Journal* 75: 357–79.

Bottoms, A.E. 1990, 'Crime prevention facing the 1990s', *Policing and Society* 1: 3–22.

Bottoms, A.E., Hay, W. and Sparks, J.R. 1995, 'Situational and social approaches to the prevention of disorder in long-term prisons', in T.J. Flanagan (ed.), *Long-Term Imprisonment*, Thousand Oaks CA, Sage, pp. 186–96.

Bowker, L. H. 1980, *Prison Victimization*, New York, Elsevier.

——— 1982, 'Victimizers and victims in American correctional institutions', in R. Johnson and H. Toch (eds.), *The Pains of Imprisonment*, Beverly Hills CA, Sage, pp. 63–76.

——— 1985, 'An essay on prison violence', in M. Braswell, S. Dillingham and R. Montgomery (eds.), *Prison Violence in America*, Cincinnati OH, Anderson, pp. 7–17.

Brehm, J.W. 1966, *A Theory of Psychological Reactance*, New York, Academic Press.

Brodsky, S.L. and Fowler, R.D. (1979), 'The social psychological consequences of confinement', in L.R. Abt and I.R. Stuart (eds.), *Social Psychology and Discretionary Law*, New York, Van Nostrand Reinhold, pp. 260–9.

Brown, B.J., Druce, N.R. and Sawyer, C.E. 1978, 'Individual differences and absconding behaviour', *British Journal of Criminology* 18: 62–70.

Brown, B.S. and Spevacek, J.D. 1971, 'Disciplinary offenses and offenders at two differing correctional institutions', *Corrective Psychiatry and Journal of Social Therapy* 17: 48–56.

Brown, K.A. 1994, 'California officers quell prison melee, prevent widespread injury', *Corrections Today* 56: 22.

Buchanan, R.A., Unger, C.A. and Whitlow, K.L. 1988, *Disruptive Maximum Security Inmate Management Guide*, Washington DC, National Institute of Corrections.

Calhoun, J.B. 1962, 'Population density and social pathology', *Scientific American* 206: 139–48.

California Department of Corrections 1991, *Suicide Prevention in the California Department of Corrections: Annual Report – 1990*, Sacramento CA, California Department of Corrections.

1994, *Suicide Prevention in the California Department of Corrections: Annual Report – 1993*, Sacramento CA, California Department of Corrections.

Camp, G. and Camp, C. 1987, *Stopping Escapes: Perimeter Security*, Washington DC, National Institute of Justice Construction Bulletin.

Campbell, C.F. 1980, 'Co-corrections: FCI Fort Worth after three years', in J.O. Smykla (ed.), *Coed Prison*, New York, Human Sciences Press, pp. 83–109.

Carbonell, J.L., Megargee, E.I. and Moorhead, K.M. 1985, 'Predicting prison adjustment with structured personality inventories', *Journal of Consulting and Clinical Psychology* 52: 280–94.

Carlson, B.E. and Cervera, N.J. 1991, 'Inmates and their families: Conjugal visits, family contact, and family functioning', *Criminal Justice and Behavior* 18: 318–31.

Carroll, L. 1982, 'Humanitarian reform and biracial sexual assault in a maximum security prison', in M. Scacco (ed.), *Male Rape*, New York, AMS Press, pp. 121–34.

Carter, J.O. 1963, 'Absconding at Dover Borstal', *Prison Service Journal* July.

Centre for Research, Evaluation and Social Assessment 1996, *Escape Pressures. Inside Views of the Reasons for Prison Escapes*, Wellington NZ, Ministry of Justice.

Cherrington, D.J. and Cherrington, J.O. 1985, 'The climate of honesty in retail stores', in W. Terris (ed.), *Employee Theft: Research, Theory, and Applications*, Park Ridge IL, London House, pp. 27–39.

Chonco, N.R. 1989, 'Sexual assaults among male inmates: A descriptive study', *Prison Journal* 69: 72–82.

Clark, J.B. and Hollinger, R.C. 1983, *Theft by Employees in Work Organizations*, Washington DC, US Department of Justice.

Clarke, R.V. 1980, 'Absconding from residential institutions for young offenders', in L. Hersov and I. Berg (eds.), *Out of School*, Chichester England, Wiley, pp. 111–36.

1987, 'Rational choice theory and prison psychology', in B.J. McGurk, D.M. Thornton and M. Williams (eds.), *Applying Psychology to Imprisonment*, London, HMSO, pp. 117–27.

1992, 'Introduction', in R.V Clarke (ed.), *Situational Crime Prevention: Successful Case Studies*, Albany NY, Harrow and Heston, pp. 3–36.

1995, 'Opportunity-reducing crime prevention strategies and the role of motivation', in P.O. Wikstrom, R.V. Clarke and J. McCord (eds.), *Integrating Crime Prevention Strategies: Propensity and Opportunity*, Stockholm, National Council for Crime Prevention, pp. 55–67.

1997, 'Introduction', in R.V. Clarke (ed.), *Situational Crime Prevention: Successful Case Studies* (2nd edn), Albany NY, Harrow and Heston, pp. 2–43.

Clarke, R.V. and Homel, R. 1997, 'A revised classification of situational crime prevention techniques', in S.P. Lab (ed.), *Crime Prevention at the Crossroads*, Cincinnati OH, Anderson, pp. 17–27.

Clarke, R.V. and Martin, D.N. 1975, 'A study of absconding and its implications for the residential treatment of delinquents', in J. Tizzard, I.A. Sinclair and R.V. Clarke (eds.), *Varieties of Residential Experience*, London, Routledge and Kegan Paul, pp. 249–74.

Clarke, R.V. and Mayhew, P.M. 1988, 'The British gas suicide story and its criminological implications', in M. Tonry and N. Morris (eds.), *Crime and Justice* (Vol. 10), Chicago, University of Chicago Press, pp. 79–116.

Clear, T.R. 1994, *Harm in American Penology*, Albany NY, State University of New York Press.

Cohen, F. and King, K. 1987, 'Drug testing and corrections', *Criminal Law Bulletin* March-April: 151–72.

Colman, A. 1991, 'Psychological evidence in South African murder trials', *The Psychologist* November: 482–6.

Cooke, D.J. 1991, 'Violence in prisons: The influence of regime factors', *Howard Journal* 30: 95–109.

Cooley, D. 1993, 'Criminal victimization in male federal prisons', *Canadian Journal of Criminology* 35: 479–95.

Cornish, D.B. and Clarke, R.V. 1975, *Residential Treatment and its Effects on Delinquency* (Home Office Research Study No. 32), London, HMSO.

1987, 'Understanding crime displacement: An application of rational choice theory', *Criminology* 25: 933–47.

Cornish, D.B. and Clarke, R.V. (eds.) 1986, *The Reasoning Criminal. Rational Choice Perspectives on Offending*, New York, Springer-Verlag.

Correctional Service of Canada 1981, *Self-Inflicted Injuries and Suicides*, Ottawa, Bureau of Management Consulting.

Correctional Service of Canada 1989, *Contraband Control Final Report* (Vol. 1), Canada, Correctional Service of Canada.

Cotton, D.J. and Groth, A.N. 1984, 'Sexual assault in correctional institutions: Prevention and intervention', in I.R. Stuart and J.G. Greer (eds.), *Victims of Sexual Aggression: Treatment of Children, Women, and Men*, New York, Van Nostrand Reinhold, pp. 127–55.

Cotton, J.L. 1986, 'Ambient temperature and violent crime', *Journal of Applied Social Psychology* 16: 786–801.

Cox, V.C., Paulus, P.B. and McCain, G. 1984, 'Prison crowding research: The relevance for prison housing standards and a general approach regarding crowding phenomena', *American Psychologist* 39: 1148–60.

Coyle, A.G. 1987, 'The Scottish experience with small units', in A.E. Bottoms and R. Light (eds.), *Problems of Long-Term Imprisonment*, Aldershot, Gower, pp. 228–48.

Crouch, B.M. 1985, 'Pandora's box: Women guards in men's prisons', *Journal of Criminal Justice* 13: 535–48.

Czerniak, S.W. and Upchurch, J.R. 1996, 'Continuous improvement in prison security', *Corrections Today* 58: 62–3.

Dalton, V., Brown, N. and McDonald, D. 1996, *Australian Deaths in Custody and Custody-Related Police Operations, 1995*, Canberra, Australian Institute of Criminology.

Darke, S., Kaye, S. and Finlay-Jones, R. 1998, 'Drug use and injection risk-taking among prison methadone maintenance patients', *Addiction* 93: 1169–75.

Davies, W. 1991, 'Prison riots', *The Psychologist* March: 120–2.

Davies, W. and Burgess, P.W. 1988, 'Prison officers' experience as a predictor of risk of attack: An analysis within the British prison system', *Medicine, Science and the Law* 28: 135–8.

Davis, A.J. 1968, 'Sexual assaults in the Philadelphia prison system and sheriff's vans', *Trans-action* December: 8–16.

Dean, L.M., Pugh, W.M. and Gunderson, E.K. 1978, 'The behavioral effects of crowding: Definitions and methods', *Environment and Behavior* 10: 413–31.

Diener, E. 1980, 'Deindividuation: The absence of self-awareness and self-regulation in group members', in P. Paulus (ed.), *The Psychology of Group Influence*, Hillsdale NJ, Lawrence Erlbaum, pp. 209–42.

Dietz, P.E. and Rada, R.T. 1983, 'Interpersonal violence in forensic facilities', in J.R. Lion and W.H. Reid (eds.), *Assaults within Psychiatric Facilities*, New York: Grune and Stratton, pp. 47–59.

DiIulio, J.J. 1987, *Governing Prisons*, New York, Free Press.

1991a, *No Escape: The Future of American Corrections*, New York, Basic Books.

1991b, 'Understanding prisons: The new old penology', *Law and Social Inquiry* 16: 65–99.

Dillingham, S.D. and Montgomery, R.H. 1985, 'Prison riots: A correctional nightmare since 1774', in M. Braswell, S. Dillingham and R. Montgomery (eds.), *Prison Violence in America*, Cincinnati OH, Anderson, pp. 19–38.

Ditchfield, J. 1990, *Control in Prisons: A Review of the Literature* (Home Office Research Study No.118), London, HMSO.

Ditchfield, J. and Harries, R. 1996, 'Assaults on staff in male local prisons and remand centres', *Home Office Research and Statistics Directorate Research Bulletin* 38: 15–20.

Dobinson, I. and Ward, P. 1986, 'Heroin and property crime: An Australian perspective', *Journal of Drug Issues* 16: 249–62.

Dolan, K.A., Wodak, A.D. and Hall W.D. 1998, 'Methadone maintenance treatment reduces heroin injection in New South Wales prisons', *Drug and Alcohol Review* 17: 153–8.

Dollard, J., Doob, L.W., Miller, N.E., Mowrer, O.H and Sears, R.R. 1939, *Frustration and Aggression*, New Haven CT, Yale University Press.

Donaldson, S. 1995, 'Can we put an end to inmate rape?', *USA Today* May: 40–3.

Dooley, E. 1990, 'Non-natural deaths in prison', *British Journal of Criminology* 30: 229–34.

Dumond, R.W. 1992, 'The sexual assault of male inmates in incarcerated settings', *International Journal of the Sociology of Law* 20: 135–57.

Duncan, D.F. and Ellis, T.R. 1973, 'Situational variables associated with prison escapes', *American Journal of Correction* May-June: 29–30.

Dunlop, A.B. 1974, *The Approved School Experience* (Home Office Research Study No. 25), London, HMSO.

Edgar, K. and O'Donnell, I. 1998a, 'Assault in prison', *British Journal of Criminology* 38: 635–50.

1998b, *Mandatory Drug Testing in Prisons: The Relationship between MDT and the Level and Nature of Drug Misuse* (Home Office Research Study 189), London, HMSO.

Edwards, A., Curtis, S. and Sherrard, J. 1999, 'Survey of risk behaviour and HIV prevalence in an English prison', *International Journal of STD and AIDS* 10: 464–6.

Eigenberg, H.M. 1994, 'Rape in male prisons: Examining the relationship between correctional officers' attitudes towards male rape and their willingness to respond to acts of rape', in M.C. Braswell, R.H. Montgomery and L.X. Lombardo (eds.), *Prison Violence in America* (2nd edn), Cincinnati OH, Anderson, pp. 145–65.

Ekland-Olson, S. 1986, 'Crowding, social control, and prison violence: Evidence from the post-Ruiz years in Texas', *Law and Society Review* 20: 389–421.

Ekland-Olson, S., Barrick, D. and Cohen, L.E. 1983, 'Prison overcrowding and disciplinary problems: An analysis of the Texas prison system', *Journal of Applied Behavioral Science* 19: 163–76.

Ellis, D. 1984, 'Crowding and prison violence: Integration of research and theory', *Criminal Justice and Behavior* 11: 277–308.

Ellis, D., Grasmick, H.G. and Gilman, B. 1974, 'Violence in prison: A sociological analysis', *American Journal of Sociology* 80: 16–43.

Ellis, J. 1993, 'Security officer's role in reducing inmate problem behaviors', *Journal of Offender Rehabilitation* 20: 61–72.

Engel, K and Rothman, S. 1984, 'The paradox of prison reform: Rehabilitation, prisoners' rights, and violence', *Harvard Journal of Law and Public Policy* 7: 413–42.

Fairweather, L. 1994, 'Prison design in the twentieth century', in I. Spens (ed.), *Architecture of Incarceration*, London, Academy Editions, pp. 24–37.

Farbstein, J., Liebert, D. and Sigurdson, H. 1996, *Audits of Direct-Supervision Jails*, Washington DC, US Department of Justice.

Farbstein, J. and Wener, R. 1989, *A Comparison of 'Direct' and 'Indirect' Supervision Correctional Facilities, Final Report*, Washington DC, US Department of Justice.

Farbstein, J., Wener, R. and Gomez, P. 1979, *Evaluation of Correctional Environments*, Washington DC, US Department of Justice.

Farley, F.H. and Farley, S.V. 1972, 'Stimulus-seeking motivation and delinquent behavior among institutionalized delinquent girls', *Journal of Consulting and Clinical Psychology* 39: 94–7.

Farmer, J.F. 1988, 'A case study in regaining control of a violent state prison', *Federal Probation* 52: 41–7.

Farrington, D.F. and Nuttall, C.P. 1980, 'Prison size, overcrowding, prison violence, and recidivism', *Journal of Criminal Justice* 8: 221–31.

Felson, M. and Clarke, R.V. 1997, 'The ethics of situational crime prevention', in G. Newman, R.V. Clarke and S.G. Shohan (eds.), *Rational Choice and Situational Crime Prevention*, Aldershot, Ashgate Publishing, pp. 197–218.

Fine, B.J. and Kobrick, J.L. 1987, 'Effect of heat and chemical protective clothing on cognitive performance', *Aviation, Space, and Environmental Medicine* 58: 149–54.

Fitzgerald, G. 1989, *Commission of Inquiry into Possible Illegal Activities and Associated Police Misconduct*, Brisbane, Queensland Government Printer.

Fleisher, M.S. and Rison, R.H. 1999, 'Gang management in corrections', in P.M. Carlson and J.S. Garrett (eds.), *Prison and Jail Administration: Practice and Theory*, Gaithersburg MD, Aspen Publishers, pp. 232–8.

Fleming, J., McDonald, D. and Biles, D. 1992, 'Self-inflicted harm in custody', in D. Biles and D. McDonald (eds.), *Deaths in Custody Australia, 1980–1989*, Canberra, Australian Institute of Criminology, pp. 381–416.

Florida Department of Corrections 1981, *Evaluation of Uniform System of Inmate Custody Classification*, Tallahassee FL, Florida Department of Corrections.

Forst, M.L. and Brady, J.M. 1985, 'The effects of determinate sentencing on inmate misconduct in prison', in M. Braswell, S. Dillingham and R. Montgomery (eds.), *Prison Violence in America*, Cincinnati OH, Anderson, pp. 97–111.

Forsyth, D.R. 1990, *Group Dynamics* (2nd edn), Pacific Grove CA, Brooks/Cole.

Fox, V. 1971, 'Why prisoners riot', *Federal Probation* 35: 9–14.

French, L. 1978, 'The perversion of incarceration: A social-psychological perspective', *Corrective and Social Psychiatry and Journal of Behavior Technology, Methods and Therapy* 24: 16–19.

Frey, J.H. and Delaney, T. 1996, 'The role of leisure participation in prison: A report from consumers', *Journal of Offender Rehabilitation* 23: 79–89.

Fry, L.J. 1988, 'Continuities in the determination of prison overcrowding effects', *Journal of Criminal Justice* 16: 231–40.

Gaes, G.G. 1985, 'The effects of crowding in prison', in M. Tonry and N. Morris (eds.), *Crime and Justice: An Annual Review of Research* (Vol. 6), Chicago, University of Chicago Press, pp. 95–146.

1994, 'Prison crowding research reexamined', *Prison Journal* 74: 329–63.

Gaes, G.G. and McGuire, W.J. 1985, 'Prison violence: The contribution of crowding versus other determinants of prison assault rates', *Journal of Research in Crime and Delinquency* 22: 41–65.

Galle, O.R., Gove, W.R. and McPherson, J. 1972, 'Population density and pathology: What are the relations for man?', *Science* 176: 23–30.

Ganjavi, O., Scell, B. and Cachon, J. 1985, 'Geophysical variables and behavior: Impact of atmospheric conditions on occurrences of individual violence among Canadian penitentiary populations', *Perceptual and Motor Skills* 61: 259–75.

Garland, D. 1996, 'The limits of the sovereign state: Strategies of crime control in contemporary society', *British Journal of Criminology* 36: 445–71.

Geller, E.S., Koltuniak, T.A. and Shilling, J.S. 1983, 'Response avoiding prompting: A cost-effective strategy for theft deterrence', *Behavioral Counseling and Community Interventions* 3: 28–42.

Gendreau, P., Ross, R. and Izzo, R. 1985, 'Institutional misconduct: The effects of the UVIC program at Matsqui Penitentiary', *Canadian Journal of Criminology* 27: 209–17.

Gerber, J. and Fritsch, E. J. 1995, 'Adult academic and vocational correctional educational programs: A review of recent research', *Journal of Offender Rehabilitation* 22: 119–42.

Goffman, E. 1961, *Asylums*, Garden City NY, Anchor Books.

Goodstein, L., MacKenzie, D.L. and Shotland, R.L. 1984, 'Personal control and inmate adjustment to prison', *Criminology: An Interdisciplinary Journal* 22: 343–69.

Goranson, R.E. and King, D. 1970, *Rioting and Daily Temperature: Analysis of the U.S. Riots in 1967*, Toronto, York University.

Gore, S.M., Bird, A.G. and Ross, A. J. 1995, 'Prison rites: Starting to inject inside', *British Medical Journal* 311: 1135–6.

Gorta, A. and Nguyen Da Huong, M.T. 1988, *An Analysis of Interviews with Recaptured Escapees: Some Suggestions of Reasons for Escape*, Sydney, NSW Department of Corrective Services.

Gorta, A. and Sillavan, T. 1991, 'Escapes from New South Wales gaols', *Australian and New Zealand Journal of Criminology* 24: 204–18.

Gould, M.S. and Shäffer, D. 1989, 'The impact of suicide in television movies. Evidence of imitation', in R.F W. Diekstra, R. Maris, S. Platt, A. Schmidtke and G. Sonneck (eds.), *Suicide and its Prevention*, New York, E. J. Brill, pp. 331–40.

Gove, W.R., Hughs, M. and Galle, O.R. 1977, 'Overcrowding in the home: An empirical investigation of its possible pathological consequences', *American Sociological Review* 44: 59–80.

Government of Victoria 1993, *Inquiry into the Victorian Prison System*, Melbourne, L.V. North Government Printer.

Graham, F. 1981, 'Probability of detection and institutional vandalism', *British Journal of Criminology* 21: 361–5.

Graham, K. and Homel, R. 1996, 'Creating safer bars', in M Plant, E. Single and T. Stockwell (eds.), *Alcohol: Minimising the Harm*, London, Free Association Press, pp. 171–92.

Grant, A.A. 1995, *Investigation into Drugs in Prisons in South Australia, Report to the Minister for Correctional Services*, Adelaide, S.A. Government.

Greenberg, J. 1997, 'The STEAL motive. Managing the social determinants of employee theft', in R.A. Giacalone and J. Greenberg (eds.), *Antisocial Behavior in Organisations*, Thousand Oaks, CA, Sage, pp. 85–108.

Hall, W., Ward, J. and Mattick, R. 1993, 'Methadone maintenance treatment in prisons: The New South Wales experience', *Drug and Alcohol Review* 12: 193–203.

Haney, C., Banks, C. and Zimbardo, P. 1973, 'Interpersonal dynamics in a simulated prison', *International Journal of Criminology and Penology* 1: 69–97.

Haney, C. and Zimbardo, P. 1998, 'The past and future of U.S. prison policy. Twenty-five years after the Stanford prison experiment', *American Psychologist* 53: 709–27.

Harries, K.D. and Stadler, S. J. 1988, 'Heat and violence: New findings from the Dallas field data, 1980–1981', *Journal of Applied Social Psychology* 18: 129–38.

Harris, G.T. and Varney, G.W. 1986, 'A ten-year study of assaults and assaulters on a maximum security psychiatric unit', *Journal of Interpersonal Violence* 1: 175–91.

Hatty, S.E. and Walker, J.R. 1986, *A National Study of Deaths in Australian Prisons*, Canberra, Australian Institute of Criminology.

Haycock, J. 1991, 'Crime and misdemeanors: A review of recent research on suicides in prison', *Omega* 60: 85–98.

Hayes, L.M. 1983, 'And darkness closes in … A national study of jail suicides', *Criminal Justice and Behavior* 10: 461–84.

   1989, 'National study of jail suicides: Seven years later', *Psychiatric Quarterly*, 60: 7–29.

   1995, 'Prison suicide: An overview and a guide to prevention', *Prison Journal* 75: 431–56.

Hayes, L.M. and Rowan, J.R. 1988, *National Study of Jail Suicides: Seven Years Later*, Alexandria VA, National Center on Institutions and Alternatives.

Heffernan, E. and Krippel, E. 1980, 'A coed prison', in J.O. Smykla (ed.), *Coed Prison*, New York, Human Sciences Press, pp. 110–19.

Heilpern, D.M. 1998, *Fear or Favour: Sexual Assault of Young Prisoners*, Lismore NSW, Southern Cross University Press.

Hemmens, C. and Marquart, J.W. 1999, 'Straight time: Inmates' perception of violence and victimization in the prison environment', *Journal of Offender Rehabilitation* 28(3/4): 1–21.

Hepburn, J.R. 1989, 'Prison guards as agents of social control', in L. Goodstein and D.L. MacKenzie (eds.), *The American Prison: Issues in Research and Policy*, New York, Plenum, pp. 191–206.

Herrick, E. 1989, 'Survey: Inmate escapes, 1987 and 1988', *Corrections Compendium* 14: 9–20.

Hildebrand, R. J. 1969, 'The anatomy of escape', *Federal Probation* 33: 58–66.

HM Chief Inspector of Prisons for England and Wales, 1999, *Suicide Is Everyone's Concern: A Thematic Review*. London, HMSO.

Holeman, H. and Krepps-Hess, B. J. 1983, *Women Correctional Officers in the California Department of Corrections*, Sacramento, California Department of Corrections.

Hollinger, R.C. 1989, *Dishonesty in the Workplace: A Manager's Guide to Preventing Employee Theft*, Park Ridge IL, London House.

Holt, R., and Phillips, R. 1991, 'Marion: Separating fact from fiction', *Federal Prisons Journal* 2: 28–36.

Home Office 1984, *Suicides in Prison: Report by HM Chief Inspector of Prisons*, London, HMSO.

   1986, *Report of the Working Group on Suicide Prevention*, London, HMSO.

Homel, R., Hauritz, M., Wortley, R., McIlwain, G. and Carvolth, R. 1997, 'Preventing alcohol-related crime through community action: The Surfers Paradise Safety Action project', in R. Homel (ed.), *Policing for Prevention: Reducing Crime, Public Intoxication and Injury. Crime Prevention Studies* (Vol. 7), Monsey NY, Criminal Justice Press, pp. 35–90.

Hopper, C.B. 1962, 'The conjugal visit at the Mississippi State Penitentiary', *Journal of Criminal Law, Criminology and Police Science* 53: 340–4.

   1969, *Sex in Prisons*, Baton Rouge, Louisiana State University Press.

   1989, 'The evolution of conjugal visiting in Mississippi', *Prison Journal* 69: 103–9.

Horning, D.N.M. 1970, 'Blue-collar theft: Conceptions of property, attitudes towards pilfering, and work group norms in a modern industrial plant', in E.O.

Smigel and H.L. Ross (eds.), *Crimes Against Bureaucracy*, New York, Van Nostrand Reinhold, pp. 46–64.

House of Commons 1977, *Report of an Inquiry by the Chief Inspector of the Prison Service into the Cause and Circumstances of the Events at H.M. Prison Hull During the Period 31st August to 3rd September, 1976*, London, HMSO.

Hunt, G., Riegel, S., Morales, T. and Waldorf, D. 1993, 'Changes in prison culture: Prison gangs and the case of the "Pepsi generation" ', *Social Problems* 40: 398–409.

Ibrahim, A.I. 1974, 'Deviant sexual behavior in men's prisons', *Crime and Delinquency* 20: 38–44.

Inch, H., Rowlands, P. and Soliman, A. 1995, 'Deliberate self-harm in a young offenders' institution', *Journal of Forensic Psychiatry* 6: 161–71.

Inciardi, J.A., Lockwood, D. and Quinlan J.A. 1993, 'Drug use in prison: Patterns, processes, and implications for treatment', *Journal of Drug Issues* 23: 119–29.

Incorvaia, D. and Kirby, N. 1997, 'A formative evaluation of a drug-free unit in a correctional services setting', *International Journal of Offender Therapy and Comparative Criminology* 41: 231–49.

Indermaur, D. and Upton, K. 1988, 'Alcohol and drug use patterns of prisoners in Perth', *Australian and New Zealand Journal of Criminology*, 21: 144–65.

Innes, C.A. 1987, *Population Density in the State Prisons, Bureau of Justice Statistics Special Report*, Washington DC, US Department of Justice.

— 1988, *Drug Use and Crime: State Prison Inmate Survey 1986*, Washington DC, Bureau of Justice Statistics.

Jan, L. 1980, 'Overcrowding and inmate behavior. Some preliminary findings', *Criminal Justice and Behavior* 7: 293–301.

Jayewardene, C.H.S. and Doherty, P. 1985, 'Individual violence in Canadian penitentiaries', *Canadian Journal of Criminology* 27: 429–39.

Jenne, D.L. and Kersting, R.C. 1996, 'Aggression and women correctional officers in male prisons', *Prison Journal* 76: 442–60.

Jensen, G.F. 1972, 'Parents, peers, and delinquent action', *American Journal of Sociology* 78: 562–75.

Johnson, G. and Farren, E. 1996, 'An evaluation of prisoners' views about substance free zones', *Issues in Criminological and Legal Psychology* 25: 30–8.

Johnson, R. 1976, *Culture and Crisis in Confinement*, Lexington MA, Lexington Books.

Johnson, R., Lewis, J. and Young, P.G. 1978, 'The training school absconder: A preliminary assessment of antecedent problems and motives', *Juvenile and Family Court Journal* 29: 3–8.

Johnston, E. 1991, *National Report of the Royal Commission into Aboriginal Deaths in Custody*, Canberra, Australian Government Publishing Service.

Jones, E.E. 1979, 'The rocky road from acts to dispositions', *American Psychologist* 34: 107–17.

Jones, R.S. and Schmid, T.J. 1989, 'Inmates' conceptions of prison sexual assault', *Prison Journal* 69: 53–61.

Kalinich, D.B. and Stojkoviv, S. 1987, 'Prison contraband systems: Implications for prison management', *Journal of Crime and Justice* 10: 1–21.

Kantrowitz, N. 1996, *Close Control: Managing a Maximum Security Prison*, Albany NY, Harrow and Heston.

Karacki, L. 1989, 'Serious prison infractions', *Federal Prisons* 1: 31–5.

Kauffman, K. 1988, *Prison Officers and their World*, Cambridge MA, Harvard University Press.

Kelman, H.C. and Hamilton, V.L. 1989, *Crimes of Obedience*, New Haven, Yale University Press.

King, M.B. 1992, 'Male rape in institutional settings', in G.C. Mezey and M.B. King (eds.), *Male Victims of Sexual Assault*, Oxford, Oxford University Press, pp. 67–74.

King, R.D. 1987, 'New generation prisons, the prison building programme, and the future of the dispersal policy', in A. Bottoms and R. Light (eds.), *Problems of Long-Term Imprisonment*, Aldershot, Gower, pp. 115–38.

1991, 'Maximum-security custody in Britain and the USA', *British Journal of Criminology* 31: 126–52.

Knox, G.W. and Tromanhauser, E.D. 1991, 'Gangs and their control in adult correctional institutions', *Prison Journal* 71: 15–22.

Korte, T., Pykäläinen, J. and Seppälä, T. 1998, 'Drug abuse of Finnish male prisoners in 1995', *Forensic Science International* 97: 171–83.

Krasnow, P. 1995, 'Corrections architecture building for the future', *Corrections Compendium* 20: 1–5.

Kratcoski, P.C. 1988, 'The implications of research explaining prison violence and disruption', *Federal Probation* 52: 27–32.

Kunzman, E.E. 1995, 'Preventing suicide in jails', *Corrections Today* 57: 90–94.

La Vigne, N.G. 1994, 'Rational choice and inmate disputes over phone use on Rikers Island', in R.V. Clarke (ed.), *Crime Prevention Studies* (Vol. 3), Monsey NY, Criminal Justice Press, pp. 109–25.

Lambiotte, J. 1980, 'Sex role differentiation in a co-correctional setting', in J.O. Smykla (ed.), *Coed Prison*, New York, Human Sciences Press, pp. 221–47.

Langenbach, M., North, M.Y., Aagaard, L. and Chown, W. 1990, 'Televised instruction in Oklahoma prisons: A study of recidivism and disciplinary actions', *Journal of Correctional Education* 41: 87–94.

Laycock, G. 1977, *Absconding from Borstals* (Home Office Research Study No. 41), London, HMSO.

Lazarus, R.S. and Folkman, S. 1984, *Stress, Appraisal, and Coping*, New York, Springer-Verlag.

LeBeau, J.L. 1994, 'The oscillation of police calls to domestic disputes with time and the temperature humidity index', *Journal of Crime and Justice* 17: 149–61.

Lefkowitz, M., Blake, R.R. and Mouton, J.S. 1955, 'Status factors in pedestrian violation of traffic signals', *Journal of Abnormal and Social Psychology* 51: 704–5.

Lembo, J.J. 1969, 'The relationship of institutional disciplinary infractions and the inmate's personal contact with the outside community', *Criminologica* 7: 50–4.

Lester, D. 1990, 'Overcrowding in prisons and rates of suicide and homicide', *Perceptual and Motor Skills* 71: 274.

Levinson, R.B. 1982, 'Try softer', in R. Johnson and H. Toch (eds.), *The Pains of Imprisonment*, Beverly Hills CA, Sage, pp. 241–56.

Leyens, J.P., Camino, L., Parke, R.D. and Bekowitz, L. 1975, 'Effects of movie violence on aggression in a field setting as a function of group dominance and cohesion', *Journal of Personality and Social Psychology* 32: 346–60.

Liebling, A. 1992, *Suicides in Prison*, London, Routledge.

1993. 'Suicides in young prisoners: A summary', *Death Studies* 17: 381–409.

1995, 'Vulnerability and prison suicide', *British Journal of Criminology* 35: 173–87.

Liebling, A., Muir, G., Rose, G. and Bottoms, A. 1999, *Incentives and Earned Privileges for Prisoners – an Evaluation* (Research Findings No. 87), London, Home Office Research, Development and Statistics Directorate.

Light, S.C. 1990, 'The severity of assaults on prison officers: A contextual study', *Social Science Quarterly* 71: 267–84.

1991, 'Assaults on prison officers: interactional themes', *Justice Quarterly* 8: 241–61.

Lillis, J. 1994, 'Prison escapes and violence remain down', *Corrections Compendium* 19: 6–9.

Linden, R., Perry, L., Ayers, D and Parlett, T.A.A. 1984, 'An evaluation of a prison education program', *Canadian Journal of Criminology* 26: 65–73.

Lockwood, D. 1980, *Prison Sexual Violence*, New York, Elsevier.

Lombardo, L.X. 1982, 'Stress, change and collective violence in prison', in R. Johnson and H. Toch (eds.), *The Pains of Imprisonment*, Beverly Hills CA, Sage, pp. 77–93.

1989, *Guards Imprisoned: Correctional Officers at Work* (2nd edn), Cincinnati OH, Anderson.

Lyons, J.A. 1997, *Inmate Escape Incidents*, New York, New York State Department of Correctional Services.

Mabli, J., Holley, C., Patrick, J. and Walls, J. 1979, 'Age and prison violence', *Criminal Justice and Behavior* 6: 175–85.

McCain, G., Cox, V. and Paulus, P.B. 1980, *The Effect of Prison Crowding on Inmate Behavior*, Washington DC, Law Enforcement Assistance Administration.

McCorkle, R.C., Miethe, T.D. and Drass, K.A. 1995, 'The roots of prison violence: A test of the deprivation, management, and "not-so total" institution models', *Crime and Delinquency* 41: 317–31.

McDonald, D. 1992, 'Drug testing in prisons', in D. Biles and D. McDonald (eds.), *Deaths in Custody Australia, 1980–1989*, Canberra, Australian Institute of Criminology, pp. 65–84.

MacDonald, J.M. 1999, 'Violence and drug use in juvenile institutions', *Journal of Criminal Justice* 27: 33–44.

Macintyre, S. and Homel, R. 1997, 'Danger on the dance floor. A study on interior design, crowding and aggression in nightclubs', in R Homel (ed.), *Policing for Prevention: Reducing Crime, Public Intoxication and Injury. Crime Prevention Studies* (Vol. 7), Monsey NY, Criminal Justice Press, pp. 91–114.

McKenzie, I.K. 1982, 'Unlawful assembly: Riot, rout: The mechanisms of the mob', *Police Studies* 5: 40–6.

McManus, L.F. and Conner, J.C. 1994, 'Deterring escapees through comprehensive perimeter security', *Corrections Today* 56: 142–4.

Mahan, S. 1994, 'An "orgy of brutality" at Attica and the "killing ground" at Santa Fe: A comparison of prison riots', in M.C. Braswell, R.H. Montgomery and L.X. Lombardo (eds.), *Prison Violence in America* (2nd edn), Cincinnati OH, Anderson, pp. 253–64.

Mahan, S. and Lawrence, R. 1996, 'Media and mayhem in corrections: The role of the media in prison riots', *Prison Journal* 76: 420–41.

Maitland, A.S. and Sluder, R.D. 1998, 'Victimization and youthful prison inmates: An empirical analysis', *Prison Journal* 78: 55–74.

Mandaraka-Sheppard, A. 1986, *The Dynamics of Aggression in Women's Prisons in England*, Aldershot Hants, Gower.

Markus, T.A. 1994, 'Can history be a guide to the design of prisons?', in I. Spens (ed.), *Architecture of Incarceration*, London, Academy Editions, pp. 13–19.

Marlatt, G.A., Demming, B. and Reid, J.B. 1973, 'Loss of control drinking in alcoholics: An experimental analogue', *Journal of Abnormal Psychology* 81: 233–41.

Marrero, D. 1977, 'Spatial dimensions of democratic prison reform', *Prison Journal* 57: 31–42.

Marshall, W.L. 1988, 'The use of explicit sexual stimuli by rapists, child molesters and nonoffender males', *Journal of Sex Research* 25: 267–88.

Martin, D.N. 1977, 'Disruptive behaviour and staff attitudes at the St. Charles Youth Treatment Centre', *Journal of Child Psychology and Psychiatry* 18: 221–8.

Martin, F.P. and Osgood, D.W. 1987, 'Autonomy as a source of pro-social influence among incarcerated adolescents', *Journal of Applied Social Psychology* 17: 97–107.

Martin, R. and Zimmerman, S. 1990, 'A typology of the causes of prison riots and an analytical extension to the 1986 West Virginia riot', *Justice Quarterly* 7: 711–37.

Martinson, R. 1974, 'What works? Questions and answers about prison reform', *Public Interest* 35: 22–54.

Megargee, E.I. 1976, 'Population density and disruptive behavior in a prison setting', in A.K. Cohen, G.F. Cole and R.G. Bailey (eds.), *Prison Violence*, Lexington MA, D.C. Heath, pp. 135–46.

1977, 'The association of population density, reduced space, and uncomfortable temperatures with misconduct in a prison community', *American Journal of Community Psychology* 5: 289–97.

Memory, J.M., Guo, G., Parker, K. and Sutton, T. 1999, 'Comparing disciplinary infraction rates of North Carolina fair sentencing and structured sentencing inmates: A natural experiment', *The Prison Journal* 79: 45–71.

Michael, B. 1992, *An Analysis of Escapes from Prison Custody in Queensland*, Brisbane, Queensland Corrective Services Commission.

Mieczkowski, T. 1995, *Hair Analysis as a Drug Detector*, Washington DC, National Institute of Justice.

1997, *Hair Assays and Urinalysis Results for Juvenile Drug Offenders*, Washington DC, National Institute of Justice.

Mieczkowski, T. (ed.) 1999, *Drug Testing Technology: Assessment of Field Applications*, Boca Raton FL, CRC Press.

Mieczkowski, T. and Lersch, K. 1997, 'Drug testing in criminal justice: Evolving uses, emerging technologies', *National Institute of Justice Journal* December: 9–15.

Mieczkowski, T., Newel, R. and Wraight, B. 1998, 'Using hair analysis, urinalysis, and self-reports to estimate drug use in a sample of detained juveniles', *Substance Use and Misuse* 33: 1547–67.

Milgram, S. 1974, *Obedience to Authority: An Experimental View*, New York, Harper and Row.

Millham, S., Bullock, R., Hosie, K. and Frankenburg, R. 1977, 'Absconding', *Community Schools Gazette* 71: 281–91, 325–37.

Mischel, W. 1968, *Personality and Assessment*, New York, Wiley.

Money, J. and Bohmer, C. 1980, 'Prison sexology: Two personal accounts of masturbation, homosexuality, and rape', *Journal of Sex Research* 16: 258–66.

Montgomery, R.H. 1994, 'American prison riots: 1774–1991', in M.C. Braswell, R.H. Montgomery and L.X. Lombardo (eds.), *Prison Violence in America* (2nd edn), Cincinnati OH, Anderson, pp. 227–51.

—— 1997, 'Bringing the lessons of prison riots into focus', *Corrections Today* 59: 28–32.

Moos, R.H. 1968, 'Assessment of the social climates of correctional institutions', *Journal of Research in Crime and Delinquency* 5: 174–88.

Moss, C.S., Hosford, R.E. and Anderson, W.R. 1979, 'Sexual assault in prison', *Psychological Reports* 44: 823–8.

Nacci, P.L. and Kane, T.R. 1983, 'The incidence of sex and sexual aggression in federal prisons', *Federal Probation* 47: 31–6.

—— 1984, 'Inmate sexual aggression: Some evolving propositions, empirical findings, and mitigating counter-forces', *Journal of Offenders' Counseling Services and Rehabilitation* 9: 1–20.

Nacci, P.L., Teitelbaum, H.E. and Prather, J. 1977, 'Population density and inmate misconduct rates in the federal prison system', *Federal Probation* 41: 26–31.

Nagle, J.F. 1978, *Report of the Royal Commission into New South Wales Prisons*, Sydney NSW, Government Printer.

Nelles, J., Fuhrer, A. and Hirsbrunner, H.P. 1999, 'How does syringe distribution in prison affect consumption of illegal drugs by prisoners?', *Drug and Alcohol Review* 18: 133–8.

Nelson, W.R. 1993, 'New generation jails', in *Podular, Direct Supervision Jails: Information Package*, Washington DC, US Department of Justice, pp. 25–41.

Nelson, W.R. and Davis, R.M. 1995, 'Podular direct supervision: The first twenty years', *American Jails* 9: 11–22.

Newman, G. 1997, 'Introduction: Towards a theory of situational crime prevention', in G. Newman, R.V Clarke and S.G Shohan (eds.), *Rational Choice and Situational Crime Prevention*, Aldershot, Ashgate Publishing, pp. 1–24.

Newman, O. (1972), *Defensible Space: People and Design in the Violent City*, London, Architectural Press.

New York State Special Commission on Attica 1972, *Attica: The Official Report of the New York State Special Commission on Attica*, New York, Bantam Books.

O'Donnell, I. and Edgar, K. 1996, *The Extent and Dynamics of Victimisation in Prisons*, Oxford.

—— 1999, 'Fear in prison', *The Prison Journal* 79: 90–9.

Ogburn, K.R. 1993, 'Arizona officer helps end escalating kitchen melee', *Corrections Today* 55: 80.

Oliver, S.S., Roggenbuck, J.W. and Watson, A.E. 1985, 'Education to reduce impacts in forest campgrounds', *Journal of Forestry* 83: 234–6.

O'Neill, S.M. and Paluck, B.J. 1973, 'Altering territoriality through reinforcement', *Proceedings of the 81st Annual Convention of the American Psychological Association*, Montreal, Canada, pp. 901–2.

Painter, K. and Farrington, D.P. 1997, 'The crime reducing effect of improved street lighting: The Dudley project', in R.V. Clarke (ed.), *Situational Crime Prevention: Successful Case Studies*, Albany NY, Harrow and Heston, pp. 209–26.

Parmeter, J.E., Murray, D.W. and Hannum, D.V. 2000, *Guide for the Selection of Drug Detectors for Law Enforcement Applications* (NIJ Guide 601–00), Washington DC, National Institute of Justice.

Patrick, S. 1998, 'Differences in inmate-inmate and inmate-staff altercations: Examples from a medium security prison', *Social Science Journal* 35: 253–63.

Paulus, P. 1988, *Prison Crowding: A Psychological Perspective*, New York, Springer-Verlag.

Paulus, P.B. and McCain, G. 1983, 'Crowding in jails', *Basic and Applied Social Psychology* 4: 89–107.

Paulus, P.B. and Nagar, D. 1989, 'Environmental influences on groups', in P.B. Paulus (ed.), *Psychology of Group Influence* (2nd edn), Hillsdale NJ, Lawrence Erlbaum, pp. 111–140.

Pelissier, B. 1991, 'The effects of rapid increase in a prison population: A pre- and post-test study', *Criminal Justice and Behavior* 18: 427–47.

Pennsylvania Department of Corrections 1999, *National Study Reveals Ridge Administration Crackdown Has Made Pennsylvania Prisons Nearly 99 Percent Drug Free* (Press release) http://www.correctionsdrugtesting.com/pennstudy.htm

Phillips, D.P. 1989, 'Recent advances in suicidology. The study of imitative suicide', in R.F.W. Diekstra, R. Maris, S. Platt, A. Schmidtke and G. Sonneck (eds.), *Suicide and its Prevention*, New York, E. J. Brill, pp. 299–312.

Phillips, D.P. and Carstensen, L.L. 1990, 'The effects of suicide stories on various demographic groups 1968–1985', in R. Surette (ed.), *The Media and Criminal Justice Policy*, Springfield IL, Charles C Thomas, pp. 63–72.

Pilant, L. 1998, 'Smart cards: An information tool for the future', *National Institute of Justice Journal* July: 21–4.

Porporino, F.J. 1992, 'Violence and suicide in Canadian institutions: Some recent statistics', *Forum on Corrections Research* 4: 3–5.

Porporino, F.J., Doherty, PD. and Sawatsky, T. 1987, 'Characteristics of homicide victims and victimizations in prisons: A Canadian historical perspective', *International Journal of Offender Therapy and Comparative Criminology* 32: 125–35.

Porporino, F.J. and Dudley, K. 1984, *An Analysis of the Effects of Overcrowding in Canadian Penitentiaries* (Working Paper No. 6), Ottawa, Ministry of Correctional Services.

Porteous, M.A. and McLoughlin, C.S. 1974, 'A comparison of absconders and non-absconders from an assessment centre', *Community Schools Gazette* 67: 681–699.

Power, K.G., Markova, I., Rowlands, A., McKee, K.J., Anslow, P.J. and Kilfedder, C. 1991, 'Sexual behaviour in Scottish prisons', *British Medical Journal* 302: 1507–8.

Poyner, B. 1993, 'What works in crime prevention: An overview of evaluations', in R.V. Clarke (ed.), *Crime Prevention Studies* (Vol. 1), Monsey NY, Criminal Justice Press, pp. 7–34.

Prentice-Dunn, S. and Rogers, R.W. 1982, 'Effects of public and private self-awareness on deindividuation and aggression', *Journal of Personality and Social Psychology* 43: 503–13.

Prentice-Dunn, S. and Spivey, C.B. 1986, 'Extreme deindividuation in the laboratory: Its magnitude and subjective components', *Personality and Social Psychology Bulletin* 12: 206–15.

Quinsey, V.L. and Varney, G.W. 1977, 'Characteristics of assaults and assaulters in a maximum security psychiatric unit', *Crime and/et Justice* November: 212–20.

Ralph, P.H. and Marquart, J.W. 1991, 'Gang violence in Texas prisons', *Prison Journal* 71: 38–49.

Ramsay, R.F., Tanney, B.L. and Searle, C.A. 1987, 'Suicide prevention in high-risk prison populations', *Canadian Journal of Criminology* 29: 295–307.

Regoli, E.D. and Poole, R.M. 1993, 'Violence in juvenile institutions', *Criminology* 21: 213–32.

Reicher, S. 1991, 'Politics of crowd psychology', *The Psychologist* November: 487–91.

Reisig, M.D. 1998, 'Rates of disorder in higher-custody state prisons: A comparative analysis of managerial practices', *Crime and Delinquency* 44: 229–44.

Reser, J. 1992, 'The design of safe and humane police cells: A discussion of some issues relating to Aboriginal people in police custody', in D. Biles and D. McDonald (eds.), *Deaths in Custody Australia, 1980–1989*, Canberra, Australian Institute of Criminology, pp. 147–90.

Rideau, W. and Sinclair, B. 1982, 'Prison: The sexual jungle', in A.M. Scacco (ed.), *Male Rape*, New York, AMS Press, pp. 3–29.

Riley, M.W. and Cochran, D.J. 1984, 'Dexterity performance and reduced ambient temperature', *Human Factors* 26: 207–14.

Robson, R. 1989, 'Managing the long-term prisoner: A report on an Australian innovation in unit management', *Howard Journal of Criminal Justice* 28: 187–203.

Roggenbuck, J.W. 1992, 'Use of persuasion to reduce resources impacts and visitor conflicts', in M. J. Manfredo (ed.), *Influencing Human Behavior: Theory and Applications in Recreation, Tourism, and Natural Resources Management*, Champaign IL, Sagamore, pp. 149–208.

Rosenthal, N.E., Sack, D.A., Carpenter, C.J. *et al.* 1985, 'Antidepressant effects of light in seasonal affective disorder', *American Journal of Psychiatry* 142: 163–70.

Rosenthal, R. 1990, 'Media violence, antisocial behavior, and the social consequences of small effects', in R. Surette (ed.), *The Media and Criminal Justice Policy*, Springfield IL, Charles C Thomas, pp. 53–61.

Ross, L. 1977, 'The intuitive psychologist and his shortcomings: Distortions in the attribution process', in L. Berkowitz (ed.), *Advances in Experimental Psychology* (Vol. 10), New York, Academic Press, pp. 173–220.

Ross, M., Grossman, A.B., Murdoch, S., Rundey, R., Golding, J., Purchase, S., Munyard, T., Scott, M. and Bridger, A. 1994, 'Prison: Shield from threat, or threat to survival?', *British Medical Journal* 308: 1092–5.

Rothenberg, D. 1983, 'Sexual behavior in an abnormal setting', *Corrective and Social Psychiatry and Journal of Behavior Technology Methods and Therapy* 29: 78–81.

Rowan, J.R. 1990, 'Design, equipment, construction, and other blunders in detention and correctional facilities: Who is to blame?', *American Jails* July/August: 12–20.

———— 1996, 'Having more female officers reduces prisoner assaults on staff', *Overcrowded Times* 7: 2–3

Ruback, R.B. and Carr, T.S. 1984, 'Crowding in a women's prison: Attitudinal and behavioral effects', *Journal of Applied Social Psychology* 14: 57–68.

Rucker, L. 1994, 'Coercive versus cooperative environments: The collateral effects in prisons', *Prison Journal* 73: 73–92.

Salive, M.E., Smith, G.S. and Brewer, F. 1989, 'Suicide mortality in the Maryland state prison system, 1979 through 1987', *The Journal of the American Medical Association* 262: 365–9.

Saum, C.A., Surratt, H.L., Inciardi, J.A. and Bennett, R.E. 1995, 'Sex in prison: Exploring the myths and realities', *Prison Journal* 75: 413–30.

Saylor, W.G. and Gaes, G.G. 1992, *PREP Study Links UNICOR Work Experience with Successful Post-Release Outcome*, Washington DC, US Department of Justice.

Scacco, A.M. 1975, *Rape in Prison*, Springfield IL, Charles C Thomas.

1982, 'The scapegoat is almost always white', in A.M. Scacco (ed.), *Male Rape: A Casebook of Sexual Aggression*, New York, AMS Press, pp. 91–103.

Schaffer, N.E. 1991, 'Prison visiting policies and practices', *International Journal of Offender Therapy and Comparative Criminology* 35: 263–75.

Schippers, G.M., van den Hurk, A.A., Breteler, M.H.M. and Meerkerk, G. 1998, 'Effectiveness of a drug-free detention treatment program in a Dutch prison', *Substance Use and Misuse* 33: 1027–46.

Schmidtke, A. and Häfner, H. 1989, 'Public attitudes towards and effects of the massmedia on suicidal and deliberative self-harm behavior', in R.F.W. Diekstra, R. Maris, S. Platt, A. Schmidtke and G. Sonneck (eds.), *Suicide and its Prevention*, New York, E. J. Brill, pp. 313–30.

Scott, N.A., Mount, M.K. and Duffy, P.S. 1977, 'MMPI and demographic correlates and predictors of female prison escape', *Criminal Justice and Behavior* 4: 285–300.

Scott-Denoon, K. 1984, *B.C. Corrections: A Study of Suicides 1970–1980*, British Columbia, Corrections Branch.

Sechrest, D.K. 1991, 'The effects of density on jail assaults', *Journal of Criminal Justice* 19: 211–23.

Select Committee on Home Affairs 1999, *Drugs and Prison* (Home Affairs Fifth Report) http://www.parliament.the-stationery-office.co.uk/pa/cm199899/cmselect/cmhaff/363/36302.htm

Senese, J.D., Wilson, J., Evans, A.O., Aguirre, R. and Kalinich, D.B. 1992, 'Evaluating jail reform', *American Jails* September/October: 14, 23.

Shaffer, C.E., Bluoin, D. and Pettigrew, C.G. 1985, 'Assessment of prison escape risk', *Journal of Police and Criminal Psychology* 1: 42–8.

Shawver, L. and Dickover, R. 1986, 'Exploding a myth', *Corrections Today* 48: 30–4.

Shellow, R. and Roemer, D.V. 1987, 'No heaven for "Hell's Angels" ', in R.H. Turner and L.M. Killian (eds.), *Collective Behavior* (3rd edn), Englewood Cliffs NJ, Prentice-Hall, pp. 115–23.

Sherman, L. 1993, 'Defiance, deterrence and irrelevance: A theory of the criminal sanction', *Journal of Research in Crime and Delinquency* 30: 445–73.

Shewan, D., Gemmell, M. and Davies, J.B. 1994, 'Prison as a modifier of drug using behaviour', *Addiction Research* 2: 203–15.

Sigurdson, H.R. 1985, *The Manhattan House of Detention: A Study of Podular Direct Supervision*, US Department of Justice.

1987a, *Larimer County Detention Center. A Study of Podular Direct Supervision*, US Department of Justice.

1987b, *Pima County Detention Center. A Study of Podular Direct Supervision*, US Department of Justice.

Sinclair, I. and Clarke, R.V. 1982, 'Predicting, treating, and explaining delinquency: The lesson from research on institutions', in P. Feldman (ed.), *Development in the Study of Criminal Behaviour Volume 1: The Prevention and Control of Offending*, Chichester, Wiley, pp. 51–77.

Sinclair, I.A. 1971, *Hostels for Probationers* (Home Officer Research Study No. 6), London, HMSO.

Skinner, B.F. 1953, *Science and Human Behavior*, New York, Free Press.

Skovron, S.E. 1988, 'Prison crowding: The dimensions of the problem and strategies of population control', in J.E. Scott and T. Hirschi (eds.), *Controversial Issues in Crime and Justice*, Newbury Park, Sage, pp. 183–98.

Smith, R.R. and Sabatino, D.A. 1990, 'American prisoner home furloughs', *Journal of Offender Counseling* 10: 18–25.

Snyder, N.H., Broome, O.W., Kehoe, W.J., McIntyre, J.T. and Blair, K.E. 1991, *Reducing Employee Theft: A Guide to Financial and Organizational Controls*, New York, Quorum.

Sorensen, J. and Wrinkle, R.D. 1996, 'No hope for parole: Disciplinary infractions among death-sentenced and life-without-parole inmates', *Criminal Justice and Behavior* 23: 542–52.

Sparks, R., Bottoms, A. and Hay, W. 1996, *Prison and the Problem of Order*, Oxford, Clarendon.

Spertzel, J.K. 1993, 'New York officers quell dorm disturbance', *Corrections Today* 55: 34.

Stahl, A.B. 1993, 'USBD corrections officers help end major disturbance', *Corrections Today* 55: 28.

Steinke, P. 1991, 'Using situational factors to predict types of prison violence', *Journal of Offender Rehabilitation* 17: 119–32.

Stephan, J.J. 1997, *Census of State and Federal Correctional Facilities, 1995*, Washington DC, US Department of Justice.

Stevens, D.J. 1997, 'Prison regime and drugs', *The Howard Journal* 36: 14–27.

Stone, M.B. and Hoffman, P.B. 1982, 'The effects of presumptive parole dates on institutional behavior: A preliminary assessment', *Journal of Criminal Justice* 10: 282–97.

Strang, J., Heuston, J., Gossop, M., Green, J. and Maden, T. 1998, *HIV/AIDS Risk Behaviour Among Adult Male Prisoners* (Research Findings No. 82), London, Home Office Research, Development and Statistics Directorate.

Struckman-Johnson, C., Struckman-Johnson, D., Rucker, L. and Bumby, K. 1996, 'Sexual coercion reported by men and women in prison', *Journal of Sex Research* 33: 67–76.

Suedfeld, P. 1980, 'Environmental effects on violent behavior in prisons', *International Journal of Offender Therapy and Comparative Criminology* 24: 107–16.

Surette, R. 1990, 'Estimating the magnitude and mechanisms of copycat crime', in R. Surette (ed.), *The Media and Criminal Justice Policy*, Springfield IL, Charles C Thomas, pp. 87–101.

Swann, R. and James, P. 1998, 'The effect of the prison environment upon inmate drug taking behaviour', *The Howard Journal* 37: 252–65.

Sykes, G. 1958, *The Society of Captives*, Princeton NJ, Princeton University Press.

Sykes, G. and Matza, D. 1957, 'Techniques of neutralization: A theory of delinquency', *American Sociological Review* 22: 664–70.

Sylvester, S.F., Reed, J.H. and Nelson, D.O. 1977, *Prison Homicide*, New York, Spectrum.

Tewksbury, R. 1989, 'Fear of sexual assault in prison inmates', *Prison Journal* 69: 62–71.

Thomas, C.W. and Cage, R.J. 1977, 'Correlates of prison drug use: An evaluation of two conceptual models', *Criminology* 15: 193–210.

Thompson, B. 1992, *Reasons for Escape: Interviews with Recaptured Escapees* (Research Bulletin No. 17), Sydney, NSW Department of Corrective Services.

Thornton, D. and Speirs, S. 1985, 'Predicting absconding from young offenders institutions', in D.P. Farrington and R. Tarling (eds.), *Prediction in Criminology*. Albany NY, University of New York Press, pp. 119–34.

Towl, G.J and Crighton, D.A. 1998, 'Suicide in prisons in England and Wales from 1988 to 1995', *Criminal Behaviour and Mental Health* 8: 184–92.

Trace, M. 1998, 'Tackling drug use in prison: A success story', *International Journal of Drug Policy* 9: 277–82.

Trasler, G. (1986). 'Situational crime prevention and rational choice: A critique,' in K. Heal and G. Laycock (eds.), *Situational Crime Prevention: From Theory into Practice*, London, HMSO, pp. 17–42.

Travis, L.F., Latessa, E.J. and Oldendick, R.W. 1989, 'The utilization of technology in correctional institutions', *Federal Probation* 53: 35–40.

Tucker, D. 1982, 'A punk's song: View from the inside', in A.M. Scacco (ed.), *Male Rape: A Casebook of Sexual Aggression*, New York, AMS Press, pp. 58–79.

Unseem, B., Camp, C.G. and Camp, G.M. 1996, *Resolution of Prison Riots. Strategies and Policies*, New York, Oxford University Press.

Unseem, B and Kimball, P. 1989, *States of Siege. U.S. Prison Riots, 1971–1986*, New York, Oxford University Press.

US Department of Justice 1991, *Intervening with Substance-Abusing Offenders: A framework for action*, Longmont CO, National Institute of Corrections.

1992, *Fact Sheet: Drug Testing in the Criminal Justice System*, Rockville MD, Drugs and Crime Data Center and Clearinghouse.

1995, *Technology Issues in Corrections Agencies: Results of a 1995 Survey*, Longmont CO, National Institute of Corrections.

1999, *Video Surveillance Equipment Selection and Application Guide*, Washington DC, National Institute of Justice.

Vaag, J. 1994, *Prison Systems*, Oxford, Clarendon.

Vambucca, G. 1999, 'Finding a better way', *HIV/AIDS Legal Link* 10: 7–11.

van den Haag, E. 1980, 'Prisons cost too much because they are too secure', *Corrections Magazine* 6: 39–43.

van Groningen, J. 1993, 'Drugs in gaol: The responses available to prison administrators', *Keypoints* September: 13–16.

van Hoeven, K.H., Stoneburner, R.L. and Rooney, W.C. 1991, 'Drug use among New York City prison inmates: A demographic study with temporal trends', *The International Journal of the Addictions* 26: 1089–105.

Veno, A. and Davidson, M. 1977, 'Prison violence: Some different perspectives', *International Journal of Criminology and Penology* 5: 399–409.

Veno, A. and Veno, E. 1993, 'Situational prevention of public disorder at the Australian Motorcycle Grand Prix', in R.V. Clarke (ed.), *Crime Prevention Studies* (vol. 1), Monsey NY, Criminal Justice Press, pp. 157–75.

Wale, S. and Gorta, A. 1987. *View of Inmates Participating in the Pilot Prerelease Methadone Programme. Process Evaluation of the New South Wales Department of Corrective Services Methadone Programme: Study 2*, Sydney, NSW Department of Corrective Services.

Walters, G.D. 1998, 'Time series and correlational analyses of inmate-initiated assaultive incidents in a large correctional system', *International Journal of Offender Therapy and Comparative Criminology* 42: 124–32.

Warr, M. and Stafford, M. 1991, 'The influence of delinquent peers: What they think or what they do?', *Criminology* 29: 851–65.

Watson, T.S. 1996, 'A prompt plus delayed contingency procedure for reducing bathroom graffiti', *Journal of Applied Behavioral Analysis* 29: 121–4.

Wees, G. 1996, 'Violence on the rise in U.S. prisons', *Corrections Compendium* 21: 9–27.

Weiss, C. and Friar, D. 1974, *Terror in Prisons*, New York, Bobbs-Merrill.

Weiss, R.P. 1987, 'The community and prevention', in E.H. Johnson (ed.), *Handbook on Crime and Delinquency Prevention*, New York, Greenwood Press, pp. 113–36.

Welch, M. and Gunther, D. 1997, 'Jail suicide and prevention: Lessons from litigation', *Crisis Intervention* 3: 229–44.

Wener, R., Frazier, W. and Farbstein, J. 1987, 'Building better jails', *Psychology Today* 21: 40–9.

Wener, R. and Olsen, R. 1978, *User Based Assessment of the Federal Metropolitan Correctional Centers Final Report*, US Bureau of Prisons.

  1980, 'Innovative correctional environments: A user assessment', *Environment and Behavior* 12: 478–93.

Whatmore, P.B. 1987, 'Barlinnie Special Unit: An insider's view', in A.E. Bottoms and R. Light (eds.), *Problems of Long-Term Imprisonment*, Aldershot, Gower, pp. 249–60.

White, T.W. and Schimmel, D.J. 1995, 'Suicide prevention in federal prisons: A successful five-step program', in L. Hayes (ed.), *Prison Suicide: An Overview and Guide to Prevention*, Washington DC, US Department of Justice, pp. 48–59.

Wilkinson, R.A. and Unwin, T. 1999, 'Visiting in prison', in P.M. Carlson and J.S. Garrett (eds.), *Prison and Jail Administration: Practice and Theory*, Gaithersburg MD, Aspen Publishers, pp. 281–6

Wilson, D. 2000, *Drug Use, Testing, and Treatment in Jails*, Washington DC, Bureau of Justice Statistics.

Wolfgang, M.E. 1964, 'Age, adjustment and the treatment process of criminal behavior', *Psychiatry Digest* July: 21–35, August: 23–36.

Wooden, W.S. and Parker, J. 1982, *Men Behind Bars: Sexual Exploitation in Prison*, New York, Plenum.

Wooldredge, J.D. 1994, 'Inmate crime and victimization in a southwestern correctional facility', *Journal of Criminal Justice* 22: 367–81.

  1998, 'Inmate lifestyles and opportunities for victimization', *Journal of Research in Crime and Delinquency* 35: 480–502.

Woolf, Lord Justice, and Tumin, S. 1991, *Prison Disturbances April 1990*, London, HMSO.

Wortley, R. 1996, 'Guilt, shame and situational crime prevention', in R. Homel (ed.), *The Politics and Practice of Situational Crime Prevention. Crime Prevention Studies* (Vol. 5), Monsey NY, Criminal Justice Press, pp. 115–32.

  1997, 'Reconsidering the role of opportunity in situational crime prevention', in G. Newman, R.V. Clarke and S.G. Shohan (eds.), *Rational Choice and Situational Crime Prevention*, Aldershot, Ashgate Publishing, pp. 65–82.

1998, 'A two-stage model of situational crime prevention', *Studies on Crime and Crime Prevention* 7: 173–88.

Wright, K.N. 1985, 'Developing the prison environment inventory', *Journal of Research in Crime and Delinquency* 22: 257–77.

1991a, 'A study of individual environmental and interactive effects in explaining adjustment to prison', *Justice Quarterly* 8: 217–42.

1991b, 'The violent and victimized in the male prison', *Journal of Offender Rehabilitation* 16(3/4): 1–25.

1993, 'Prison environment and behavioral outcomes', *Journal of Offender Rehabilitation* 20: 95–113.

Wright, K.N. and Goodstein, L. 1989, 'Correctional environments', in L. Goodstein and D.I. MacKenzie (eds.), *The American Prison: Issues in Research and Policy*, New York, Plenum Press, pp. 253–70.

Zimbardo, P.G. 1970, 'The human choice: Individuation, reason, and order, vs deindividuation, impulse, and chaos', in W.J. Arnold and D. Levine (eds.), *Nebraska Symposium on Motivation 1969*, Lincoln NE, University of Nebraska Press, pp. 237–307.

Zimmer, L. 1987, 'How women reshape the prison guard role', *General and Society* 1: 415–31.

Zupan, L.L. 1991, *Jails: Reform and the New Generation Philosophy*, Cincinnati OH, Anderson Publishing.

Zupan, L.L. and Menke, B.A. 1991, 'The new generation jail: An overview', in J.A. Thompson and G.L. Mays (eds.), *American Jails*, Chicago, Nelson-Hall, pp. 180–94.

Index

NOTE: Page numbers in *italics* refer to figures and tables.

access control, 67
accounts, 170
administrative segregation, 144, 195
age composition, 89–90, 108, 126, 149
aggression, 27–8, 29
AIDS/HIV, 111
air conditioning, 87
anonymity, 26–7, 61–2, 74
architecture of prisons, 37–42
Asch, S. E., 22
Atlas, R., 96–7, 145
atmospheric conditions, 29–30
   see also seasonal variations; temperature
      and behaviour
Attica riot, 190, 206, 207–8

Bandura, A., 21
Bayens, G. J., 86
behaviour, and situations, 3–4, 6–8
behaviour theory, 15–18
benefits of disorder, denying, 70
Berkowitz, L., 28
Binda, H., 132
blind spots, 39, 87, 108, 125
Bottoms, A. E., 215–17
Bowker, L. H., 121
Brady, J. M., 133–4
Brehm, J. W., 25
Buchanan, R. A., 75
building-tender system, 92, 131–2, 202

Calhoun, J. B., 31
CCTV, 147, 224
cells, 37, 39–40, 65
   self-harm in, 142, 143–4, 145–7

violence and assaults in, 84–5, 106, 107,
      123
Clarke, R. V., 32, 66, 176–7, 178, 180, 182,
      183, 185, 187
co-correctional facilities, 90–1, 109
coercion, 127
cognitive disengagement, 20–2, 62
collective disorder
   controlling, *209*; physical environment,
      196–9; population characteristics,
      199–200; prison regime, 200–8
   nature of, 190–6
   research limitations, 208
commands, 119–20, 127
compliance, 25–6, 61
concentration, of high security prisoners, 47
conditioning, 15–17
conformity, 22–3, 47, 60
conjugal visits, 109–10
consensual model of prison regime, 51–2
consequences, clarifying, 63
consequent determinants, 17–18
contraband, control of, 203–4
control model of prison regime, 49–50
Cornish, D. B., 32, 183
costs of disorder, increasing, 71
counselling, 186–7
counterproductive control, 72–6, 221–3
   and drug use, 164, 166, 169, 172
   and sexual assaults, 116
   and violence, 93–4, 98, 100, 135
crowding, 30–2, 44–5, 218
   and collective disorder, 199–200
   and escapes, 182
   reducing, 64–5

and self-harm, 148
and violence, 88–9, 125–6
see also deindividuation
cues (environmental), 16–17

defiance, 25
deflecting offenders from disorder, 67–8
deindividuation, 26–7, 61–2, 74
density of population, 31–2, 44–5, 88, 89
deprivation model, 8–9, 48, 214–17
see also situational precipitators
design of prisons, 37–43, 198
determinate sentencing, 133–4
deterrence, from escape, 184–5
DiIulio, J. J., 49, 50, 51–2, 193–4, 197, 200–1, 204
discipline, 183–4
discriminative stimuli, 16–17
dispersal, of high security prisoners, 47
dogs, drug searches by, 166
Dollard, J., 27
dormitories, 84–5, 106, 107, 123, 180
drug searches, 163, 165–6
drug testing, 156, 163–5
drug trafficking, 158, 161, 162–3, 166–8
drug use
    controlling, *171*; physical environment, 161; population characteristics, 161–2; prison regime, 162–70; research and initiatives, 170, 172
    nature of, 155–60
drug-free units (DFUs), 169–70

effort of disorder, increasing, 67–8
Ekland-Olson, S., 131–2, 202
electronic aids *see* technological aids
eliciting stimuli, 16
employees *see* staff
entry-exit screening, 68
environment *see* physical environment and control; situational context
environmental cues, 16–17
environmental irritants, 65
environmental psychology, 28–32
environmental stress model, 28–9, 44–5
escapes
    controlling, *188*; physical environment, 180–2; population characteristics, 182; prison regime, 182–7
    nature of, 173–80
    research on, 173, 188
expectancy effects, 19–20
expressive assaults, 81

facilitators of disorder, 68
family
    and escapes, 187

leave to visit *see* furloughs
visits from, 96, 109–10, 152
Farbstein, J., 85–6
force, used by staff, 128, 207–8
formal surveillance, 68
Forst, M. L., 133–4
frustration, 27–8, 64, 75
functional units, 216
    architecture of, 41, 42
    and collective disorder, 197–8
    and drug use, 161
    escapes from, 180–1
    management of, 41, 42, 63, 124, 125, 198, 218, 221
    natural surveillance in, 69
    and self-harm, 147
    and sexual assaults, 107–8
    social condemnation in, 71
    and violence, 85–6, 88, 124–5
fundamental attributional error, 6–7
furloughs, 109–10, 152, 179, 187

gangs, 46, 52, 60, 92–3, 105, 108–9, 132–3
gender issues, 90–1, 109, 131, 157
Goffman, 214–15
grievance mechanisms, 205
guards *see* staff

hard control
    and soft control, 76, 219–23
    too hard control, 72–5, 193–4
    see also opportunity-reduction model; situational regulators
Heilpern, D. M., 101
heterogeneous prison populations, 46–7
high security *see* security level
Hilderbrand, R. J., 178, 181
home visits *see* furloughs
Homel, R., 66
homicides, 80, 82, 83, 93
homogeneous prison populations, 46–7
homosexual behaviour, 113
    see also sexual assaults
housing type, 84–5, 107, 143–4

identification of property, 70
imitation *see* modelling and imitation
incentives, 97–8, 164
inducements, 127
injuries, 119
inmates *see* prisoners
instrumental assaults, 81
interventions, labelling of, 218–19
isolation, 144
    see also segregation

Jan, L., 182

Kane, T. R., 106, 109, 113
Kauffman, K., 121, 127–8
Kimball, P., 202, 210
King, R. D., 86
Kratcoski, P. C., 119, 122, 129, 130, 131

La Vigne, N. G., 94–5, 213
Lawrence, R., 205–7
Laycock, G., 174, 183, 184
layout of prisons, 37, 39–42, 199
legitimacy, 203, 223
Liebling, A., 97–8, 139
Light, S. C., 118, 119–21, 126, 128
location
    of collective disorder, 195–6
    prior to escape, 180
    of self-harm, 142–3
    of sexual assaults, 106–7
    of violence, 83–4, 122–4
Lockwood, D., 106
Lucasville riot, 206

Mabli, J., 89–90
McCorkle, R. C., 92
Mahan, S., 205–7
making an example, 72, 185
management approach, 48–9
    see also functional units; prison regime
        and control
manipulation, 127, 139
Matza, D., 21
maximum security see security level
media management, 205–7
medication, 170
Megargee, E. I., 88–9
mental illness, 139
methadone programmes, 168–9
Milgram, S., 24
minimum security see security level
Mischel, W., 7–8
mixed-gender prisons, 90–1, 109
modelling and imitation, 18–19, 47, 59, 184
Montgomery, R. H., 191, 192, 195, 204, 205
motivation
    for collective disorder, 192–5
    for drug use, 158–60
    for escape, 175–7, 185
    for self-harm, 139–40
    for sexual assaults, 105–6, 114
    for violence, 80–1, 119–21, 128
murders see homicides

Nacci, P. L., 106, 109, 113
natural surveillance, 69
needle distribution, 169
neutralisation theory, 21, 62, 74
New Mexico riot, 194, 202, 206

obedience, 23–4, 60–1
offenders
    deflecting from disorder, 67–8
    see also prisoners
opportunity-reduction model, 33, 55, 65–6,
        140, 212–14
    see also situational regulators
overcontrol see counterproductive control

parole, 96–7
patterned spontaneous attacks, 121
perimeter security, 161, 181–2
permissibility, 62–4, 74
personal possessions, 94–5, 151
persuasion, 25, 127
physical environment and control, 36–43
    of collective disorder, 196–9
    of drug use, 161
    of escapes, 180–2
    of self-harm, 143–7
    of sexual assaults, 107–8
    of violence, 84–7, 124–5
population see prison population
positive expectations, 60
precipitators see situational precipitators
Prentice-Dunn, S., 27
prescribed medication, 170
pressures, 60–2, 73–4
prison control see counterproductive control;
        situational prison control
prison leave see furloughs
prison officers see staff
prison population, 43–7
    age composition, 89–90, 108, 126, 149
    crowding see crowding
    density, 31–2, 44–5, 88, 89
    gender composition, 90–1, 109
    involved in collective disorder, 199–200
    involved in drug use, 161–2
    involved in escapes, 182
    involved in self-harm, 148–9
    involved in sexual assaults, 108–9
    involved in violence, 87–91, 125–7
    racial composition, 46, 90, 108–9, 126–7,
        200
    size, 43–4, 87–8, 125, 161–2, 199
    turnover, 45–6, 91, 127, 149, 162
    see also prisoners
prison regime and control, 47–9
    of collective disorder, 200–8
    of drug use, 162–70
    of escapes, 182–7
    models of, 49–52
    of self-harm, 149–52
    of sexual assaults, 109–14
    of violence, 91–8, 127–34
prisoner–prisoner violence

controlling, *99–100*; physical
  environment, 84–7; population
  characteristics, 87–91; prison regime,
  91–8
nature of, 79–84
research limitations, 98
see also sexual assaults
prisoner–staff ratio, 92, 129–30, 201
prisoner–staff relations, 41, 42, 127–9, 166,
  202–3
prisoner–staff violence
controlling, *134*; physical environment,
  124–5; population characteristics,
  125–7; prison regime, 127–34
nature of, 117–24
prisoners
drug testing of, 156, 163–5
monitoring accounts of, 170
protection of vulnerable, 94, 113–14
reactions to sexual assault of others,
  110–11
reducing numbers of, 45
relations between and escape of, 185
segregation of, 94, 113–14, 143, 144, 195
transfer of, 204–5
see also prison population
prisons
age of, 196–7
conditions in, 194, 204
discipline in, 183–4
evolution of, 37–42
layout of, 37, 39–42, 199
research on new-generation, 224
size of, 43–4, 87–8, 125, 161–2, 199
theories of misbehaviour in, 8–9
privacy, 30, 146–7
privileges, removing, 71
programme availability, 95–6, 113, 133, 151,
  186, 204
prompts, 58–60, 73
property (personal), 94–5, 151
protection
of prisoners, 94, 113–14, 185
of staff, 53–4
provocation, 64–5, 74–5, 128
punishment, 17–18, 20, 70–2

racial composition
of prisoners, 46, 90, 108–9, 126–7, 200
of staff, 92, 130, 201
racial dimensions, of sexual assaults, 103, 105
rape, 102, 103
rational-choice perspective, 32–3, 55, 212
reactance, 25–6, 74
regime *see* prison regime and control
regulators *see* situational regulators
reinforcement, 17–18, 20

Reisig, M. D., 48
reminders, 59
remission, 96–7
Reser, J., 146, 147
responsibility, clarifying, 62–3
responsibility model of prison regime, 50–1
rewards of disorder, reducing, 69–70
riots *see* collective disorder
risks of disorder, increasing, 68–9
Ruiz trial, 92–3, 131–2, 202
rule setting, 62

searches, 68, 120, 163, 165–6
seasonal variations, 29, 81–2, 121, 140,
  178, 195
security
evolution of, 39, 40
perimeter security, 161, 181–2
security crackdowns, 92–4, 132–3, 218
security firebreaks, 198
security level
and collective disorder, 195
and drug use, 160
and escapes, 179, 182–3, 189
high-security prisoners, 47
and self-harm, 141
and sexual assaults, 106
and violence, 82, 121–2
security protocols, 203
segregation, 94, 113–14, 143, 144, 195
self-awareness, 26–7
self-harm
controlling, *153*; physical environment,
  143–7; population characteristics,
  148–9; prison regime, 149–52
nature of, 137–43
research approaches to, 136
self-report data on drug use, 156
Senese, J. D., 86
sentence
length of, 46–7
security reduced during, 182–3
stage of, 106, 141, 177–8
sentencing (determinate), 133–4
sexual assaults
controlling, *115*; physical environment,
  107–8; population characteristics,
  108–9; prison regime, 109–14
nature of, 101–7
research limitations, 114
victim responses to, 116
situational context
of collective disorder, 195–6
of drug use, 160
of escapes, 177–80
location, 83–4, 106–7, 122–4, 142–3, 180,
  195–6

situational context (*cont.*)
  seasonal variations, 81–2, 121, 140, 178, 195
  security level *see* security level
  of self-harm, 140–3
  of sexual assaults, 106–7
  stage of sentence, 106, 141, 177–8
  time, 82, 122, 142, 160, 179–80, 195–6
  of violence, 81–4, 121–4
situational precipitators, 34–5, 55–6, 57
  controlling pressures, 60–2
  controlling prompts, 58–60
  reducing permissibility, 62–4
  reducing provocations, 64–5
  and regulators, 54, 55–6, 76, 219–23
  specific control strategies, *99–100, 115, 134, 153, 171, 188, 209*
  see also deprivation model
situational prevention, 3–5, 12
  compared with social prevention, 216
  criticisms of, 5–6, 9
situational prison control
  efficacy of, 5–9
  methods of: dimensions of, 52–4; physical environment, 36–43; prison population, 43–7; prison regime, 47–52
  model of, 56, *57*; counterproductive control, 72–6; situational precipitators, 57–65; situational regulators, 65–72; utility of two-stage model, 217–23
  necessity of, 211–12
  need for more research, 223–5
  propriety of, 9–11
  versus deprivation approach, 214–17
  versus traditional approaches, 212–14
situational regulators, 34–5, 55–6, 65–7
  increasing anticipated punishments, 70–2
  increasing perceived effort, 67–8
  increasing perceived risks, 68–9
  and precipitators, 54, 55–6, 76, 219–23
  reducing anticipated rewards, 69–70
  specific control strategies, *99–100, 115, 134, 153, 171, 188, 209*
  see also opportunity-reduction model
situational theories of prison behaviour
  behaviour theory, 15–18
  dimensions of, 33–4
  environmental psychology, 28–32
  frustration–aggression hypothesis, 27–8
  rational-choice perspective, 32–3
  social-learning theory, 18–22
  theories of social influence, 22–7
situations, link with behaviour, 3–4, 6–8
social climate, 48
social condemnation, 71–2, 111
social influence theories, 22–7

social pressures, 60–2, 73
social prevention, 215–16
social reinforcement, 20
social-learning theory, 18–22
soft control
  and hard control, 76, 219–23
  too-soft control, 75–6, 193–4
  see also deprivation model; situational precipitators
sport, 133
staff
  authority of, 131–2
  counselling by, 186–7
  experience of, 91, 129, 201
  gender composition of, 131
  protection of, 53–4
  racial composition of, 92, 130, 201
  reducing anonymity of, 61
  reducing inappropriate obedience, 61
  responses to self-harm, 149–50
  responses to sexual assaults, 111–12
  screening for drugs, 162–3
  surveillance by, 69
  violence against lone, 130
staff training, 112, 128–9, 150, 200–1
staff turnover, 201
staff–prisoner ratio, 92, 129–30, 201
staff–prisoner relations, 41, 42, 127–9, 166, 202–3
  see also prisoner–staff violence
staffing levels, 162
stimuli, 16–17, 18, 58
stress, environmental, 29
substance-free zones (SFZs), 169–70
suicide *see* self-harm
surveillance, 68–9, 146–7
  blind spots, 39, 87, 108, 125
  evolution of, 39, 40, 41, 42, 43
surveillance protocols, 150–1
Sykes, G., 21, 214, 215

target hardening, 67
target removal, 69–70
technological aids, 42–3, 147, 165–6, 224
telephones, disputes related to, 94–5, 213–14
temperature and behaviour, 29, 81–2, 87, 121, 140, 178
temptation, reducing, 70
territory, 30, 65, 75, 123
theft, 69–70, 94
Thompson, B., 175, 176, 185, 187
time
  of collective disorder, 195–6
  of drug use, 160
  of escapes, 179–80

of self-harm, 142
of violence, 82, 122
time-bomb view of prison riots, 193
too-hard control, 72–5, 193–4
too-soft control, 75–6, 193–4
trace-detection equipment, 165–6
training *see* staff training
transfers, 204–5
triggers, 59
turnover *see* prison population; staff turnover

unexpected attacks, 121
uniforms, 59, 73, 74, 75
units *see* functional units
Unseem, B., 202, 203, 210

van den Haag, E., 189
vandalism, reducing, 63
vicarious punishment (making an example),
    72, 185

vicarious reinforcement, 20
victims
    personalising, 63–4
    of sexual assaults, 103–4, 116
    see also prisoner–prisoner violence;
        vulnerable prisoners
violence *see* collective disorder;
        prisoner–prisoner violence;
        prisoner–staff violence; sexual
        assaults
violent prisoners, 94
visits, 96, 109–10, 152, 166–8, 179, 187
vulnerable prisoners, 94, 113–14

weapons, 59, 73, 80, 119, 123, 126
weather *see* seasonal variations
Wener, R., 85–6

Zimbardo, P. G., 23, 26–7